THE PITS

AND

THE MULSANNE

Robin Donovan

"The experience of covering the length of a football pitch every second, sometimes in the dark and pouring rain, lap after lap, will remain with me forever."

Robin Donovan

CONTENTS

Dedication

Dedicated to everyone who has made my life as full as it has been. They know who they are. I thank them all immensely.

About the Author

Robin Donovan competed in no less than fourteen Le Mans 24-Hour races, including driving alongside five-time winner Derek Bell MBE in the 235mph Gulf Kremer Porsche back in 1994.

As an artist at heart, Robin chose to live in his own picture painted by his passion for competing in the world's greatest Sportscar race, the legendary 24 Heures du Mans. This compelling, poignant, and inspiring memoir provides a uniquely intimate view of everything from his journey there to what it actually feels like racing at over 200mph.

Prologue

It's all rather difficult to explain why I spent so many years pursuing a dream to be a race driver. I never had that much self-confidence, was not technically savvy and indeed was not interested in cars that much. At least to begin with. And the fact that apart from a few memorable ones, I can't declare any great major victories, which might make any reader ask why I am even attempting to put this all down to begin with, let alone have the front to invite you to spend a few hours of your valuable time, ploughing through this. Autobiographical books, racers in particular, are all about winning over all the odds. You know the score, how 'X' had to sell his house, divorce his wife, broke his neck but overcame all to become a world champion.

Sadly, this is not about any of those things. It's more about one person's desire to do something a little more out of the ordinary than most and how often this can turn into the pits. Dreams can be, and often are, smashed. Not everyone gets to celebrate the ultimate prize. I would argue that most who try don't.

What does that mean? Are they a failure? Does that mean their journey was of no importance?

What about the tales they can reveal, the fun and the upsets they had along the way?

Motor racing was my dream. When I was a kid, I had two aspirational posters hanging up on my bedroom wall. One was of Formula One, the other Le Mans. Both held equal status in my mind's eye. Brought up in an era when, in the '70s, racers lost their lives on a regular basis, come the 80s, racing myself; the odds were better but nowhere as close to what they are now. We lived in a different world, a special world where safety and money were not the first priorities. The thrills and spills, the partying and visiting far-off destinations were.

Through these pages, I wanted to outline one person's experience attempting to find that holy grail. This is not about major successes. And it's certainly not about BHP, Turbo boosts, roll bar settings or tyre pressures. As an artist, more than anything, I wanted to share a life spent within what I perceived to be a wonderfully colourful, all-encompassing picture. A picture, I thought, specifically drawn for me.

Intro

I had never been to Le Mans. All my racing pals had and had tried to get me there. They said how I would not comprehend the sheer enormity and magnificence of the event until I had been to see it first-hand. To witness the electrifying, what was then 50, now 65 car start. To experience the surreal atmosphere that descends as dusk falls and the unrivalled spectacle as the greatest sports car marques on earth, headlights blazing, screaming into the night at speeds topping 230mph. They told me of all the incredible adventures they had camping with the masses, the beer mountains, midnight parties and 'American Graffiti' moments.

It all sounded incredible, but still, I didn't want to take on what, for many, was a much-celebrated annual trip. Quite simply, I didn't want to go until I was racing there myself. My girlfriend thought I was barmy. Most friends just laughed. A few gave a 'tongue in cheek' good luck with that, then.

Therefore, it was with great excitement I finally made my way up the old concrete steps behind the iconic landmark of the Le Mans pits. At the top, I marvelled at the view that befell me: the start/finish line of the most legendary of all sports car circuits in the world: the Circuit de la Sarthe, home to the mighty 'Vingt-Quatre Heures du Mans'. This was as close to an epiphany as I have ever experienced. Laid out before me was where I was meant to be. It was here, on this hallowed ground, that all my heroes had chivalrously screamed past at some stage in the past.

Just in my own lifetime, first, we would have Stirling Moss, where his Mercedes 300 SLR, battled it out with Mike Hawthorn's Jaguar D-Type in the '50s. Then came the likes of John Surtees, Lorenzo Bandini and Jochen Rindt as they grappled with their muscular, blood-red Ferraris in the early 60's. This was only to be overcome by the awesome Ford GT 40s later in the decade when my boyhood heroes, such as Bruce McLaren, Chris Amon, Dan Gurney and Pedro Rodriguez, took centre stage. After that, there was the rise of the iconic, near 250mph Porsche's 917 running with the names of Richard Atwood, Jo Siffert, Jackie Oliver and Brian Redman behind the wheel. This was before Graham Hill and Henri Pescarolo gave Matra their first win in '72. The mighty Kremer Porsche team win saw out the 70s before, within no time at all, came the indomitable Porsche 956, dauntlessly steered by the likes of Derek Bell, Jackie Ickx and Hans Stuck.

The year was 1986, and as a piece of wastepaper blew aimlessly across the empty track like a tumbleweed in a western movie, my heroes all began to disintegrate in front of me as the realisation came that within a couple of days, it was finally my turn.

Derek Bell:

Derek holds legendary status throughout the world. Considered to be the greatest British racing driver ever to compete in endurance racing, he won the Le Mans 24 Hours five times, the Daytona 24 Hours three times and the World Sportscar Championship twice.

Foreword by Derek Bell MBE:

I have known Robin for a long time now. I must have been in my early twenties at the time when, still in school shorts, he was there, sitting in the front row as I gave a local talk about my Formula 3 career. He's appeared in my life on and off ever since. Being local to me and so keen on motorsport, I took him to Silverstone when I was competing in the four-wheel-drive McLaren at the British Grand Prix. This was long before he had a driving license of his own.

Years later, I must say I was a little surprised to bump into him again at the Shah Alam circuit in Malaysia at the end of 1985 for the last round of that year's World Endurance Championship. It was a first time for both of us, as it was the first-ever World Championship round Robin competed in and the first World Championship I managed to secure. Almost a decade later, we eventually competed together at Le Mans in the Gulf-sponsored Kremer Porsche K8. In more recent years, we have worked together at Le Mans, where he enables his VIP guests to fully experience this legendary race with the people who did it.

Perhaps not always gaining the overall results his obvious dedication and passion deserved, Robin always worked very hard to display his obvious talents in whatever car he could get his hands on. Sadly, not all were the best. A quiet and honourable character throughout, he tells his refreshingly different, slightly unconventional, and poignant story in the same spirit. The highs and lows of his time as a racing driver are sometimes breathtakingly descriptive, sometimes very funny. However, his journey is told with his usual humility, honesty, and candour.

It perhaps goes without saying that, as well as representing British motorsport extremely highly throughout his career, Robin never did disappoint behind the wheel when circumstance allowed.

Chapter One
Pedal Power

I was told I was born in a hospital, in bed, at a very young age. Apparently, my mother was there with me at the time. Apart from this bit of hearsay, the first two years of my life went by in a blur until I reached my third birthday. Now, **this** I do remember. The year was 1958, and as has happened regularly ever since, my birthday falls on December 18th, exactly a week before Christmas. Without my brother, he was to arrive five years later; I lived in a tiny old cottage in the seaside town of Bognor Regis with just my mum and dad. The day was particularly cold, but the present they gave me for this grand occasion was particularly big. With little room indoors, I was taken out, furniture-free, into the similarly sized tiny garden to unwrap it. After tearing the birthday paper away, to my absolute delight, I was presented with a magnificent red pedal car. I remember it being big, bright, and very shiny. In no time at all, I was firmly sat behind the wheel …and stayed there much of the day. My parents, concerned about the temperature, made moves to remove me, but I wasn't having any of it. I yelled and screamed whenever they tried to bring me in. As time went by, they brought me out gloves, extra jumpers to wear and even a sandwich. I just pedalled around to my heart's content until it got dark. You could say the scene was set.

Later on, we moved to a newly built house on a large modern estate, all the rage in the 60's. A time for building go-karts out of apple boxes and pram wheels, learning to ride and then race our bicycles around the many pathways that linked various parts of the estate together and going to schoolboy scrambles with my best pal at the time. Paul lived around the corner, and unlike mine, he was in the enviable position of having a far more enthusiastic father who bought him a proper scrambling bike. Oh, and there was a bit of school in between.

School was ok. I was a quiet chap. Small for my age, I resorted to getting a little kudos from the teachers, at least, for always coming first in class for art and providing fine, overdone illustrations to my schoolwork in history, geography and sometimes science. Without the need to indulge in any form of drawing skills, I struggled in maths. This was a problem, as I always wanted to be a pilot, where maths was an essential element at the time.

My dad was a well-decorated WWII pilot. He skippered bombers in the war. After receiving his wings at the training school at RAF Cranwell in 1941, he endured a first tour flying Wellington bombers before going on to complete two more tours on Lancasters. Few pilots in bomber command ever made it through three tours. He was one of the lucky ones. Therefore, just by being there in the end, I was one too.

From around five years old, when mum was out doing extra jobs to bump up the small amount of housekeeping money coming in, I spent many an evening positioned on a stool in the corner of the local RAF club. I sat there with a glass of orange squash and a Milky Way in hand and watched on as my dad would wolf down copious amounts of scotch whilst regaling stories of past endeavours with his mostly moustachioed compatriots. Nevertheless, I wanted to be like him. Indeed, quietly looking up towards the club ceiling with all the many immaculately made Airfix models dangling down on the cotton string, I really wanted to be a Spitfire pilot. I wanted to fly solo. At worst, crash and burn. At best, come home to pick up all the girls and free beer. Not that I had really discovered what was so special about girls or beer then, but I had still figured out that this was the life for me.

I must have been around eight when my relatively poor parents splashed out on a trip to Guernsey. My first foray into what I felt at the time was foreign shores. We were only there for a week, but on one of the days there, we went to the local kart circuit. There was no actual racing that day; all the participants were mostly day trippers or the odd weekend racers getting in a few mid-week laps. I had never driven a powered go-kart before, but I just took to it like a duck to water. Within three laps, I had lapped everyone on the circuit; within six laps, I had lapped them twice. Odd, because at my tender age, it had come so easily to me. Indeed, I wondered what everyone else was doing. Suffice to say, I came away buzzing and didn't get much sleep that night, thinking I was another Jim Clark in the making.

Coming home, I started to worship my new heroes of the day. With no real money to speak of, my dad bought a vintage Rolls Royce. He thought it gave him some prestige, but I was embarrassed when he took me to school in it. I always insisted he drop me off at the corner and not take me to the actual gate. Every month, he would buy 'Motorsport' magazine, which had their Rolls Royce buying and selling pages towards the back. Of course, the magazine was mostly dedicated to motorsport, where my new heroes leapt out of the pages, particularly the big black and white photographs in the centre. I cut out all these pictures and sellotaped them up on my bedroom wall when he had finished with the mag. Here, we had all the Grand Prix stars of the day. Jim Clark and Graham Hill. Jack Brabham and John Surtees. Chris Amon and Jo Bonnier. Dan Gurney and Lorenzo Bandini. I later found out that all these new Grand Prix heroes of mine competed at Le Mans as well.

It was at this time that my dad took me to a talk Derek Bell was delivering at the local Pagham-based Scout Hut. Still in shorts, I sat in awe in the front row as the young Derek told of his exciting exploits in Formula Three. All the time, his Super 8mm projector providing full colour, albeit rather wobbly, evidence of his magnificent escapades in the category. I sat there fully entranced from start to finish and, of course, asked for his sacred autograph before I left.

Not long afterwards, my dad, in what was possibly the last thing big thing he really did for me motor racing-wise, took me to see the film 'Grand Prix' at our local Odean cinema. I had been there a few times before. First, I went to see Lawrence of Arabia with him and again with my mum in tow, to see Mary Poppins and the Sound of Music, but 'Grand Prix' was something else. This movie, directed by John Frankenheimer, photographed in Super Panavision 70 and presented in 70mm Cinerama, had screen superstars of the time, such as James Garner and Yves Montand, replicating my newly found, real-life heroes. Again, I was in awe, simply spellbound as I witnessed the dangerous lives they lived unfold in full Technicolor: the danger, the excitement, the rewards.

It came as a bit of a revelation that suddenly, I realised that I didn't have to join the RAF to become a pilot (I was too short anyway) because here I had modern-day Spitfires happily racing around on the ground during peacetime, crashing and burning with all the heroes left to celebrate with all the best girls. And apart from any height issue, you didn't need a degree in maths to compete! All good stuff, but where was I to go from here?

Chapter Two
Growing up Pains

One of the first missions to undertake was to write to my local hero, Derek Bell. I told him I wanted to be a racing driver and needed him to give me all the advice he could offer to become one. I hand-wrote this very important, life-changing note in the best script possible and gave it to my dad to post as I didn't have his address. Burning to get going as soon as possible, it took what seemed a lifetime for him to respond. He eventually did respond but not in the way I had hoped for. He told me that the life of a racing driver was like that of an actor. You can spend as much time out of work as in work, and how it would be much better to go and get a degree in the real world before contemplating alternative options. He told me how good I was at art and how I should consider this as a way forward to begin with. How did he know I was good at art? Could it be that whilst passing on my note, my dad also added a few words of his own that he wanted to share with Derek? I will never know for sure; my dad would never say; Derek never did either, but feeling a little scuppered, my destiny as a full-blooded race driver took a sideways turn, and I wasn't even 12 yet.

1968 arrived, and I was taken to the British Grand Prix at Brands Hatch. I had looked forward to it every day since my dad promised me the trip on my birthday the previous December. Sadly, Jim Clark, my very first racing hero, would not be there. The British Grand Prix was held in July, and Jim Clark died in a fairly insignificant Formula Two race at Hockenheim, Germany, three months before.

Come July, my dad parked up on freshly mown grass, and we made our way up over the hill to view the track on the other side. I had never been to a motor race before, and the excitement I felt was immeasurable. As we approached the top of the rise, I could hear the profound noise and smell the Castrol R the cars left hanging pungently in the air. I could not believe I was actually going to witness all my heroes in the flesh. Now, here, laid out before me, was the arena where my chosen gladiators would battle it out.

After the very swift and nimble Formula Ford cars, we were treated to the powerful saloons, and then it was the lunchtime break before the Grand Prix cars came out. I could not wait but neither could my bladder. I hastily made my way to the outer paddock, where I was told the nearest toilets were. It was not long before the Grand Prix cars were about to take to the track, so I peed as fast as I could to run back the 100 yards or so to where Dad was opening up the picnic basket. The men's toilets consisted of nothing more than a metal trough, but next to me, one of my favourite F1 heroes was also delivering his wares. Indeed, he had hardly put himself away when I asked for his autograph. I then ran back to my picnic and rather proudly said to my Dad I had just had a pee with Pedro Rodriguez, who was then a huge Grand Prix star. It was a big deal for me, although I'm not sure how impressed my dad was. Suffice to say, it wasn't long before the silence was broken by the roar of the mighty F1 engines and the crackle and spit of their exhausts. After their warmup lap, it became silent as the out-of-view grid was formed, and then, with an almost unbelievable sound and a cloud of lingering smoke, they opened up and rushed through the first corner, Paddock Hill Bend, and came towards us. Eagerly awaiting their arrival at the approach to Druids Bend, I felt I was in heaven. There was no place on earth I would have preferred to be as they all blasted past.

Jo Siffert, a big star at the time in both Formula One and World Sportscars, would win the Grand Prix that day. He would die three years later on the same track in a Formula One BRM. Ferraris would come 2nd and 3rd. Pole sitter Graham Hill and now my pee mate, Pedro Rodriguez, would be amongst the many retirements.

I could not have been more inspired as we took the long drive home. And with the intent of doing something about it, I eventually managed to get an old Villiers kart with my own paper round pocket money and that of a few friends. I painted it dark blue and bright orange. I hardly knew how to change a spark plug but the kart at least looked like the bee's knees.

My Dad was now running a pub in Chichester and although he had no real intentions to help with my aspirations, he did talk to a couple of young local beer drinkers, Tim and Rob. He talked them into taking me to an old, dilapidated karting circuit that was made within the boundaries of an abandoned WW11 airfield about 15 miles away. I had made a trailer out of spare wood and old wheels. Carefully, with white emulsion, I painted the car's number plate onto a board I had painted matt black that was nailed to the rear end. I'm not sure it was legal even back then, but they regularly took me anyway and allowed me to drone around for hours on end. It wasn't exactly Silverstone, as the old concrete slabs that made up the track were heavily cracked, and the weeds grew high, but I felt thoroughly at home in my own little world. My crew seemed very happy to sit in the sun, smoke endless Guards cigarettes, drown down the odd tinny, and chat about dating girls.

I can't remember what broke beyond repair first. It could have been the old, greasy Villiers engine, or it could have been the rather frail wooden trailer, but as the summer drew to an end, it was time to consider joining a proper kart club. With the help of Tim and Rob, I managed to get hold of a Birel Komet K33 kart and joined the Chichester Karting Club. They didn't have a track of their own, but we visited others, and then every five to six weeks, they would be allowed to take over a portion of the city's main car park. In that first year, I took enough wins and runner-up spots in the junior category to take the club title. After a few successes, the following year, I was asked to be considered for the Junior National team. The first of the runoffs back then was to be held at Worcester Park Raceway, Surbiton. Armed with a set of brand-new tyres, fully adjusted spark plugs, and a new, finely tuned Tillotson carburettor, I thought nothing could stop me from proving my race talents.

The big day came, and after the heats, we lined up for the big final. Having been caught out in the rain earlier, I was in 6th spot on the grid but knew I could get up to the sharp end in a lap or two. Running 4th on my second lap we raced into the fast corner at the end of the back straight when all hell broke loose. The first two places clashed wheels, and as the chap running third braked hard, I hit his kart. My kart flew up in the air as I fell on my back, kart-less, onto the tarmac. My kart then came back down as my legs were flailing skywards and crashed back down to hit my left foot square on. The result? A trip to the hospital where a slipped epiphysis was diagnosed. Basically, my hip had been totally disjointed.

The surgery involved placing 3 five-inch pins into the hip to connect me all back together again. Then, after weeks on crutches with more weeks following them, they took them out. I was now 15, and whilst the other boys in the class suddenly discovered the delights of dating girls, I was left to hobble around much of the spring and summer on my four legs, two of which [the metal ones] were definitely an unwanted addition. Once again, my racing life was scuppered. I never kissed the girls that season or ever sat in a go-kart again.

However, a week or so after I was let out of hospital for the first time after the accident, I was taken to Goodwood. My dad knew an executive who worked for Girling Brakes, which was going to an important Formula One test at the circuit. My dad was invited to bring me along as I was obviously in need of a little well-earned distraction.

That morning, we arrived at the circuit during a torrential rainstorm. A Formula One car was there, half covered over by a tarpaulin but no sign of anyone else. With an umbrella up, my dad fought his way around the back of the paddock. Here, a lone mechanic sat in the cab of the only transporter on site, eating a sandwich. Firstly, hesitant to wind down his window in the downpour the reluctant mechanic told him they had all cleared off to the Chichester Park Hotel. He said he had no idea when they would be back.

As the hotel was less than 5 minutes up the road, we made our way there and found what was obviously a race team sitting back in the deep leather sofas of the reception lounge, drinking copious cups of coffee. The Girling Brakes chap told us they had all but given up on the day. It was nearly noon; the new driver had not arrived, and the rain was getting worse.

We were about to bid our farewells to the team and head off home when a tall man with long blonde hair confidently strode in. He wore black flared trousers and a matching black polo neck top with a gold chain around his neck and a striking gold watch around his wrist. Although this was the early spring of 1970, and things all around were beginning to look a little hipper, I must say he stood out from the doleful, badged-up, anorak-wearing team members.

What I did not know in the hotel was that this person was Ronnie Petersen, here for his first Formula One test. In later years, he would become known as the Super Swede. Driving for March, Tyrell, and Lotus, he would take part in 123 Grand Prix events in total, of which he would win 10 of them. Like so many other race drivers in the 70's, he would meet his end in a race car. His time came in 1978 at the start of the Italian Grand Prix at Monza.

Outside, the rain kept coming down as Ronnie made his way over to me and, in a quiet, husky voice, asked why I was on crutches. I duly told him and asked whether there was any likelihood of him getting out on the circuit today. In his then Pidgin English, he said, hell yes and then said he was going straight to the circuit and did I want a ride. Leaving the others behind, I clambered into his BMW 2800 CS along with my crutches as he tore off at breakneck speed along the tree-lined lanes toward Goodwood. On arrival and without stopping to find an official, not that there was anyone brave enough to stand around in such conditions, he proceeded to go straight onto and then lap the circuit. The tyres squealed in anguish on the far edges of adhesion as he made light of the ongoing rain, mist, and puddles. He casually took it all in his stride as I held on for what seemed like dear life while he learned the circuit. A simply awesome experience.

Come the afternoon, the clouds dispersed, and the sun shone a little. My dad and I sat in the run-down pits while we witnessed what would become one of the world's most renowned grandmasters, showing off just how fast a Formula One Grand Prix car could travel on a glistening, damp track. After that day, I never saw him again to actually speak to, but I will never forget our laps of the circuit minutes before he drove a Grand Prix car for the first time.

All great stuff, but what was I to do to step up onto the next rung of my own ladder?

Chapter Three

The Artful Dodger

The rest of 1970 came and went in a flash. Bruce McLaren: F1 Grand Prix, Can-Am, and Indianapolis 500 winner, race car constructor, and also winner of the 1966 Le Mans 24 hours lost his life at Goodwood testing in June of that year. While I was back in hospital again, having the pins in my hip taken out, September saw the Austrian Lotus Grand Prix driver Jochen Rindt killed in practice for the Italian Grand Prix. He would be the only F1 driver ever to win a World Championship posthumously.

In that year, a drinking friend of my dad's took me at breakneck speed in his new Ford Capri to Thruxton. I don't know what remains in my memory the most: risking life and limb as his passenger or Jochen Rindt's Formula Two win and my hero Derek Bell coming home an excellent 3rd place just behind Jackie Stewart at the circuit.

Later that year, I was also to visit the Crystal Palace circuit to witness the greats again in the European Formula Two Championship. This was in the days when many competing in F1 also raced in F2. Jackie won the first heat and Jochen Rindt the second. This was also the day when the debonair, and soon to become legendary, Francois Cevert signed up for the Tyrell World Championship winning squad competing in Formula One. His meteoric rise to fame that day ended in 1973 against the fatally hard barriers he hit in qualifying during the last round of the 1973 Grand Prix calendar at Watkins Glen in the USA. Cevert's teammate, the World Champion Jackie Stewart, totally distraught, retired on the spot before that final race of the season. A race that would have been Stewart's 100th Grand Prix.

In January of 1971, my dad took me to the racing car show in Olympia, where I had a crack on what was a fairly primitive racing car simulator set back in a corner of one of the exhibition halls. Here, after a long wait for my turn, I was allowed to do a set number of timed laps after providing my name, age, and address. I didn't think much more of the experience until, to my surprise, a note came through the post a few weeks later to say I had won first prize. The award was a fully paid initial trial at the Motor Racing School stables at Brands Hatch.

Given a lift from Sussex to the Kentish circuit, as I was not old enough to have a driving license, I sat there behind the wheel of a race car for the first time. It was an old Lotus 61 Formula Ford. Although not even competitive outside the racing school world, I felt entirely in my element: the directness of the steering, the open wheels, the light fibreglass body, the simple 4-speed gear shift, and the tempered growl of the race engine. It was a device to do exactly what it said on the tin. A car built solely for the racetrack, nothing else.

Overseen by the wonderfully amiable race school director Brian Jones, later to become a top motorsports commentator known as "The Voice of Brands Hatch", I went out for my first exploratory laps. As I began to build up speed, everything became perfect in my world. Had it not been for the race helmet, I could have almost sworn I felt the wind in my hair as the tarmac rushed up towards me. I was alone and free. For once in my short life, I felt totally in charge.

As my given number of laps came to an end, I focused on the road ahead. I don't think I even saw my designated chequered flag being waved from the pit wall. Continuing to pound around the circuit, it wasn't until a very upset chief instructor took it upon himself to stand on the actual circuit, frantically waving at me to slow down, that I noticed my time had come to an end. As disinclined as I was, I reluctantly made my way back to the pits. The chief instructor at the time was a charismatic local racing superstar, Tony Lanfranchi. Like a naughty schoolboy, Tony practically manhandled me up to the top of the control tower for a reprimand from Brian Jones. Fortunately for me, both Brian and Tony started to laugh halfway through their blistering lambasting. They agreed that although I had taken liberties, the speed of this total beginner standing in front of them was clear to see. I was let off the hook until the next time.

In the following couple of years, I had all but given up on my then addiction to being a Grand Prix driver, had discovered girls, and had begun dating. A wonderfully lovely girl named Christine was the first real love of my life. She was very pretty, always happy and funny, and I loved her to bits. She was born a year later than me, a week before Christmas on the very same date. Married years ago now, to this day on my birthday, she still sends a card with a handwritten note summing up her year, wishing me a happy birthday and a Merry Christmas. No other contact, no emails during the year, but the note is always very special. Every year, I, of course, always send her the same.

As suggested by Derek Bell years earlier, in 1972, I enrolled to do a BA in Art and Design at the West Sussex College of Art & Design. This institute had a college annexe in my then hometown of Worthing and a University annexe in the far-trendier city of Brighton just down the road.

As a full-blooded student in the early 70s, I wore my hair long, donned wide flares, and a very smelly Afghan coat. Later, the Afghan coat was exchanged for a less rancid RAF great coat. In the early days of the likes of David Bowie, Elton John, and Mott the Hoople, all the rage then was also the heavily stacked shoes of the glam rock era. At 5'4 in stockinged feet, I got to tower over most of the old ladies that slowly ambulated along the Worthing promenade, but all the more regular height students also wore such platform footwear. So, no ultimate gain was made there.

However, something was exciting about all the freedom given to a student. I could now visit the pub for a pint, smoke the odd joint, and go to all the many rock concerts that visited the college and the nearby concert halls.

By then, my Mum had sought companionship elsewhere, had moved out of the pub, and was undertaking divorce proceedings. At 17, I was still there living with my dad and 12-year-old brother. Even if I had wanted to, I couldn't move out as I would always spend the entire proceeds of my student grant on the day it arrived. The funds would immedietely go on to the next stage of the Brands Hatch racing school. Cashless, I would then have to do anything required in the pub to earn pocket money to get by. This included cleaning out the loos and polishing the brass pipes that linked each urinal together. Each morning before leaving for the college, I did the bottling-up and hoovered all the pub carpets. When I got back, I would work behind the bar, underage as I was to begin with. At the weekends, I worked in the kitchen helping to prepare the bar snacks sold at the time, the ploughman's lunches, scampi in a basket, and cheese and tomato toasties.

It was during this time I dodged my first encounter with the great white bearded man above. My grandmother had given me her old car. An old, well-worn Hillman Imp. To my delight, I had actual road wheels for the very first time. However, without a full license at the time, the car had to be emblazoned with learners L plates, and

24

I had to enlist the help of more qualified student friends to legally oversee my driving from the passenger seat. Nevertheless, I spent many a happy hour roaring around, upsetting the neighbours with my derring-do.

One day, three of us students decided to go up to London to see a band. There was Tony, older than me with long curly hair and bum fluff, a lead guitarist in the college band, and the qualified driver up-front in the passenger seat next to me. Little Andy was in the back. Andy was the college comedian. At 5', and that was with his platforms on, this outgoing, characterful chap guaranteed a laugh a minute. We had our only pint of the evening before we went into the concert hall and left early as the band was not up to much.

Uneventful as it was, we were happy and sang and chatted on the way home as I progressed down the A24 as far as my little wheels would carry us. It was a dark night, but the lights on the dual carriage shone brightly. Suddenly, they didn't as we hurtled into the far more bendy countryside near Southwater. With no thought for slowing down to match the darkness encountered, I got a wheel off the road as I went into one of the tighter bends. The little car dug in as it hit the bottom of a ditch and began to bounce forward end over end multiple times before barrel-rolling to a murky stop.

As the car was often upside down doing its own thing and without any of us wearing safety belts, I can remember at the time having two competing parallel thoughts. One was, oh dear, I'm about to die. Nothing was upsetting about it, just a calmness and resignation that it was all about to come to an end. In complete conflict with this was my other thought: how funny Andy was in the back. He was screaming out loud as over and over we went. He was flying around, sometimes near the roof in full view as my head rolled back, other times out of view as my head rolled forward.

Finally, silence. The car was on four wheels the right way up. The car lights burned through the mist. Although glass was everywhere, none of it was left in the windows. Although broken all around the pillars, the roof was still on. We all sat there quietly in the dark. Finally, Tony broke the silence, 'ooh' he said, I've lost my feet. Looking down, all that had happened was both his platforms had fallen off as his limp body had just spent a few seconds, which felt like a lifetime, flailing around. He quietly put his boots back on and proceeded to get out of the broken car. I did the same through the driver's door that was virtually hanging off anyway. My only injury was stinging my hands on the huge nettles that surrounded us as I got out.

But now we have a big problem. We couldn't find Andy. He wasn't in the back of the car. We could only think that he must have been eventually thrown out of the back window. We fought our way through the nettles to visit the route the car took when it left the road to find him. Nothing, he was nowhere to be seen. He had just disappeared. With Tony and me having managed to survive fully intact with no harm done, we were worried that my silly escapade off the road had indeed ended in tragedy. Then we heard a muffled groan. It seemed to be coming from the car, but we had already seen there was no one in the car. We headed back and again peered in the back. Nothing, or was there? On closer inspection, all was revealed. Andy was fine, just hidden under the back seat. The back seat had obviously worked its way loose, and when we went end over end, Andy was either high in the sky or the seat was. When it all came to rest the seat had come down on top of him. Whew, we both thought.

In those days, there were no mobile phones, so just a little bit shaken but fully intact we all walked along the dark road until we found a house. Explaining our situation, we were given a cup of tea and phoned Tony's parents. His dad came out to pick us up. The only thing salvageable from the whole wreck was the jack, which we put in his boot. As the big boot came down, Andy was in the way, and it cracked down right on his head. He passed out like a light. Tony and I both chuckled. We thought a small price to pay for such excitement.

On returning home, my dad chose not to speak to me for a week. It wasn't until later on, through chatting to locals in the pub, that I discovered that in the same week as my trip to the weeds, my dad had turned over his Jaguar MK 2 after a heavy session in the pub. The car had similarly rolled, and as a landlord with a license, he chose to run away and hide in the local Chinese restaurant he regularly frequented. Indeed, he hid in the kitchens when the local constabulary came by to make inquiries as to the marooned car at the end of the windy road close to the premises. Mmm, I thought. Perhaps he was not only cross with me for being too carefree and writing off my own car but cross with himself for similar reasons. As it happened, I was charged with dangerous driving. My dad said he would represent me. I initially said no, but on the day, my father, this good upright citizen, local landlord, and member of the county council, was superb, and I got away with the lesser charge of careless driving. Not bad, albeit I still had not even passed my driving license by then.

After three attempts, I finally passed my driving test. I think I failed the first time as I thought taking driving tests was better than taking lessons. Also, my hair had grown pretty long by then, and the old chap taking the test obviously did not like my hippie approach to something so serious. The second attempt was held in the pouring rain. The instructor told me to do an emergency stop when he hit his newspaper on the dashboard. I did this so fast that as I screeched to a halt in lightning time, all the while keeping the rear of the car from not overtaking the front, the instructor was within inches of going through the windscreen. Another fail came short and swift.

Finally, armed with my new license and with the summer holidays fast approaching, I thought I would try a summer job driving. I friend I knew put in a good word with a local kitchen dealer that specialised in industrial-sized units for restaurants and the like. He had a showroom and, most importantly, a Bedford van. My job was to pick up and deliver the smaller-sized parts. The first job, however, was to pick up his Jaguar engine. He had just had it specialist tuned by a local supplier. With help from the workers at the tuners, we got the gleaming engine carefully covered in cloths into the back of the van, and I headed back to the showroom.

It began to drizzle. I had two choices. I could go straight down the road on the dual carriageway for 2 or 3 miles, turn right at the roundabout, and then I only had a couple of miles on an equally boring main road back to the showroom. My other option was to turn off and go cross-country. The narrow and windy country road was much more fun, especially on a greasy, wet surface. I chose the latter. I was in my element as the little van wheels squealed and slithered around the country farm lanes, desperate to hold traction. Although I didn't know the road, I was even making up time as I came to a humpback bridge. No problem, I thought as I hardly slowed down. Of course, I had completely forgotten the precious cargo I was carrying in the back of the van. Over the bridge, I went only to see that the road veered sharply to the left straight afterward. The engine in the back must have been a couple of inches in the air as I desperately tried to steady the van in line with the road. The engine must have then slammed to the right of the cab, the weight of which threw the small van to the other side of the road. Nine times out of ten, I would have been ok with this, but the van slammed head-on into an oncoming transit van, the first vehicle I had seen since I left the main road.

There was a huge crashing sound as the front of my van was virtually destroyed on impact. The first thing of great concern was I thought the glass from the completely shattered windscreen had blinded me. With my eyes fully open, I could not see a thing. Wiping my eyes, everything slowly began to come back into vision. The blood from three large gashes in my forehead had drenched my whole body down to my knees in red. I sat there for a time, bewildered at my stupidity. I could not get out as the dashboard was firmly wrapped around me, with the steering wheel now only two inches from my chest. Fortunately, the transit van driver fared better. His vehicle was bigger, stronger, and set higher off the road. Nursing a broken thumb, the driver was nice enough, considering what I had just put him through. Checking if I was ok, he then made his way to the nearby farmhouse to get help. A lovely lady, who in later years reminded me of Ma Larkin in the Darling Buds of May, appeared. She brought me a cup of tea and a cake she had just baked while we waited for the services to arrive. The Fire Brigade duly cut the roof off the van and released me enough for the awaiting Ambulance to take me a few miles south to Worthing General Hospital.

The funny thing was that after the Ambulance had sped to the hospital with its blues and twos going crazy and delivered me to the A&E department, I was sent to their waiting room. I sat there for two hours as all manner of injuries were seen first. I remember one chap sat further up the queue with his forefinger in a bandage. I must have looked like a ghastly sight with dried red blood down to my knees, but other than a nurse popping over to check my head and to ask if anything else hurt, I sat there waiting my turn until seen.

After stitching me up, I was released and made my way home by cab. I went upstairs into the lounge and with a sore head, I quietly contemplated being out of work again and what the police would charge me with. My brother Simon came into the room and put the TV on. As is his usual way, he did not say a word to me other than asking if there was anything I particularly wanted to watch. We must have both sat there for at least two hours, with me looking like Frankenstein before he noticed. I love my brother.

You tend to go through periods in your life when you can be very insular. This is particularly true when growing up. I think we were both in our own separate worlds at the time. In future years, Simon attended Le Mans many times to spur me on along with his mates. Although we don't catch up often, we always have fun when we do.

Going back to my little head-on, in due course I was to receive a charge of careless driving again. It could have been much worse. The kitchen dealer did not request damages for his written-off van but never wanted to see me again. In between my pub work, I tried to spend the rest of the summer working on a local mushroom farm.

My job was to water them. I spent the first week or two doing exactly what I was told to do, armed with only a water spray gun as company. The mushrooms were housed in vast sheds that resembled those of a WWII prison camp. The sheds were dark and musty filled with row after row of these mushroom beds four bunks high. The farmers said you had to spray the water at a certain speed and consistency and should be able to do four sheds per day. After a while, I figured I could do four sheds in no time at all if I sped up the water and rushed through the process. After each shed, I could then slip out the back, take off my tee shirt, and indulge in a few rays for half an hour at a time. What I had not bargained on was the harder and quicker you deliver the water, the more likely these fragile white mushrooms mottle, turn brown, and die. It took about a week before I was rumbled. It was back to the drawing board in more ways than one.

My last dodge from getting to heaven too early came a year or so later. On this occasion, I was not in my car at the time. In fact, I had only just gotten out of it. My girlfriend at the time was Jane. She was a couple of years younger than me. Beautiful and blonde, she was a well-photographed student model. Jane lived with her Mum, Stepfather, and sister in a bungalow halfway down a very high hill in the local village of Sompting. We had a passionate, spark-filled relationship. For some reason, we often seemed to have more than our fair share of altercations, many of these being caused by her overbearing and very strict Stepfather.

It was quite late this particular evening when I parked up the road where she lived. On this occasion, it was my turn to make up, albeit I was running behind time. I never noticed it was closer to midnight than 11 when I drew to a halt on the hill. At the time, I had an old '66 MGB Roadster. It was a great car, British Racing Green, soft top, wire wheels with more rust than bodywork in places. The lock on the driver's side didn't work, and the handbrake was pretty suspect, so I parked a little further up the hill on the left under a streetlamp. I was told that someone was less likely to try and nick it if it was in full view as opposed to a darker area. I started to stroll down the hill, trying to figure out what I was going to say. The view ahead was the road falling away in front of me and the tops of the bungalows peeking out from the pavements on either side. The bungalows were quite a lot lower than the road. At right angles to the road, their individual driveways went down to each dwelling. Each had a small front garden that was almost like a pit with a high front wall.

As I approached her bungalow on the right, I heard a trundling sound. I turned round to see my MGB rolling down the road, picking up speed. To my amazement, it seemed to be coming straight for me. Instantly, I dived down on all fours onto the pavement as the car leaned right, mounted the pavement, and headed straight for me and her house. I will never know why, out of all the bungalows in the road, it chose hers. Swiping past me, my last memory of looking on at ground level was of the car leaving the pavement and, in the sudden piercing silence that followed, launching itself into thin air, aiming for the family's roof.

Fortunately, gravity prevailed, and it crashed down into their garden, flattening a couple of garden gnomes and a small decorative wooden wheelbarrow on landing. Again, silence. I looked around. Most of the house lights in the neighbourhood had gone off. It was later than I thought. There were definitely no lights on in Jane's house. It was a quiet, dark evening. No one came to the door. Everything remained calm. The only strange thing was an MGB sitting there quietly in her front garden.

It took a few minutes to build up enough courage to ring the doorbell. What seemed like a dozen times, I put my finger up to the bell but could not ring it. However, there was no way out. I had to hit that bell. Finally, I rang. No answer. I rang again. Obviously, no one was up. After what seemed like a lifetime, Jane's Stepfather answered the door while tying a knot in his newly donned dressing gown. He shouted, 'What time do you call this, Jane isn't speaking to you at the moment and even if she was, she's had gone to bed'. He was about to carry on with his tirade when, aghast, he suddenly saw beyond my apologetic face into his front garden. He walked past me and looked on, not saying a thing. I trembled as I pathetically tried to explain. Still, nothing came from his mouth. The poor man was in total disbelief.

After some time, he let out the biggest grin and began to chuckle. He still didn't say a single thing to me but rushed back into the house and shouted, 'Hey girls, get up, come, and see this'. In no time at all, Jane, her sister, and her Mum came out into the dark garden. Lights went on next door, and the next-door neighbours quickly joined the late-night garden party. One of the neighbours had a Polaroid camera and started to take photographs of them all sitting on the bonnet. It was like they had just hunted down a lion in the Savanna. Finally, the Stepfather turned to me and said, 'I always hated that stupid little wheelbarrow'.

As an epilogue to this story, I had to come out the next day with a mobile crane I had to hire. This was the only way I could retrieve the car from the garden. I remember it cost £75. Bearing in mind that my second-hand MGB cost a total of £280 back then, £75 was a lot of money in the 70's. To my delight, I found that when the car finally got back home, there was little damage done, albeit I have to say the tracking was a bit out.

Chapter Four
Cops & Quarries

Life continued at college. In the first foundation year, we were tasked with all manner of disciplines. From fine art, graphics, fashion, textile design, and print. We also covered photography and movie-making. One of my favourites was conceptual. The next three years were spent specialising in graphic design. We had a range of weird and wonderful tutors.

Jake, our principal, was larger than life. With gay abandon, he used to arrive very late each morning in his pristine white, open-top Triumph Spitfire. With his Balbo's beard, he wore self-made, garishly coloured tops and bottoms with a large matching musketeer hat. Always by his side were his three pink miniature poodles.

There was the delectable Jenny, head of fashion. She had short hair, was very pretty, and always beautifully turned out. Before too long, and to our dismay, we found out that Jenny was going out with Brian Ferry, the lead singer in Roxy Music. He would pop by on occasion to pick her up. Immaculately turned out in his short, sharp, floppy haircut, two-tone suit, and brogues, he put all our obvious 70's style fashions to shame.

Terrance was our fine art tutor. In his late fifties, with bulging blood-red eyes, stained yellow smokers' fingers, and terribly wrinkled face, he always wore the same old pair of brown corduroy trousers and matching jacket while he held court for hours on Van Gogh, Picasso, and Rembrandt. When the lights dimmed down, and the slide projector clicked to life, he would slip out a small whisky flask and take a quick swig when he thought no one was looking. Of course, everyone was.

Another tutor who stood out was Peter, in charge of photography. Short, bespectacled, and bearded with a large, pronounced waistline, he was the ever-friendly one. Always caring and helpful, Peter often joined us in the pub after the day's work.

After college, I often went with friends, and the occasional tutor to a seedy old pub called the Devil's Kitchen. Here we nursed our pints while we spent many a happy hour just watching the other locals. Quite a few were more into their drug habits than eager beer drinkers. Some tended to prop the bar up while chatting away at great speed, hardly sipping from their pint mugs. You could instantly tell these were the ones on amphetamines. You then had the odd glassy-eyed hippy sitting alone, staring into his ashtray for what seemed like hours at a time. His choice would have been marijuana or LSD. Tucked into the corner, you would get both the cops and the hippies busily doing business.

In those days, you could hardly tell the cops and the civvies apart. With their long hair, flared jeans, and beards, they all looked pretty similar. Earlier on in the week, the police, whose main station was just down the road, would often nick them and confiscate their illegal wares. Later, these upright members of the constabulary would come to the pub and sell back the goods they had previously taken at a discount price and personally pocket the funds.

With the little spare time I had when I wasn't working in my dad's pub, we went to the college dances, where we were often visited by bands such as Atomic Rooster, Medicine Head, and the Pink Fairies. Many times, we saw Hawkwind and Argent, who tended to do the local concert hall circuit, and then, on occasion, we would travel to Brighton or Portsmouth to see the more established bands such as Genesis, Yes, and Pink Floyd.

After the loss of my Hillman Imp, I lashed out £80 for a sit-up and beg Ford Popular. It only had three forward gears, and the windscreen wipers never worked. It was green, but I hand-painted the rusty bodywork dark blue and the wheels bright orange, just like my old Villiers kart. However good I thought the go faster colours were, it did nothing for the speed, which maxed out around the 50mph mark. One weekend, we travelled five-up along the coastal road to Brighton to see the band Family. In torrential rain, it was again Andy in the front passenger seat, who boldly hung out the window and manually moved the wipers. The car really was not for this earth, and one fine day soon afterward, my nonstudent pal Tom and I took it to the hilltop of a local quarry. In true James Dean style, we let the handbrake off, rolled it down the hill, and both jumped out at the last minute as it plunged over the top. We thought this was a fitting grand final moment for such a motor. We then hitched a lift home.

From Ford Popular, I went on to get an old Triumph Herald Estate and then a bright red Triumph Spitfire. It was only in the last couple of years at college I bought my British Racing Green MGB roadster. I loved that car with a passion, as did the girls.

While trying to be a good student, the inbuilt fever for racing never really subsided. With ever-diminishing funds, I was still journeying up to Brands Hatch whenever I could afford to pay for another step up the school ladder. We had what was called our Class 2 test. This consisted of timed laps of the Brands Hatch circuit heading off in an anticlockwise direction. A totally different circuit when you do it the wrong way round. Because the barriers were all in the wrong place for such an activity, it just wouldn't be allowed today.

However, back then, it was, and again, I came first with the fastest lap. Passing your Class 2 test allowed you into the racing school's own championship. From straightforward timed lapping in Formula Ford cars, we could now actually race against each other in the school's fleet of Ford Escort GT cars. Privately held at the circuit with no paying spectators, these races were great fun but often ended in tears as there was always the odd rollover or T-Bone. Many ended up with severe damage. With my college grant in hand, I managed to do the second season in full. It was sponsored by Men Only magazine. The final race of the year was held on a proper open race day, where I managed to take the laurels for winning both the race and the school championship. My prize was a peck on the cheek from Men Only centrefold model Fiona Richmond, as she handed over my winners' cup and, better still, a fully sponsored Formula Ford race at the public Easter Monday meeting the following year.

My inaugural Formula Ford race was certainly an experience. The Formula Ford 1600 school car sponsored by Rolatruc was a couple of years old, so not one of the best. Added to the mix, there were faster Formula Ford 2000 cars including a works Van Diemen entry for a certain Ayrton Senna da Silva. As the flag fell, Ayrton disappeared from us all and, within 3 or 4 circuits, was lapping us all. I held on, didn't make any mistakes, and was quite happy to bring the car home in one piece in a solid midfield position. Not the most auspicious start but at least I had held my own and competed in my first public single-seater race.

My last race in the school cars was a public racing school v celebrities race at Brands Hatch. Half the grid was made up of the top racing school students and half of the likes of TV presenter Noel Edmunds and boxing champ Henry Cooper. The celebrities were despatched first, followed by the pupils. A grinning Brian Jones, who tried to tell me off when I first started at the school, awarded me the garland and the cup for winning the race. The last I was going to see for a while.

Chapter Five
Pastis & Panorama

College life was drawing to a close. We had our final exhibition, where we all displayed our best and all looked forward to the big end-of-term party. I would have not missed this for the world had it not been for a call I received from Peter Duker [formerly Deuchcar], who was casually working as a part-time independent foreign correspondent for cycle race magazines. Knowing of my yearning to race cars, Peter, now living in the South of France near Antibes, invited me to join him as he had tickets for the Monaco Grand Prix just down the road. Towering well over six feet, Peter was outspoken, jocular, and forever cheerful. This larger-than-life character was known as the Big Duke.

He was a long-time friend of my dad's and played banjo with his band in the pub whenever he was in town. Heir to the James Deuchar brewery in Newcastle-upon-Tyne the only interest he had in beer was drinking it. The only other passions he had were professionally playing jazz & blues and amateur cycle racing. When he was in his early twenties, he set up his first trad-jazz band before finding success as Big Pete Deuchars New Orleans Jazz band playing with Ginger Baker. The band name changed to Big Pete Deuchar and his Professors of Ragtime as he did stints in both Germany and the U.S.A. Recording several albums and the odd local TV show along the way he also played with Chris Barber and Ken Colyer.

Once while going home to Sussex to make sure his second wife was still breathing, he leafed through an old, well-worn Marquee Club program from the early 60's with me. Here, he proudly pointed out where he starred as the headline act and, far more importantly, the Rolling Stones featured as a mere support band. The boom or bust lifestyle of a jazz player was put on hold in 1970 when, out of the blue, he decided to get into the Guinness Book of Records for cycling around the world in the fastest time. While out training near Goodwood, he was knocked down on his bike by a hit-and-run motorist. The never-to-be-caught driver managed to drive right across Pete's head. After six weeks in a coma and ten long months of reconstructive surgery, the once fairly good-looking chap did what he set out to do. After pedalling around the world and fully bearded, in an attempt to cover up a multitude of scars, he came home to pen his first published book 'Sting in the Tail'.

I hesitantly declared to my still girlfriend at the time, Jane, that I would head off to the South of France, see the Grand Prix, and be back the following week. I came home two months later.

On arrival at the train station in Nice, I was met by the Big Duke. After our hellos and with nothing more than a rucksack in hand, I took my place as pillion on his motorbike. With some surprise, I was roared to the first hairdresser he could find where he demanded my hair be cut nice and short. Feeling unduly clean-cut, I walked out to join him in a bar a few metres down the road. In the ten minutes we stayed there, I had a beer, and he had at least three Paul Ricard drinks known as Pastis. Apprehensively, I got back onto the back of the bike for the half-hour ride back to Antibes. Here, we went to his favourite harbourside drinking hole, where he introduced me to the locals. More pastis was consumed as the sun started to go down. Finally, we rode up a dark, winding hill into the mountains to his dwelling, a small two-bed caravan. I felt strangely at home with the strong smell of the surrounding pine trees, the amazing blood-red sunset, and the panoramic view of the harbour lights starting to twinkle way down below. That evening, we whiled away the hours with Big Pete holding court with numerous colourful stories of his past. These tales included everything from hiring Ginger Baker, later to become the drummer of Cream, to traversing the continents on his bicycle, often half-cut, getting into lots of booze-ups and punch-ups along the way. Intermittently, he would play his beloved banjo as we chuckled our way into the wee small hours.

It took little time to get into the swing of life on the Cote d'Azur. With a never completely sober Big Pete riding everywhere on his trusty BMW R90S, the butterflies I first felt being his pillion soon subsided.

The first weekend there, we went to the Monaco Grand Prix. It was hot and sunny and exceptionally colourful, with the eager fan-filled grandstands facing down to the harbour where the super yachts bobbed up and down in the light wind. What was so outstanding was the noise as the amplified sound of the engines ricocheted off the walls of the surrounding buildings of this tiny principality. It was 1976, the legendary year of the titanic battle between Niki Lauda and James Hunt. This was three races before Lauda's life-changing Nurburgring accident when he was at the height of his powers. In his bright red Ferrari, Niki confidently strode at leisure to a comfortable win that further extended his title defence. Fortunately, from our harbour side seats between Tabac Corner and the swimming pool complex, there was plenty more to see. James Hunt blew up at the harbour chicane, and Clay Regazzoni skated up the escape road on the oil, and then later on, Ronnie Petersen crashed at Tabac. Not that I knew it at the time, but a few years later, I was to co-drive with other Grand Prix stars competing that day. Namely Jean-Pierre Jarier and Arturo Merzario.

After accepting Big Pete's offer of an extended stay, I was promoted to being his official photographer for the southern stages of the Tour de France. We headed down the coast to the start of Stage 12 at Port Barcarès and stayed with the tour over the Pyrenees and then north through Pau, Langon, and Lacunau. We didn't leave until the tour reached stage 18 at Bordeaux.

The days were spent amidst the hustle and bustle of a multitude of other reporters on motorbikes vying for the best photo opportunities alongside the stream of competing riders. We would try our hardest not to get in the way of the team managers, who would also drive alongside their riders, shouting out instructions. On the steeper climbs, meandering uphill slowly, you could feel the motorbike wobble underneath you to hold steady. Cresting the summit was altogether different as the cycle riders would then burst into life as they careered downhill at speeds of 110kph, leaving the motorbike reporters in their wake.

On occasion, there would be a breakaway when one rider would sprint ahead of the group. Trying to steady myself on the small footrests provided on the back of the bike, I would stand up to photograph him when I could grab a clear view over Big Pete's head. I often tried using the same method with the leading riders as we raced across the finish line. A good shot really depended on how sober Pete was and, therefore, how brave I felt at the time to take it.

As the large 60-vehicle publicity caravan that precedes the racing was already there at the end of each stage, the central square of every town had already burst into life by the time we arrived. While the riders, their soigneurs, and managers would quickly retreat to their hotels, all the bars and restaurants would be filled with a hoarding mass of strangers. These many race reporters, photographers, and fans would then party and make merry until the wee small hours. By morning, they would all be gone until the next time.

After one such stage, Big Pete found a back street bar where the locals, not particularly interested in the race, were playing pool. He challenged them to a game and then another. He lost more than he won but then upped the stakes with a grand four-man final. Not until after I was drafted in to partner Big Pete, did he share the fact that this would be strip pool. Fortunately, this focused his skills, and we left the bar fully clothed while our opponents were left down to their underpants.

By now, Pete was a little worse for wear as we staggered our way across the town square enroute back to the hotel. Halfway across, we bumped into a group of motorcycle Gendarmes who had just fallen out of a nearby bar. By day, they acted as the very strict police escorts for the tour. Still in their super-smart uniforms, by night, they obviously liked to party as much as everyone else. As it was beyond midnight, I thought our extracurricular activities were over for the day, but not Pete. He challenged them to swim across the centrally located fountain, the first to the other side, touching the fountain statue in the middle, the winner. Again, with no great personal gain to be made, I was begrudgingly forced into being his sidekick on this alcohol-induced endeavour. Yet again, we came out tops and felt very pleased with ourselves as we chuckled and squelched our way back to the hotel, leaving puddles in the lift that took us up to our rooms. All harmless, if a little silly fun, but now I was feeling the need to get back to some form of reality. After all, I had jobs to find, a waiting girlfriend to somehow recompense, and the possibility of even cars to race. My time here was done.

A couple of years later, for some strange reason only known to him, Big Pete was to get married to a grumpy German lady. He called her 'Her Hitler'. They lived back in the UK, and she bore him a much-wanted first son. He worshipped his little boy but still struggling with his alcohol consumption, his wife went home to Germany and legally prevented him from seeing his son. Hugely depressed, very sadly, he got up one day and caught the 7.25 from Market Harborough on the nose. The Big Duke cashed out in much the same way he lived; unconventionally.

I arrived back on UK shores just in time to witness the British Grand Prix at Brands Hatch. Clay Regazzoni collided with his Ferrari teammate, 1975 world champion Niki Lauda, at the start of entering the infamous Paddock Hill Bend. Home favourite James Hunt being launched into the air and breaking his suspension in the resulting mayhem. Amidst the confusion the race was stopped as James managed to drive his stricken McLaren to a back road leading to the pits. Having not completed a full lap, Hunt was technically out, and anyway, there was no time for his car to be put together in time to make the restart. As the Grand Prix field got together without this new British hero, the crowd took things into their own hands. Reaching a fever pitch, the fans broke into chants of 'We want Hunt, we want Hunt' before launching every manner of projectile into the sky. Bottles and beer cans rained down onto the circuit as the McLaren boys frantically worked to mend Hunt's broken car. By the time the starting Union Jack fell half an hour later [no green lights in those days], Hunt was back and taking the restart duly took the cheers of the UK spectators to heart by chasing down Niki Lauda. It took Hunt 44 laps to pass before dominating the rest of the laps to win by a massive 52 seconds. Sadly, two months later, Ferrari would win their appeal against the result but 'hey' what a race.

It was not long afterwards, at the height of the hottest summer on record, I was traipsing through the streets of London with portfolio in hand, looking for a job. The long hair, pinstripe jacket with matching flared trousers, and white clogs did not help with either the sizzling temperatures or the beleaguered feeling of anxiety baking out of every step taken. I had given myself a week to find a job and had parked up my old Triumph banger at Scratchwood service station where, sleeping in the back, I could at least wash before taking the train into town. My final interview of my last day had me meeting the chairman of Fordham Sadler Advertising which was just behind the London Palladium. To my delight and horror, I was hired on the spot and with feet now blistering, was sent across the road to their art department.

I slept in the studio cupboard for two nights before being discovered and nicely whisked away to be looked after by the chairman and his kindly wife for a week or two in his deluxe Radlett-based homestead. I fitted in well; my work was up to scratch, and within a short amount of time, I was offered the studio director's job after the outgoing one was fired. All was going well. I was suddenly earning good money. I found a new girlfriend, Corinne, who was again unbelievably pretty (I always managed to have a fair amount of luck there), communicative, and intelligent. To later on become a well-accomplished private school teacher, Corrine went to University in South London.

Within no time, we had set up a home in Winchmore Hill. I spent most of my weekend's spanner rattling and pit boarding for a Formula Ford racing team based at Brands Hatch. The work was free, but I was having fun even though I didn't have much clue about the mechanics of it all. All I was really interested in was getting behind the wheel, and although I kept telling the race team owner, I was good, the closest I ever got to drive the cars was taking them back to the paddock at 20mph after a race. In the end, Tony Douglas, the owner of DPL Racing [Douglas Print Racing], gave me a proclamation.

If I was that good and that committed, I should come and work for him. By then, I was only nine or ten months into a flourishing career in graphic design. Was I really going to drop it all and leave the bright lights of the West End to work in the then-dodgy East End for a dull print company? Perhaps I was young or stupid or both, but yes I did. I gave up all the promise of a fruitful career in the advertising world to deliver print in a rusty old van to follow a dream. A dream he said that would allow me all the time off I needed to test and race one of his cars. Oh well, why the hell not, I thought.

Taking home a third of the wages I had before, the days were long and pretty boring. If I was not out tackling the London traffic doing print deliveries, I was left to guillotine the print on the factory floor or sent into solitary confinement for hours on end to the finishing room to machine fold thousands of brochures.

Within a few months, I was elevated to print manager. Here, armed with folders of Heidelburg printing plates, each morning, I was given the unenviable task of briefing disgruntled East End printers, twice my age and with ten times my foul language capacity, to work on one urgent job or another. Sometimes, I even had to ask them to work on well into the night. Now, that was scary!

All the while, I still worked with their racing team at weekends, but my dream of stepping into a race car did not seem immediately forthcoming.

Chapter Six

Bangs & Chips

I'm not sure if the regular driver of the Douglas Print Racing car left or was pushed, but my hard work finally paid off, and I was elevated to the position of race driver for the DPL team. Not the most competitive drive on the planet, with a two-year-old Crossle 32F, but absolute heaven to me. An experience to behold as the power-to-weight ratio of these simple single-seater racing cars offers any fledgling newcomer all the tools to begin a career in motorsport. That is if the driver's talent and the gods allowed. Indeed, Formula Ford was THE stepping stone for many, including the likes of Ayrton Senna, Nigel Mansell, and Michael Schumacher. The races were all close and fraught with a mass of overtaking as these open-wheeled cars, all with simple steel space-frame chassis, no wings to give aerodynamic downforce, and relatively narrow, one-make Dunlop tyres, all made for very open competition.

Here, Britain led the way with burgeoning grids in numerous UK Formula Ford Championships. Quite often, there could be over one hundred entries for any one race, which often meant multiple qualifying sessions with a novice race for the slowest, at least two heats for the rest, with a grand finale for the cream of the pack.

The butterflies really began and finished with the standing starts. There was so much to do in the cockpit that once the flag dropped, the nerves instantly fell aside. So, there you sat, waiting for the start. Full-face helmet on, all strapped up and cocooned in, with a pounding heart you could hear your heavy breath on the visor even above the engine. Lined up in qualifying position on what were huge grids that often disappeared around the corner on small start/finish straights such as Brands Hatch, you stared intently at the man with the starter's flag. There was no red/green light system in those days. You would crunch the small gear stick into first and constantly rev the engine. As the starter would raise his flag, you held the revs up high, and as the engine noise reached a crescendo, you hoped you timed it right as the flag fell. In that very second, you would release the clutch and, often with wheels spinning, you would then take off in an almighty cloud of smoke and dust.

If you managed to scrabble through the first few corners without hitting anyone or they you, there was half a chance you could make it to the end. They were normally only ten to fifteen-lap scratch races, but so much could happen in those twenty-plus minutes due to the pure adrenalin overload. At any moment, a car could barrel roll in front of you, or you could bash your tyres with another that could bring one or both of you off or, quite simply, leave your braking too late and, in a fragment of a second, loose the back end and spin-off towards the uninviting barriers.

As Formula Ford was such a great apprenticeship for learning your trade, the pals I had now gotten to know, who were mostly drivers, mechanics, and engineers, all just talked, ate, and slept racing. It was as if the very early 80s, with all its music, fashion, and culture, all ran in another parallel universe. We missed the big hair and even bigger shoulder pads. Because we were at one track or another most weekends, we even missed out on the many concerts and even the marriage of Prince Charles to Lady Diana. We all just lived for racing.

The DPL Racing team was based at Brands Hatch. Tony Douglas, the quiet, ultra-hardworking and straightforward owner of the print works and the race team, rented a pit garage at the circuit. It was ours to use as we wanted. Like many, we prepared our race cars here and used the Kentagon, the then, new five-sided clubhouse bar, as our local. Having indulged in the odd too many beers, sometimes I took to staying overnight at the circuit. Most pit garages had a converted coach parked up behind that doubled up as both transporter and race accommodation. The rear of each coach was for the race cars; the middle normally had a quite often badly built, de-briefing office of sorts, and close to the front end were equally badly put together bunk beds. With the seats of the office used as additional beds, you could put up at least six people while away racing.

For one season, I chose to live in one of these coaches full-time with another overly dedicated Formula Ford driver - Steve. He worked full time on his car while I had to commute back to London.

However, with more time allowed away from the day job for testing and racing, I thought it was great to be on the front line, actually in the trenches, as it were. Although Steve managed a three-year stint, too many smelly socks and a lack of proper shower facilities limited my calling to one season – but boy, we did have some fun.

One summers day, a wealthy amateur popped by the garage looking for someone who could prepare his classic Dulon Formula Ford It required a full gearbox overhaul, new dampers, and some work to the braking system. Never being really into the mechanics in any big way, it was Steve who had the time, the inclination, and the know-how to get his hands dirty. He had a generous three-week deadline as the chap was away sailing on some far-off Caribbean trip.

Steve got to grips with the job in hand in no time at all and, by polishing off the gleaming fibre glass bodywork, just to give it that extra touch, had everything ready within a fortnight. With the work completed, the now immaculate car sat in a corner, ready for collection. Job done; we thought. That was until the mid-week test session came around. With a twinkle in his eye, Steve said why don't we take it out for a spin. Shake it down. What harm could that do? And anyway, it would be a good chance to see if the new components he had put on the car all held together. Within no time at all, I had donned my overalls and helmet and was off down the pit lane and out onto the track.

Although basic, everything worked well in this older car that would soon be consigned to the historic Formula Ford championship, and as I settled in, the lap times quickly came down. What fun, I thought, as I accelerated down the hill from the Druids hairpin and rounded Graham Hill Bend. On the limits of adhesion, there was little I could do about the scene in front of me. Thomas Lauda, a cousin of Niki, had got it all wrong and was spinning like a top. Should I go for the left or the right? Where he was in that one-hundredth of a second wouldn't be where he was in the next. I obviously chose the wrong direction as; with a huge bang I collected him broadside.

What a mess. The nose of this car was completely demolished, and the front wheel was hanging off, as was half the front suspension. As the marshals placed the car on the back of one of the designated Brands Hatch pickup trucks, I thought of all the problems we were about to face. In the first place, we should never have taken the Dulon out on the track without the owner's permission. Secondly, this was a historic car, parts would be hard to find. On top of that, the owner would be collecting the car in under a week.

Steve got to work straight away, stripping the car. He procured a few parts locally, and a friendly machinist around the corner made a few more. I was given the unenviable task of heading up North in our unreliable, rusty old transit van to pick up a nosecone he had surprisingly managed to source. We both worked flat out for four days rebuilding the car and our *pièce de resistance* was a new spray job of the entire bodywork, compliments of another pal who had a paint spray workshop nearby.

With the collection of the now flawless car scheduled for the following day, it was time to celebrate our endeavours. We had done it. We retired to the Kentagon bar, where we met up with a couple of friends who had helped us. They also rented a pit a few stops down and lived in another coach behind the garage. We all made merry until the thought of eating something came up. Apart from the odd sandwich, we had forgotten food for the last few days, and now, with the job done, we were starving. With the bar food long since finished for the evening, we decided to head for the local fish & chip shop in West Kingsdown.

Since it was getting dark, our first stop was to pick up our trusty Transit behind the pits. Of course, try as we might, the bloody thing wouldn't start. To make matters worse, our friend's car was being used that evening by their race driver out on a promise. As the fish & chip shop was to close in the next 15 minutes, what were we to do? Go without or…... Steve looked at me, and I looked at Steve, the same scary thought was going through our minds. Take the race car! We could have used the Crossle, the one I raced but decided on the Dulon. Somehow, all four of us managed to clamber onto this relatively small, cigar-shaped single-seater. Cramped at the very front of the small cockpit, I sat up straight and drove while Steve squeezed into a standing position behind me, holding on to the rollover bar. The two other guys sat awkwardly on either side of the open rear suspension struts with their legs flailing upwards to get some purchase on the bodywork.

With everyone aboard, we fired it up and drove past the pit garages, through the tunnel under the track, and carried on behind the towering grandstands to the back gate. Here, Steve had to undo the padlock and open the big iron gates. With no headlights, the skies seemed darker than ever before as we clocked up the one-mile distance down the A20 to the West Kingsdown turn-off. All the while, the race engine coughed and spat as I tried to keep the revs down so as not to make too much noise. Apart from noticing the rear lights of some cars up ahead as they disappeared into the distance, gratefully, it was a traffic-less run. To our delight, the fish & chip shop was still open, and we feasted ourselves outside before, the last of the chips still in hand, decided we should get back before we ran out of courage, somewhat brought on by the earlier beer intake.

Looking back, we would have had the entire book thrown at us if caught. Drunk driving in a non-road-going car with no headlights, let alone MOT, four up! Nevertheless, our trip back was uneventful, and all of us at least slept on full stomachs.

The following morning, the portly figure of the Dulon owner approached down the pit lane. He was met by the striking sight of his Dulon, resplendent in its revitalised paint job, sitting proudly outside our garage. We stood there with the sincerest smiles we could muster wrapped around our faces, out of view of our tightly crossed fingers behind us. To our surprise and delight, he was overwhelmed with the obvious work we had put in, saying the additional spray job was over and beyond the call of duty. Paying us handsomely, we then helped him load the car onto his trailer and waved him goodbye.

Although we competed in many of the national championships of the time, we didn't really have enough money to do a full season, from start to finish, in any of them. We kind of dipped in and dipped out. We attacked a few of the Dunlop Star of Tomorrow, Esso, and the Towsend Thoresen championship rounds, as well as a few more of the local Champion of Brands races. However, towards the end of that season, I finally won my first Formula Ford race.

Against the might of the ever-evolving-brand new Van Diemen cars, our old Crossle unexpectedly passed the line first. I had managed to get the old car in third place with just a few laps to go. In the closing laps, I could see a tremendous scrap taking place ahead of me between the two front runners. As we approached the infamous Paddock Hill Bend, they clashed wheels, the first-placed car spinning wildly off as the second-placed car hit his back wheels and dramatically barrel-rolled up and over him. Both landed up in the barriers, one upside down.

For the first time, I was leading a major Formula Ford race. In some ways, it was quite unsettling. As a result, my lap times descended perilously downhill. The fourth-positioned car, now quickly promoted to second, over which I had initially built a little leeway, made up ground increasingly quickly. I seemed to have more eyes on my mirrors than on the clear road ahead. Always endeavouring to win, my brains had all but turned to mush as we passed the finish line almost side by side. Nevertheless, I had won.

I would go on to win quite a few races in this category, but it was that first success that still stands out. Probably for all the wrong reasons, but the result of standing first on that podium being warmly interviewed by Brian Jones was incredible.

Of course, not all those races went as well. Still not being able to afford a Van Dieman, we went from a two-year-old Crossle 32F to a one-year-old Royale RP26 for the next season. My Dad, who had practically disowned me for throwing away a good career in advertising to take up racing, announced he was going to attend one of my races at Brands Hatch. He had never been to any of my races before. I would have preferred David Bowie, the Prime Minister, or even God, to have been there then display my efforts in front of my father. Little did I know that he was only coming because he was now chairman of the RREC [Rolls Royce Enthusiasts Club], and along with his comrades, he had taken an invitation to take their old Rollers on a slow lap of the circuit at lunchtime.

The day came, and we slithered our way around on the warmup lap as a recent downpour had left the track sodden and glistening. As we lined up for the start, my nerves tingled more than usual. Not so much because of the waterlogged tarmac, I was good in the wet. However, the presence of my father's eyes somewhere out there kept boring into me. As the flag began to fall and wheels spun, I lowered the revs slightly and gathered some grip. By the time we had plunged down Paddock Hill Bend and raced up to Druids Hairpin, I was in the leading bunch. Tentatively rounding the hairpin and skittering down to Bottom Bend, I was up to third before a huge thwack came from behind. David Hunt, brother of James Hunt, in his heavily Cossack-sponsored Van Diemen, launched himself over the top of my car. Smashing down from the sky, his car skated along the track in front of me upside down in a dramatic shower of sparks coming from his roll over hoop.

With a very bent rear suspension, I came to a halt, crashing into the barrier behind the pits. I was stuck inside the car as my girlfriend came rushing over and shouted out through the net wire fencing. She thought I had hurt myself, and amidst the rain and the noise and, of course, my full-face helmet, she could not hear me shout back that I was fine. I just couldn't get out of the wreck only because I had done my safety belts up the wrong way. Obviously, not concentrating when the nerves got the better of me before the start. By the time the marshals had got me out and I had shared an ambulance with Dave to the medical centre for a quick check-over, a good forty minutes had passed. Finally making my way back to the paddock, my dad had long since departed.

That aside, come the summer, I had begun to make my mark as a front-runner in as many of the races as we could afford to enter. Although a mismatch as far as a championship was concerned, I was now mixing it with the best up-and-comers in the country and doing well. As with any Formula Ford racer, we all had eyes firmly fixed on the big Formula Ford Festival at the end of the year. Here, hundreds from far and wide across the world would enter a three-day festival of racing with heats, semi-finals, and a grand final for the fastest 40 cars.

And so, it was in late August that I clashed with Roberto Moreno and was again sent onward towards the barriers. This time, however, the car had not slung sideways but was speeding at full momentum for an undiluted head-on attack with the Armco. I am forever intrigued by the amount of information you can calculate in a split second. In no more than perhaps one and a half seconds to impact, I had concluded that I could very easily break both my ankles and that I would be laid up in hospital for a couple of weeks and on crutches for at least six more. My whole recovery would take about two to two and half months, but I should be fit enough to do the renowned Formula Ford Festival in late November. As it happened, at the last moment, the car slung to the right and then slammed into the barriers sideways. This led to two missing wheels but not two broken ankles.

Having been in similar positions before and indeed since I still find it amazing just how the mind works as everything slows down in those fractions of a second before the inevitable crunch.

Having got to the Formula Ford Festival, I was hoping for great things. I knew we could never match the big budget of the works-factory teams, but we had steadfastly progressed throughout the season, and by the time the festival came around, we had a solid package with a good, albeit slightly second-rank car. Always held at Brands Hatch, one of the first important tricks was to stay out of trouble at the start. The top end of the grid was slightly uphill on the approach to one of the great bends in UK national motorsport, the notorious Paddock Hill Bend. You enter the bend practically on the crest of the hill before plummeting down what is a very steep section. Only at the end of this long sweeping right-hand corner do you start travelling back uphill to the hairpin.

Being at the end of the main start/ finish straight, you approach what is to begin with a blind corner at speed. Only when you are on it, and the corner falls away in front of you, can you see the rest. Many mishaps have occurred here. One of the most renowned was the clash of the Ferraris on the first lap of the British Grand Prix way back in 1976, the famous incident that took out James Hunt's McLaren.

Unknown to many, there was a secret Formula Ford Club, simply called the Paddock Hill Club. The only endorsement for entry to this exclusive club was to barrel roll off here. Most quick drivers had done it at least once, but I had not. Sadly, it had to be the Formula Ford Festival, where I finally got my turn as we crested Paddock Hill. Having accomplished practice without a scrape, it was early on in one of the first heats that, in the middle of the leading pack, one of the front runners clashed and began to wildly spin backward. Collecting another car in his wake, I was faced with nowhere to go other than up and over. The car hit one of the spinning wheels and immediately launched me into a series of cartwheels before barrel-rolling down the hill and into the bank. Again, in that split second, I first thought, 'Oh my god, I'm about to kill myself'. Feeling as though I had been put in an open tumble dryer that could see both sky and tarmac, my second thought was, 'But if I don't, I've joined the club'!

Chapter Seven
1000 to 1

Racing was my life, but I wasn't progressing. I had a test in the works Van Diemen Formula Ford car at Snetterton and was as quick as any of their factory drivers, but we didn't have the funds to exploit anything as the manufacturer, Ralph Firman, suggested. Formula Three was beckoning but that was treble the cost of a season in Formula Ford. I took a long, hard look at my situation. I was now in my mid-twenties, old even then to become an F1 star. I was still working at the printers, and racing prospects were becoming bleaker by the minute. Perhaps now was the time to look at other options.

I particularly remember reaching a decision after the success of a certain John Crichton-Stuart, 7th Marquess [formerly Earl] of Bute. We all knew him as plain old Johnny Dumfries. He was racing in Formula Ford at the same time as us with much the same standard race car. A likeable and certainly unpretentious chap, he was, at best, a mid-field runner. Looking through the entry list prior to any race, he was not someone you would be concerned about if his name was featured. Then, in my last Formula Ford season, he came into money. Who knows, but I guess it might have been something to do with him getting to his 21st Birthday and really being an Earl. Anyhow, he was then able to run with a top team in a brand-new race car and immediately started to do surprisingly well.

Indeed, later in 1984, long after my decision was made, he went on to dominate the British Formula Three championship, taking home an exceptional 14 victories. From here, he ended up partnering Ayrton Senna at Lotus Formula One in 1986 before winning Le Mans outright in 1988 with the Silk Cut Jaguar Team. Through no fault of his own, the early successes Johnny made were enough to reason that without the funds, you were on a hiding to nothing. With that, I hung up my helmet and walked away. I just couldn't compete.

Armed with my faithful, somewhat dated portfolio, I trod the boards in pursuit of a proper London-based graphic design job again. Now, not in the same league as my old companions, I eventually found gainful employment in a village-based studio in Rickmansworth. Hannibal Graphics was the name, and 'mad Hannibal' was the characterful owner. Tall, gangly, and most of the time very funny, Gerald Hannibal was a carbon copy of Basil Fawlty in Fawlty Towers, the British TV sitcom character played by Monty Python's John Cleese.

We were closing in on the mid-eighties by now, and while hard-working, the studio staff used to try singing along to things such as Malcolm McLaren's Buffalo Girls and a weird cocktail of Hannibal offerings that included any form of obscure, foreign pop cassette tapes. The hard work became harder when suddenly Gerald's temper got lost, and everything from rubber plants to the much-used stereo would head through one of the six second-floor windows we had. At the same time, he would also kick in the plasterboard fittings around the reception area. Fortunately, his temper used to subside as quickly as it grew. To make things better, there was a special handyman, understanding of Gerald's ways, who always had pre-measured and made windows and plaster boards ready for immediate delivery and replacement.

Overall, the studio worked well. Gerald, the boss, was normally a fun guy. But apart from practically racing his new Sunbeam Lotus to the pub, often under a one-lane bridge where wing mirrors got seriously compromised, I was bored. Where was the real fun?

Still living with the lovely Corrine, now a new schoolteacher, I would occasionally visit our local supermarket. This time, I spied on the first Weetabix packet I had designed. Standing out in all its glory from the shelf. I felt a lot better seeing my design printed and boxed on the shelves. By the second and third time, that small euphoric feeling soon wore off.

At much the same time, my Dad, happier now that I had a proper job, invited me to the States. We descended on his greatest pal, Frank Cooke, chairman of the Rolls Royce Club of America, who lived in a small village called North Brookfield in Massachusetts. After being met and greeted at his grand mansion house, we soon departed to his far more basic and much more friendly summer retreat in South Brookfield just a couple of miles down the road. Much more to my liking, this old, strong, pine-smelling wooden building was where I spent my evenings armed with a bag of pretzels and supping gin & tonic. A great sight as the sun went down over the horizon of the Quaboag Pond. The pond is actually a big, picturesque lake, and on the hot summer days, I spent my time learning how to sail and specifically tack on one of the boats Frank owned, quayside. With the wind behind me, managing to sail across the lake was no problem. The effort came getting back. Lost in the swampy end and bitten to bits by bugs, it did not take long to figure out how to tack back.

All good fun, but I was still bored. What was I to do? Almost as an epiphany, it came to me as I bobbed around on gentle waves. Keep my graphic design job and engineer some kind of amateur racing I could do. Maybe the Classic Formula Ford 2000 championship, mostly based at Lydden Hill, a small circuit based in Kent.

With this in mind, I headed back to the UK with all cylinders firing. Once at home, I set about the idea of capturing the imagination of anyone who would listen to sponsoring an old championship for out-dated cars. Hmm, to my surprise, no one did.

A couple of weeks later, I saw that 'Thundersports' was taking off in a really big way. Having replaced the National Aurora Formula One series a couple of years before, the cars were big, spectacular, and noisy. The hour-long races included three separate classes and always had two drivers per car that swapped over around halfway through with a compulsory pit stop. Not only were they often the feature race of the day, but they were also the main support race for the British Grand Prix. And, of course, the two drivers only had to find half the sponsorship budget each. Now, this was something to get my teeth into.

Using my graphic skills and my associations with cheap, friendly printers, I had 1000 brochures printed off in no time at all. With no internet back then, it was harder to find appropriate names and addresses. Nevertheless, in time, I had secured at least around 700 and duly set about mailing them all off together with a personalised cover letter. Indeed, typing up the individual names and addresses with an old typewriter purchased from the local junk shop took longer than anything else. Exhausted by my recent endeavours, I finally popped the last batch into the letter box and sat back and waited for all the responses to come back in. And waited. And waited. And waited.

A week went by. Then another week. On the third week, I had three or four 'due to the economic climate' replies filter through. Now feeling disillusioned, I mustered up just about enough enthusiasm to find another 300 addresses. These mostly to the home construction and DIY industries that had seemed to be particularly thriving in the 80s. I again typed up a cover letter for each and mailed out the remaining brochures I had. Again, I waited only to procure another 'due to the economic climate' note.

When I thought all was lost, I then received three more letters. One asked for more details; another one asked me to come in to see them personally. And then, unbelievably, the following day, yet another note fell on my doorstep again, asking me to come into their offices. Suddenly, I felt as if I was back in business.

Having immediately responded to the interested parties, I went about purchasing several white, 1:18 toy models of a BMW M1 [one of the cars that race in the series] and carefully set about painting the first two up, each in the corporate colour scheme and branding of the potential sponsors. I secured clear Perspex display boxes to provide that final touch.

All set and fully suited and booted, I brought my wares to the only leads I had mustered. First to the Bellway Homes construction company and then to British Gypsum, a company better known at the time for its brand, Artex.

Barrett Homes were sent further details but didn't reply. Bellway Homes, seen first, said they were interested in my proposal, but it came to nothing. However, British Gypsum immediately sent me over to meet the new marketing director of their latest brand, Blue Hawk.

This chap was all fired up when he saw the model of the proposed race car in 3D and, particularly by one of the pictures in my presentation, that of the then-winning Texas Homecaresponsored Thundersports car. You could almost see the cogs in his brain begin to whirl around and how he could make his mark.

He had been given command of a fair-sized marketing budget, not big enough for all the races in the top category, but you could see he was committed to making an impression. In doing so, he wanted the old fuddy-duddy set that had run British Gypsum for an age to sit up and see how he could launch this new, up-and-coming brand firmly into the later part of the 20th century. What could be better than sponsoring a race car, especially one that was competing on British Grand Prix Day? Just short of saying yes there and then, I was sent home to re-work my figures and come back with a plan that had to include all the races and VIP guest hospitality at select races, including the British Grand Prix.

I knew of one driver and racing entrepreneur who could potentially help, Mike O'Brien. Temperamental but ultimately a really nice guy, Mike ran a business called Speedsport Promotions. He had been a challenger in the highly competitive world of Formula 3 and had also recently won the British Sports 2000 championship. He was considering doing the Thundersports series with his race-winning Shrike P15 Sports 2000 car. This was in the lowest class, but together, we could afford to enter all the races. It was perceived not only as a potential winner in its own category but one that could do very well overall on a good day. He also had in his charge, two VIP suites for entertaining his guests and sponsors at the races. One at Silverstone and one at Brands Hatch. We could do the entire series together and use his suites. I was almost home on my figures when Blue Hawk threw a curved ball. Don't come to us, we'll come to you.

Although I said 'certainly', what day, what time? - that was a problem. I had already told the marketing director of Blue Hawk I was a fully-fledged racing driver working out of my own offices called RMD Racing Promotions. What I really was was an equally fully-fledged, disillusioned graphic designer working from a drawing table at Hannibal Graphics.

What could I do but share my dilemma with Gerald Hannibal? And although completely mad most of the time, he understood, and we spent the week changing around the entire studio. All the nice, squashy seats in the reception area, along with the trendy furniture in his office, became mine for the day. Race car posters suddenly appeared everywhere, and we even put up an RMD sign on the front door.

The big day arrived. The chap was offered coffee on arrival from Cherrie. She was really, a graphic design intern, but was handed over to me for the day as my secretary. I had a pre-typed-up contract in hand and by the end of the hour-long meeting, his signature lay firmly fixed on the last sheet.

Let the adventure begin, I said to myself as we bid our farewells.

Chapter Eight
Thundering On

As soon we launched the new race car, fully emblazoned in Blue Hawk livery, with the painted helmet and branded racing overalls stitched to match, I became the Blue Hawk poster boy. My face appeared all over the ads and posters directed towards the DIY market.

I felt I was in the big time, although I hadn't even done more than a handful of testing laps. Time to get my head sorted. Mike brought me down to earth. He tutored me on quick changeovers during pit stops and how valuable seconds, hard-earned on the track, could so easily be lost in the pits. How slowly connecting your safety belts was quicker than nervously fumbling around in the heat of a pit stop. We spent hours practising even before we got to the first race.

By the time the first race came around at Brands Hatch, we were as fully prepared as we could be. The well-presented car looked immaculate. The Blue Hawk boss was down with us in the pits whilst dozens of executive guests from DIY stores stared enthusiastically down at us from their VIP suite overlooking the start line. No pressure, I thought to myself.

Held over the Easter Bank holiday weekend, the Thundersports race was the main event of the day. The sight of all these big cars lining up before their grand rolling start, engines spitting and gurgling like racehorses at the gate awaiting to unleash all their power, was unnerving.

Standing against the pit wall, all I could do was anxiously look on as Mike took the start. The pace car led the field away as the cars made zigzag weaving movements behind to bring their cold tyres up to temperature. At the end of the lap, the pace car steamrolled into the pits as the cars, still trying to keep their individual grid positions, thundered towards the start line. As the still red lights turned to green, at least 15,000 horsepower was fully discharged as each driver's right foot were all firmly planted to the floor. The race was on.

Mike was third in class, but as the laps counted down, he had made his way to the front. I had that uneasy feeling in the pit of my stomach as it was soon my time to don my helmet and restlessly await the mid-distance pit stop. Cars began to roar into the pitlane and amid lots of noise and dust, drivers frantically went about changing over. Trying to keep the butterflies at bay and be as composed as possible, I systematically went through everything Mike had taught me.

Mike was one of the last to come in. I'm sure he was happy leading and wanted to maintain the buffer against second place as long as he could. After all, he had won many races, and I was the new boy on the block he had to hand over his hard-earned lead to.

Having waited for what seemed an eternity, suddenly, the car was there beside me, heat pouring out of the well-used brakes. In the blink of an eye, Mike was getting out the left-hand side as I was getting in from the right. All the pre-race pit-stop practice instilled into me by Mike worked like clockwork in the heat of that important moment. I was soon out on the track and up to speed. Maybe the car in second place was a little closer to me towards the end but as the chequered flag fell, I had done my job and managed to hold on to first position. 'Wow', we had won a Sportscar endurance race!

I felt as if I could have been the winning goal scorer in the World Cup as, getting out of the car, everyone in the team embraced each other. As the congratulations subsided, we made our way to the podium for our interview over the loudspeaker delivered through the familiar, cheery tones of our very own Brian Jones.

By the time we made it up to the VIP suite, the sponsor party was in full swing. For the first time that day, all the nerves and adrenalin had finally dissipated, and as I sat back, the first beer of the day in hand, I reflected on the journey I had been on over the last few months. Quietly, at least in my head, I gave myself a pat on the back.

Of course, we were only at the beginning of this eight-race series, so there was no time to rest on our laurels. Thundersports would head out of the confines of Brands Hatch to other top national circuits such as Oulton Park, Thruxton, and Snetterton, but I would cover even more miles visiting DIY stores on non-race weekends.

Here, the car would go on display, and all dressed up in my racing gear, I had to stand around all day handing out leaflets and escorting children in and out of the small cockpit. With Blue Hawk products now going onto the shelves of every big DIY store, including B&Q, Homebase, Texas, etc. I was gainfully employed, spending as much time helping to get those products off the shelves and into people's homes as I was racing. On the track, we did well and were the team to beat. Out of the 8 races we did, we won our class 5 times, collecting some strong overall positions along the way. We had another memorable win at the British Grand Prix meeting, again held at Brands Hatch, and we easily secured the class series championship. Blue Hawk was happy with us, and by the close of the 1985 season, the ink was already dry on the '86 contract.

Not as many, but some good results also came in 1986. Perhaps due to my focus changing in my eagerness to explore getting into bigger, more high-powered cars. At the same time, I had left Hannibal Graphics and set up my own company specialising in VIP entertainment, including the big national races such as the British Grand Prix and the new, short-lived Birmingham Superprix. I was one of the first to see the potential at the Superprix, and early talks with the organiser led me to rent prime spots, including all the offices over the Ford dealership that stretched the entire length of the pit lane and the school on the first corner along with its grounds. The company offered VIP hospitality for corporate groups, both at the Ford dealership venue and at the school. Here we had a grandstand built in the grounds on the first corner and offered hospitality to different companies in various VIP caterer-prepared classrooms. We sold out to everyone from the Royal Bank of Scotland to Q8, a Kuwait oil company and Formula 3000 sponsor.

I participated in the '86 round in qualifying, but sadly, the actual race was rained off. I just loved the feel of street racing. Being so close to the barriers, the car was left with marks on the side of its rear end as, using all the available road, it was easier to tap the Armco to get the best time coming out of a couple of the tighter corners. Nice war trophies to have if you managed a good time.

As well as the big spectator events, my company offered private track experience days to companies including Blue Hawk. It was on one of these days that I was indirectly introduced to the world of International Sportscar racing.

Chapter Nine
Hospitals and Sultans

So, there I was, propping up my local bar in St Albans, quietly sipping a beer, when a chap I have forever since called Dr Clive walked in. Also standing alone, we soon got chatting. Recently made redundant, but at least with a hefty pay out, Clive Calcutt had a doctorate in pharmacology. I quickly learned that before university, he was brought up on the Suffolk/Norfolk borders and used to visit the Snetterton circuit to witness his heroes at the time, legends such as Stirling Moss and a young Jim Clark, compete there.

Bearded and bespectacled, had there been a Harry Potter novel back then, he could so easily have been one of the main characters coming straight out of a J.K. Rowling book. Intrigued by his knowledge of almost everything in the world and his obvious enthusiasm for motorsport, I invited him along to a track day I had organised at Mallory Park.

At much the same time of year, I had been speaking to John Bartlett. John was an engaging, clever man, if not a tad complex. Not only did he occasionally compete in Thundersports, but he had set up a fledgling team competing in rounds of the World Endurance Sportscar Championship. Now, too old to become a Formula 1 star, that championship was where I wanted to be. He had casually offered me a seat in his Chevron B62 C2 car for the last round of the championship in Malaysia, but I had no idea how to find the budget. I just kept him as sharp as possible, knowing my time would come, somehow, someday.

Coming back to what I was actually doing, rather than what I hoped to do in the future, Dr Clive duly turned up at the same time as all the other guests to attend my Mallory Park Racing Experience. Here guests learned the course in a saloon car, experienced solo laps in a single-seat race car, and ended the day having high-speed passenger laps in the Blue Hawk Sports 2000 car. I could not afford a non-paying stranger to go through the process of all these elements, but I could at least let Dr Clive out on the circuit for high-speed passenger laps.

As well as the Sports 2000 car, we had invited a few other drivers to bring their own cars. They would receive a free test session in return for providing a handful of passenger rides. Unfortunately, my old boss, Gerald Hannibal 'mad Hannibal', was chosen to take the Dr out in his new, race-prepared Renault Turbo. What could possibly go wrong?

Well, a lot. On his third and final lap, Gerald went into Gerrard's, the very fast, sweeping corner after the start/finish line, far too quickly. Not that I personally saw the oncoming bang and crash, but the result was that Dr Clive through no fault of his own, had landed up concussed somewhere in the back of an obliterated Renault Turbo.

Not keen on stopping the track-action, I rushed him immediately to the Leicester Royal Infirmary rather than having the on-circuit ambulance deployed. Arriving, still in my racing overalls, I was asked to take a seat whilst their new patient was fully checked over. With no mobiles in those days, I was surprised when reception called me over to say that a certain John Bartlett had called and left his number. They said the payphones were in the corner. Calling back, John babbled away at me. He said how difficult it had been to get hold of me, asked what the hell I was doing in a Leicester hospital, and, in the same breath, demanded that I make a decision regarding competing in the Malaysian race.

He had offered me a place on the team for £2,500 including the flight. The hotel was one of the sponsors. You must remember that although this was cheap, it was still a lot of money in 1985. As I only had 500 quid to my name, I should have already said no weeks before when he first asked. I was about to stop prevaricating, just come clean and put him out of his misery, when I had one of those light bulb moments. I said I'd call him back.

Dr Clive looked slightly second-hand as he lay there uncomfortably in a hospital bed. I'm sure they had given him something, as he was still very groggy. They wanted to keep him in overnight just to be on the safe side while he wanted to go home there and then. However, I had to take my chance and mentioned in passing to the still bleary-eyed Dr Clive as casually as I could, whether he wanted to join us all in Malaysia as a member of a World Sportscar team. I would pay for his flight and there was no catch other than it would be great if he could lend me £2,500!

Well, Clive wasn't doing anything at the time. He had been made redundant and, as such, wasn't short of cash. He also had a passion for motorsport. Two weeks later, we boarded a 747 bound for Kuala Lumpur. Game on.

Hot, steamy, and rainy, with a stop-off in Bangkok enroute, Malaysia was the most exotic country I had ever visited. While my fellow college students had all gone on to secure great jobs in the advertising world and had travelled due to their income, I had not. I had spent all that time poor in the UK competing at venues such as Brands Hatch. Maybe it was my turn.

We first picked up our new Malaysian Proton cars. Every team competing was offered three each as part of the championship deal. The next stop was to go to the circuit to meet the Sultan of Selangor. We were not particularly well-behaved with the free hire cars provided and, at speed, banged bumpers with fellow participants on our way. At the circuit, we were met by two lovely Malaysian girls who were tasked with generally looking after our team throughout our stay and providing translation whenever and wherever necessary. I was beginning to like this new World Sportscar status and I hadn't even got to the hotel yet. The girls explained that we were about to meet Royalty and had to behave accordingly. They told us to all line up at the start/finish in our racing overalls, not to shake hands, but to bow to a certain level.

Waiting on the windswept circuit for what seemed an age, the Sultan of Selangor finally arrived. Amidst a lot of chanting from close followers, an enclosed, elaborate gold sedan chair, held up by servants, was laid down before us. I must admit, I was expecting some old, turban-wearing King to appear, emblazoned either in state uniform with medals and a sash or a colourful, equally extravagant cultural outfit. He popped out in a black T-shirt and matching baseball cap. From then on, I knew I was going to enjoy this experience.

This was in the now revered era of Group C sports cars. Split into two categories, C1 and C2; these were big and muscular. Set at a minimum weight of just 800kg and 700kg, respectively, they were lighter than a Ford Fiesta, although at least twice the size. They looked similar to Formula One Grand Prix cars and had much the same size engine bolted in the back at the time but had fully enclosed bodywork. Not one bore any resemblance to a regular road car. For us, the team had entered a Goodmans Sound Chevron B62 in the C2 class. Stars of the C1 field then were the likes of the dominating Rothmans Porsches, forever fighting for supremacy over their arch-rivals, the always threatening Silk Cut Jaguars. Known simply as the Silk Cats.

Come the first practice day, we were short of a race part and a mechanic and I went up the pit lane garages to find one to borrow. We landed up in the very top end and it was the famous Rothmans Porsche team who had exactly what we needed and were happy to help. Not something you could consider doing these days. It was here, so long after my school days, that I again met my hero, Derek Bell who had just finished chatting to one his fellow Rothmans drivers, Jackie Ickx. Slightly discombobulated, he asked what I was doing in Malaysia. I confidently replied, racing against you, Derek.

I must admit, I can't remember much of the 800km race itself now. I remember how hot and humid it was. I had never worn three-layer fireproof Nomex overalls, underwear, gloves, and a full-face helmet in 35-degree heat before. There was also my own virgin experience of having so much unbridled power to hand and how I had to very quickly learn how to release the throttle quickly but carefully to not spend most of my time facing the wrong way. The grunt I had never experienced before coming from the 400+bhp plus Ford Cosworth DFV engine right behind me. This was the same power plant that had been used so successfully in Formula One for many years.

Towards the end of the race, I was in the cockpit when a tropical rainstorm suddenly descended with great force. The team signalled to me to stay out. Not easy on slick, non-treaded tyres, but uncomfortably slithering around I made up ground as others stormed into the pits for wets. Our driver line-up of Swede Kenneth Leim, fellow Brit Robin Smith, and myself finally came home 5th in the C2 class. Not an outstanding result, but a result all the same. In his last race before retiring, 6-time outright Le Mans winner Jackie Ickx, along with Jochen Mass, would win the race for the Rothmans Porsche team. And although Derek Bell and Hans Stuck, running in the sister Porsche 956 would fail to finish, they ultimately secured the World Championship that weekend on cumulative points scored over the season.

After the podium celebrations, a much-welcome shower, and a quick change out of sweaty overalls, all the teams were invited by the Sultan to attend his 'end of race' party. This was held in his grand Shah Alam palace, which stood obtrusively large and proud on a hilltop overlooking the circuit. Here, we all indulged in a palatial spread of fine cuisine and waiter-served champagne and partied into the wee small hours. We also bore witness to the championship-winning Rothmans Porsche team taking to the stage above the dance floor and treating us all to their version of the funky chicken.

To me, it was a fine set of firsts. First time abroad anywhere other than a camping trip to St Tropez. My first time racing in such extraordinary heat. A first time competing on the world stage in an international status, the World Sportscar Championship round, and the first time driving a 400+bhp racing car. I loved it. I wanted more. What next?

Chapter Ten
The Road to Le Mans

It all seemed to come about so fast in 1986. John Bartlett and I went to the opening round of the World Sportscar Championship at Monza. Set just outside of Milan, the Italian 'Temple of Speed', Monza was where the Chevron was to compete next in the hands of a different driver line-up. The outing was disastrous; the car was unprepared and uncompetitive, and after a huge row with the boss of Chevron, we flew home early. On the plane back, we devised a crazy plan to 'somehow' purchase the Arundel Group C sports car. As we belted up, I quipped that taking both our surnames, we could rename it the 'Donbar'. For obvious reasons, John preferred the 'Bardon'.

The brainchild of Eddie Arundel, now formally known as Edward Fitzalan-Howard, 18th Duke of Norfolk, had commissioned its build after competing in numerous other makes and obviously liked the thought of competing in a car personally named after him. Raced by the likes of big Sportscar names such as James Weaver and Jonathan Palmer, John had heard this pretty car, again powered by a Cosworth DFV, was now up for sale.

With the help of John's main sponsor, Goodmans Sound, and with further input from my own fledgling company, loans, and sponsors, we somehow managed to purchase the car. First to run in the Silverstone 1000kms, an entry was secured for the Le Mans 24 Hour race. A few weeks later, all resplendent in its new livery and to great fanfare, we launched our attack on Le Mans at the Dorchester Hotel.

We first had to drop the car off the transporter around the back entrance of the hotel onto double yellow lines. This to the delight of a couple of Mayfair traffic wardens delivering the chance to take some great pictures of us duly being awarded a parking ticket. Oh, what fun we could have had if Facebook, Instagram, or TikTok were available back then.

We rolled the car into the hotel's ornately decorated ballroom and centrally positioned it next to the podium. Making sure white sheets covered the car from top to toe, awaiting press and sponsors, followed by our own families and friends, were invited through the gigantic entrance doors. With a glass of champagne in hand, a hubbub of enthusiastic chatter filled the air. Then, to the haunting sounds from the famous Jean-Michelle Jarre album *Rendezvous*, the lights dramatically began to dim.

Dr Clive stepped up to the podium while waiters quietly filled up half-empty glasses. Only when the whole chamber lay silent Dr Clive in his extremely articulate and commanding voice, began. He thanked everyone for attending and gave his introductory patter. And then, timed to perfection, he authoritatively announced, 'Ladies and Gentlemen, I give you the Bardon', just as the bikini-clad

Goodmans girls swished away the covers, unveiling to all our fearsome Le Mans' challenger. What would we ever have done without the Doctor?

What a great day, but I had to take time out to collect all my thoughts. Was I dreaming? We were about to compete in THE most legendary of all sports car races on the planet on the hallowed ground, known throughout the globe as Le Mans.

The next stop was pretty much where I started the story. Climbing up those famed steps above the pits.

Chapter Eleven
Tragedy and Jubilation

The first big recollection of that highly memorable week was towards the beginning of it. Our all-British driver line-up consisted of me, Nick Adams, and a cheery chap called Richard Jones. Richard was already a seasoned campaigner at Le Mans and, as such, chose to take me under his wing. As the transporter was being unloaded and the mechanics busied, making everything as ship-shape as possible within the confines of the then small box pits, Richard took me on a recce of the track.

I couldn't be more excited. Having missed the test weekend a couple of weeks previously, this would be my very first ever glimpse of the nearly 13.5km circuit, one if not the most legendary in the world. With two-thirds of the lap on public roads closed later before practice started, we slowly drove around, making sure we weren't hit by all the passing commuters or trucks busily getting on with their normal Tuesday work. Constantly stopping our little Renault 5 hire car, we would then walk the track where he felt the most crucial or dangerous parts were.

Having told me the best approach to and out of the celebrated Tertre Rouge corner, we headed onto the infamous Mulsanne Straight, the fabled 3.7 miles/ 6km Hunaudieres. In those days, before the chicanes, and not that I understood this at the time, you would travel end to end in under a minute. Just sit back and think about that.

We then quietly droned our way along this rather narrow, truck-pitted piece of tarmac, the N1, now the D338 to Tours, for what seemed like an age. Richard explained shifting up the gearbox from 3rd to 4th to 5th.

Three-quarters of the way down, he pulled off to the side of the road. Getting out of the car, he illustrated that I would have been flat out for a relatively long time and pointed out that where we had now stopped, there was a slight hump in the road. In the far distance, the straight veered right. He then revealed that when I hit this hump at speed, I should count to 3 and turn. I had no idea what he was really talking about because it felt that you needed binoculars to even make out the slight kink in the road that still seemed so far ahead.

Then he delivered those words I will never forget. Believe me, he said, at over 200mph, that little kink ahead is a BEND. Not allowed to lift, by the time you have counted three, you will be there right on that bend ahead, and if you didn't steer the wheel slightly right, you would miss the apex but possibly not the trees.

Of course, he knew that although I had been pretty successful in national races, I had never travelled anywhere approaching 200mph before. And certainly not taken a bend flat out at that speed. Having been casual with my homework and not honestly knowing that he was talking about the notorious kink on the Mulsanne Straight, I could see then that I was quickly verging towards being with the big boys, and this was going to be a whole new ball game.

I suppose, in total, we must have must have spent a good two hours or more going around, exploring that lap. Taking notes along the way. However, to put a racing lap into perspective, Hans Stuck delivered the fastest lap the year before in a Porsche 962. He lapped the entire 13.5km circuit in 3 minutes 14 seconds. That's an average speed of 156mph/251kmh. Average.

The first daytime practice held on a Wednesday afternoon was a fiasco. We had all sorts of clutch and gearbox problems. Being the rookie driver of the team, I was third in line to take the wheel. With all these time-consuming issues taking priority, my first chance to experience the circuit in full daylight never came.

We were still working on the car when the night-time session began. I'm just sat there in the car, all belted up, patiently waiting for the crew to finish off. As dusk begins to fall, a certain additional aura creeps over the place. Big shadows appear across the pit lane, and the flashes from the intrusive press cameras become ever more prominent as the light fades.

With ear plugs in and a full-face helmet strapped on, you can hear your respiration as it fights its way through the fireproof balaclava that also covers everything other than your eyes. Exterior sound, however; the pit lane sirens, the quick lift air jacks, and the commentators booming out the latest news over the speakers, all become quiet and muffled.

With the rear bodywork back on, catches snapped into place, and the crew chief signalling me to fire up the engine. The whole car vibrates as the Cosworth DFV engine bursts into life. It's almost a final reminder that you're now about to leave the safety of all that has come before and head out into dark, unknown territory.

As I crunch in first gear, blip the engine, and rumble out of the pit lane and onto the track, the apprehensions of the day, indeed the week, subside. This is it. Only now do I feel as if I am really a competitor in this magical event. But, blimey, I thought, it's dark out here, and I don't really know where I'm going.

The power comes in a rush straight away. The beautiful, undeniable noise punched out by the iconic Cosworth 3-litre V8 behind me seems to disappear over my gasping. The high pitch is still there, but other than the engine note itself, I don't listen. Concentrating like hell, eyes glued to the road, I find my way down the hill to the Esses. A short squirt on the power, and in seconds, you arrive at the illustrious Tertre Rouge corner, the right-hand bend that leads on to the revered Mulsanne Straight. Crucially important to get right in so many ways. Too slow in means you'll be too slow out. Too fast in, and you're likely to be sideways coming out. Either way, any fraction of a second you lose here will have magnified to seconds by the end of the nearly 4 miles straight. Carrying the speed in, feeding the power on through the apex, and drifting to the left-hand side on exit is the only way.

That said, on my first lap ever, in the dark, this was not so much about perfect laps but just getting around. At least I had got as far as the Mulsanne. At home, I had keenly watched the helicopter TV footage of cars blasting down here. The cars would go faster than the choppers, but they managed to keep up for a little while before the race blistered away in the distance. Now, it was my turn. Snatching quickly up through the gears, was there no end in sight to what seemed like an ever-narrowing piece of road? Added to this, if you were to assume a Straight is where you can loosen up a little, check your dials, and relax clenched hands, you would be wrong. Driving a low-slung, stiffly suspended car over the truck-pitted grooves of what is normally a public road compelled the making of constant steering adjustments. This was particularly prominent in changing lanes when, on occasion, you had to move over to pass or be passed.

I was now travelling faster than I had ever been before in my life, and the car was still accelerating. On and on, both the dispatch of power and the speed continued.

Now flat out, the blazing lights in my very small rear-view mirrors were of top category C1 cars fast approaching. In my C2 car, I am now travelling at over 200mph, but these guys are coming up on me at 230. Passing at a good 20 mph faster, I try to steady myself and the car as I see them pass, taillights glowing.

It seems like I have been on this scary straight for half an hour. In reality, it has been 30 seconds. But where was this hump I was supposed to come across? The one Richard had told me all about. Would I be able to pick it out? My eyes must have been on stalks as I passed by blurred, eerie outlines of houses and trees to each side, totally focused on the road ahead. Suddenly, it's there in front of me. I count to three as told and turn. The apex of the kink, very much a bend as he declared, thunders past my right-hand wheels in a split second, and I'm around and safely on my way toward the end of the straight. I somehow get through my three practice laps and come in. Relieved and feeling good that at least the unknown was known. Well, to a certain extent.

Releasing my safety belts and awkwardly clambering out of the cockpit, I notice how the steam rises from my head in the colder evening air as I take off my sweat-drenched helmet. Sternly, the crew chief immediately gives me my debrief. He tells me I was nearly a minute too slow. The team is not allowed to compete with just two drivers, so he says that if I didn't address the situation quite dramatically next time out, they would all have to go home. Now, a few seconds off is slow. A minute is a lifetime! To make it worse, I thought I had done ok. Jeez.

As I finally put my head to the pillow, long after the midnight finish of practice, my sleep was to be unsettled and restless. This was not a good start. Had I braked far too early or taken too many confidence lifts? Maybe I didn't plant the power on quickly enough coming out of the fast sweepers. Could I have gotten too sideways coming out of the slow corners, or could I have cut that apex finer? So much to take in and evaluate with so little time. We had just one daylight and one night-time session to go. All three drivers to qualify. And that was tomorrow. I would then be responsible for the entire effort coming to nothing. Everyone going home. The massive expense of the entry, bringing over the transporter, car, the tyres, engines, and all the equipment, let alone the crew, their wages, accommodation, and sustenance. No pressure, I thought, as I finally drifted into some form of listless doze.

Anxiously, I tried to have breakfast but just idly moved the bacon around the plate. This was going to be a big day, and I thought that maybe I was just not up to this. Le Mans is big in every way.

Much later on in my career, through a pal, I met Allan McNish straight after his very first exploratory laps of Le Mans. First, as a F1 test driver, he went on to race for Toyota in Formula One, as well as winning no less than three Le Mans 24 Hour races outright. Well, on that day, he was behind the Le Mans pits, white as a feather and completely speechless. Finally, he managed to murmur that in all the years on top of his game, including six seasons in the top category Formula 3000 championship, he had never, ever been anywhere so fast, so narrow, and so lacking in run-off areas.

Had I known even the very best could be blown away by this place ten years earlier, it might have given me more assurance. Of course, I didn't, but nevertheless, I headed off back to the circuit, determined not to let the side down. For one thing, the whole team had booked that week away, and for another, I would have come across as a complete and total bell-end. Never to draw breath around any piece of racing tarmac again.

Fortunately for me, the last day of qualifying was kinder to me. I carried a little more speed onto the Mulsanne and kept totally flat through the kink. This, together with the act of braking a bit later, keeping myself clean and tidy through the slower corners, and accelerating harder and faster out of the sweeping bends, got me, indeed all of us, into the race. I had qualified. We had qualified!

Granted, we were still in a fairly lowly position. But this was an unknown car put together in just a few weeks. We were one of the private teams set against the works teams; we were running a 225mph max C2 car as opposed to a 245mph max C1 car, but we were in the bloody race. The most mythical Sportscar race on the planet.

On Friday, we partied. For the engineers and mechanics, it was a day to fettle the cars, if necessary, change the engines, and put all the final sponsor decals in place. For the drivers, it was a day to relax and enjoy, looking forward to an early night and a good sleep before the big day ahead. Oh, how I wished it ended up thus. In fact, we ended up in a restaurant famous for being where HRH Queen Elizabeth II dined and whose complimentary note and signature lay proudly in the visitor's book. Not one to usually have more than a beer, Richard introduced me to the delights of a good, very expensive red wine. I can't remember much about the return to our B&B accommodation, but I was duly on parade first thing in the morning. Albeit, feeling slightly worse for wear.

Race day had arrived. What an amazing experience it was. Close to 200,000 fans crammed into the packed arena of giant start-line grandstands. While a further nearly 100,000 perch themselves in prime positions around the rest of the circuit. Much of the pre-race action is centred on the start line. Here, marching bands strut up and down the main straight, powerfully pumping out the French national anthem, while bikini-clad promotional girls, quite often surrounded by an army of press and photographers, wave enthusiastically to the crowds. Up in the skies, the Patrouille Aerobatique de France [the French equivalent of the Red Arrows] put on a stunning aerobatic display before their final low-level dash along the pit straight. As they make their final run, the crowd cheers as they roar past, leaving a smoke trail of red, white, and blue.

Long before the downtown Friday 'Grand Parade des Pilotes', drivers were presented to the public on the startline race day. All geared up in freshly cleaned race overalls, we waited our turn to step up onto the back of one of the circuit's cabriolets. Bums on the rear shelf with feet lightly purchased on the back seat, the three of us were then taken slowly along the pit straight, waving to the throngs who had congregated to cheer us on before taking to their seats for the start. The parade car would then go up onto a high ramp set in front of the huge main ACO grandstand. Here we were all interviewed in English, which was then translated back into French, both translations going out to everyone around the circuit by loudspeaker.

Parade over, to great applause, the race cars are now quietly wheeled out by their crews. These monster 200mph+ machines, standing proud in their polished colour schemes, each emblazoned with a multitude of sponsors, all dazzle and glitter in the afternoon sunshine.

They are placed in custom 'ear of corn' formation. A tradition that goes back to when drivers lined up and ran across the track to their cars at the start. The grid now opens up to TV crews, journalists, and photographers who descend upon this elite group of contenders whilst circuit VIPs and celebrities look on. It's now our turn to join our cars on the grid for the final festivities, giving interviews, signing autographs, posing for photographs, and accepting well wishes from friends and sponsors. We are joined by our own 'Goodmans Girls' who strategically pose around the car as further pictures are taken.

The atmosphere becomes ever more electrifying as with 30 minutes to go, the grid is cleared of everyone. The teams moved their cars onto their grid positions. 20 minutes to go, the choice starting driver for each team, usually the one who qualified the fastest, dons his helmet and is belted in. Nick Adams in our case, sits there as the latches are snapped when the doors go down.

Pit lane sirens ring out as the grid is fully cleared. I apprehensively stand on the pit wall, together with the likes of Dr Clive setting up his timing watches, waiting anxiously for the start. 15 minutes to go, and a complete cacophony of engine sounds crack and burst into life. The track vibrates to the deafening din of 50 cars erupting, ready for the off.

Pace car lights flashing, the 10-minute sign goes up. Engines revving, smoke fills the air as the entire grid moves off behind the pace car. Then, as the formation drones away into the distance, silence. As the cars make their way around the pace lap, you can even hear the babble from the stands adjacent. This slow lap will take time. The cars weave along the Mulsanne as they add heat to their cold tyres. They do the same through the Porsche Curves and then nervously crystallise back into a pattern as they make their way to the start. The clock turns to 4 pm as the entire field, holding their grid positions, heads towards the start line lights. As the pace car peels pitward, the red lights turn green. In a surge of unadulterated power, clouds of smoke, and deafening sound, the cars roar by and into the first corner. The race is on.

Having thought we were falling into some kind of natural rhythm; we were then engaged in a number of time-consuming pit stops. A crack in the windshield, caused by one of our lovely Goodmans girls sitting on it before the start, got bigger. As it was the only one we had, we just had to tank tape it up. The accelerator pedal kept sticking and had to be adjusted. We had to change the battery terminal and fix the exhaust manifold. At one point, we even journeyed out to the Mulsanne when Nick broke down. We could show our support and shout from the Armco but weren't allowed by the rules to physically help in any way. Any outside service is an instant disqualification. Armed with only the spanners that had been previously tank taped to the inside the cockpit, he somehow got the car going again.

My first stint, however, goes to plan. At least I can see where I'm going. A week before, I had a bad cold. As I sped down the Mulsanne at the length of a football pitch a second, I wondered how far I would cover if I sneezed. Concentrate, I thought.

Within what felt like no time, I was signalled that my turn had come to an end. In those days, there was no speed limit in the pit lane. Rushing in, pit-lane siren signalling that I was arriving, I think I ran over at least two or three photographers' stray toes. If you wandered about as cars came in, it became part of the course back then.

Already loosening my belts, arriving in the pit lane, I search for the team box. I then see our black pit signal board with a bright yellow STOP sign and downward arrow. Fully unbelted, I jump out as Nick gets in. A chaotic cocktail of noise follows as quick lift jacks push the car up and wheels are changed by mechanics armed with pneumatic guns. All the while, the outgoing driver is shouting to the incoming driver anything he may have learned through full-face helmets as another mechanic is cleaning the fly-ridden windscreen. Doors slam shut, engine fires up. First gear found, and with a little wheelspin the car blasts back out.

The brilliance of the day was now fading as the clouds naturally darkened. A fluorescent glow appears from the pits as night-time beckons. The lights of the adjacent grandstands come on one by one as the colours of the funfair begin to sparkle in the distance. The smell of brake dust, exhaust fumes, and burning rubber is forever present in the air. Headlights begin to blaze a path into the night as these 200mph monster machines still scream past at unabated speed. Anxiously waiting in the wings, I ponder what the night might demand from us.

Close to three in the morning, and it's my turn again. Leaving the lights of the funfair and the late-night camera flashes behind me, I once again head out onto the Mulsanne. With a blackened sky and little light, I hurtle along, shifting ever up through the gearbox. Then just as I snatch top gear, I suddenly hit stones and debris that have just spewed right across the track. I see a huge ball of flame to my right. Someone has obviously gone off. And gone off in a very big way.

Looking back, it's bad to recount, but I was in racing mode, not humane mode. Pumping with adrenaline, my first thoughts were, 'he could have ruined my tyres. Maybe I should pit to have them checked out.' Halfway around the lap, marshals begin to frantically wave yellow flags. Pace cars come out to slow down and shepherd the field as the race is effectively neutralised. I decide to stay out and join the end of the closest crocodile tail.

While the pace car drives at full speed, squealing through the corners on the limits of adhesion, the race cars lazily drone around behind. Touching little more than 100mph on the straights, engine temperatures begin to bubble up. It seems to take forever to lap the course. Reaching the same spot, the car is still ablaze, but fire crews are already on the scene, and I can make out dark figures moving about in the forest. A line of marshals stand in the middle of the road, keeping us to the left-hand side of the track. Their hands push downwards to signal, keeping our speeds slow and steady.

A car had obviously launched itself over the barriers, and the outcome for the driver looked far from good. In the darkness and night-time mist, everything seemed to be happening in slow motion.

All felt murky. The figures are blurred. An eerie sense of foreboding descends.

I stay out for another hour, just following the pace car. Eyes forever on the temperature dials, I can hear the engine uncomfortably burble as I make out the fast-approaching dawn. With each slow lap that passes, the events of the night unfold before me. First, the service vehicles arrive, the blaze is put out, then the ambulance departs, and engineers start to rebuild over 100 meters of barriers destroyed in the accident. First, one side, then the other.

It wasn't until later, when I was out of the car, that the news filtered through that 32-year-old Jo Gartner, driving a Kremer Porsche 962, had been killed. It was reported that just after 3 am, as he was just snatching top gear on the Mulsanne at around 320kmph, the Porsche suddenly swerved left and violently hit the guardrail. The barriers gave way, and on forcefully hitting a concrete wall that lay behind, the car ricocheted back across the track before somersaulting over the barriers on the right. Disintegrating over 200 metres, the remains of the Porsche landed upside down as its fuel tank exploded.

To this day, the cause of the accident remains unclear. One eyewitness said he thought he saw the brake lights very briefly light up just before he swerved. This would suggest he came across a stray animal or hit a lost piece of debris from another race car. Some believe it was a drastic suspension or gearbox malfunction.

Although never substantiated, another mooted the idea that he came across kids running across the track, playing dare. Something that was apparently witnessed earlier on that night.

As dusk broke, nearly three hours under pace car conditions, the race was back on. Having got through the night, a barrage of technical problems befell us again. We lost time in the pits, bleeding the worrisome clutch, changing the battery, and lubricating the transmission. This all culminated in a two-hour stop for a full clutch change. With no chance of even being classified now, it would have been better to retire. However, having hauled the car around into the dying hours, shouting and screaming, everyone wanted to see us take the chequered flag. I was back in the car for the last stint. The sun was now shining. The track was relatively empty. A number of journeyed cars were looking less than healthy, but ours, for a change, was fully on song again. It was great to be alive and living these moments.

With just three laps to go, everything changed yet again. A pit signal was thrown at me saying 'IN'. In those days, the team signallers were based on Mulsanne Corner, the halfway point around the circuit. Telephone messages were relayed to them by the pits.

In, I thought. With three laps to go, you want me in? I'll just ignore that and see if it's really true when I come around again. With two laps to go, the same board came out. To hell with that. We're going to take that bloody chequered flag, come what may. I was determined to finish my first Le Mans. With one lap to go, I didn't even bother to look at the pit boards as I blasted out of Mulsanne Corner.

Sure enough, the chequered flag came down. It was elaborately waved for the winner and held steady as the rest of us crossed the start/finish line for the final time. Indeed, it was my childhood hero, Derek Bell, who crossed the line in first place. His 4th Le Mans win. But 'hey', we had got to the end. And what do they say, everyone who gets to the finish of a 24-hour race is a winner. I was on top of the moon.

As we went around on our slowing down lap, hundreds of smiling marshals jumped the Armco and lined up on the actual track itself to congratulate us. Just leaving us enough room to file past, they all waved, clapped, blew their horns or vigorously swayed their coloured flags from side to side. It was like the whole world had come out to celebrate the achievements of everyone who had finished. Years on, it was something that I will never forget.

At the end, we were directed to Parc Ferme. A supposedly closed area for stewards to check the cars over to make sure they have kept racing regulations before releasing them back to the teams. However, before I had even gotten out of the car, both wing mirrors were torn off by random souvenir hunters. Another group of bystanders began dismantling the rear wing before the officials turned up. Ah, at least finishing showed we were contenders.

Walking back to the pits, I was greeted by more admirers of our recent endeavours. We were certainly not winners, but by just finishing, we felt accomplished. I guess they did as well. We had done it. My back and shoulders must have been joyfully slapped a hundred times before I got to our garage. There, to greet me was the team, Nick, and Richard. They enthusiastically explained why I had been told to pit in those final laps. The side-mounted battery had fallen out of its compartment. It was trailing along the circuit, only held on to the car by its leads. Apparently, the spark trail it was leaving behind was as good as any New Year's firework display.

Blissfully pleased that I had ignored the signal, the drivers proceeded to haul me up above their shoulders and paraded me around. Brave of them, I thought, as I must have smelled beyond rank. That first year, I had one set of race overalls to last the entire race. It was wet and clammy after my very first stint. After 24 hours, I am sure it could have walked back to our B&B by itself.

We were staying in a rather tired bar-come restaurant with rooms in Connerre, a little village outside Le Mans. After a hot shower, I was feeling almost human again as I joined the others downstairs in the bar. The team, a few sponsors, and even my dad were there. All geared up ready to party the night away, we began by clinking our beer bottles in toast of our recent adventure. After two or three beers, we then took seats in the rather pokey dining room the establishment had. Around twenty-five of us ordered all three courses off the very best menu the unshaven and generally unkempt proprietor had to offer. Wine flowed all around as we waited while he beavered away in the kitchen. The soup arrived first. Uncontrollably bowing down, my head fell slowly and quietly straight into the soup. My party was over. A deep, deep sleep was beckoning.

The next day, I came down to see the place in total disarray. Obviously, a party had been enjoyed. Plates of half-eaten food remained on the tables. Empty beer bottles and wine glasses lay all around on the tables, in the bar, and on the floor. Three sponsors were still up and sat huddled together in a corner, still nursing the remains of the red wine. My pal, Mini-Malc, I found uncomfortably passed out on the football table. Having been allocated a room, for some unknown reason, my dad was discovered snoring away in the back seat of his own motor in the car park.

Of the 50 cars that started the race on Saturday, 27 fell abandoned by the wayside. Only 23 made it to the end. Save the odd pee stop, our very own Dr Clive spent all 24 Hours on the pit wall armed with his trusty stopwatch and time sheets. Out of respect, Kremer called in their second Porsche, driven by Yver, Striebig, and Cohen-Olivar, at 3.30 am that morning. It wasn't until I got back to the UK, and the adrenaline had been fully erased from my veins, did the human impact of that tragic night hit home. Six years later, I was to drive for the mighty Kremer Porsche team, but I'll leave that story for another chapter.

Birthday boy. A three-year-old full of pedal power

A few years later, with a little more pedal power, in the Gulf Kremer Porsche K8 at Le Mans

Early 80's days competing in Formula Ford 1600. Royale RP23 and before Crossle 32F

Shell Oils

From desperately seeking a sponsor in Formula Ford to eventually securing a great one with the British Gypsum brand 'Blue Hawk' for Thundersports

Thundersports: Racing and winning in the Blue Hawk sponsored Shrike P15, Class III, in 1985 & 86 and with the Arrows F1 based Harrier LR5, Class II, in 1987

My first World Sportscar Championship race at the Shah Alam circuit in Malaysia 1985

Dr Clive on the grid at Fuji Speedway, Japan

Looking all hot and bothered in Jerez, Spain, with my then girlfriend Corrine

My first Le Mans outing, driving the Bardon DB1 in 1986

And then racing into what would be a dramatic night ahead

Celebrating finishing my first Le Mans with helping hands from Nick and Richard

01

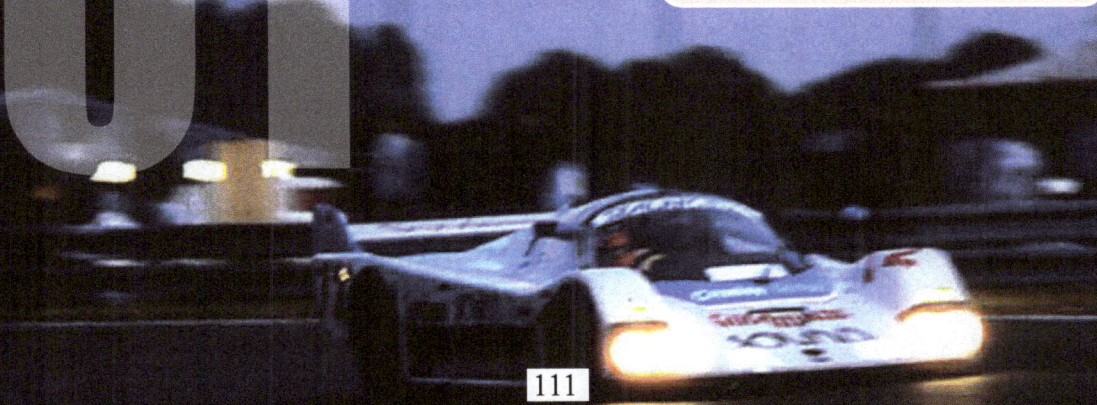

02

1997 and my second Le Mans participation in the Penthouse Bardon DB2

My third was in the Lucky Strike Argo JM 19C in 1988

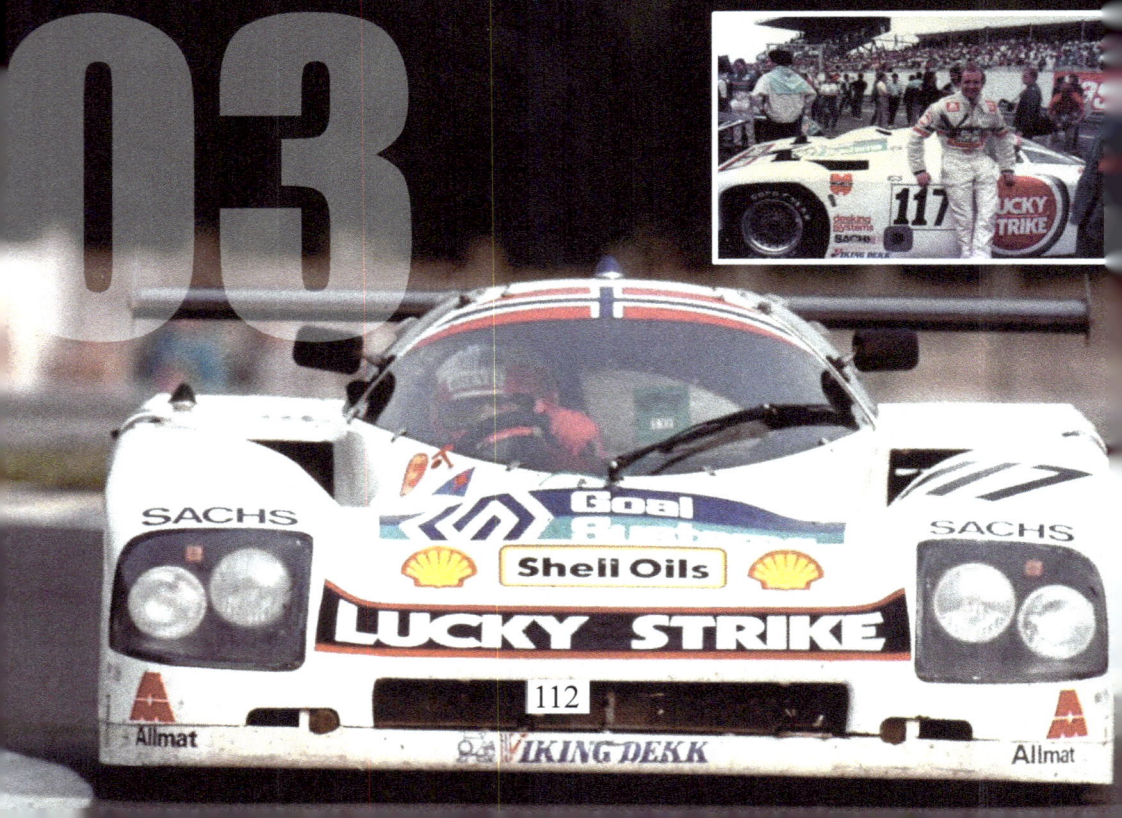

03

112

And winning Class A in the Willhire 24 Hours 1990

113

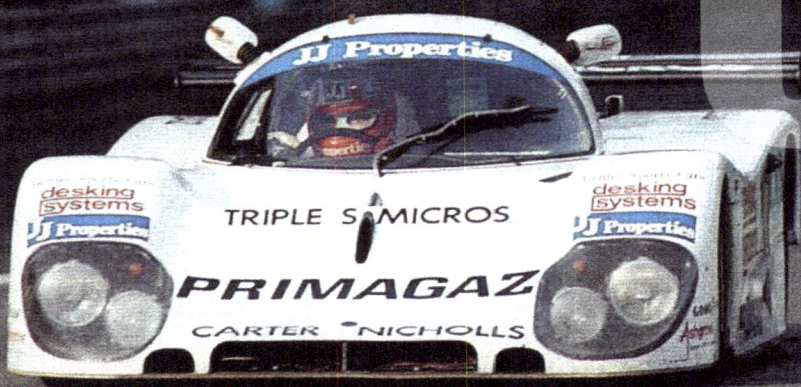

Thundering down the Mulsanne in 1989 in the works factory Tiga GC289

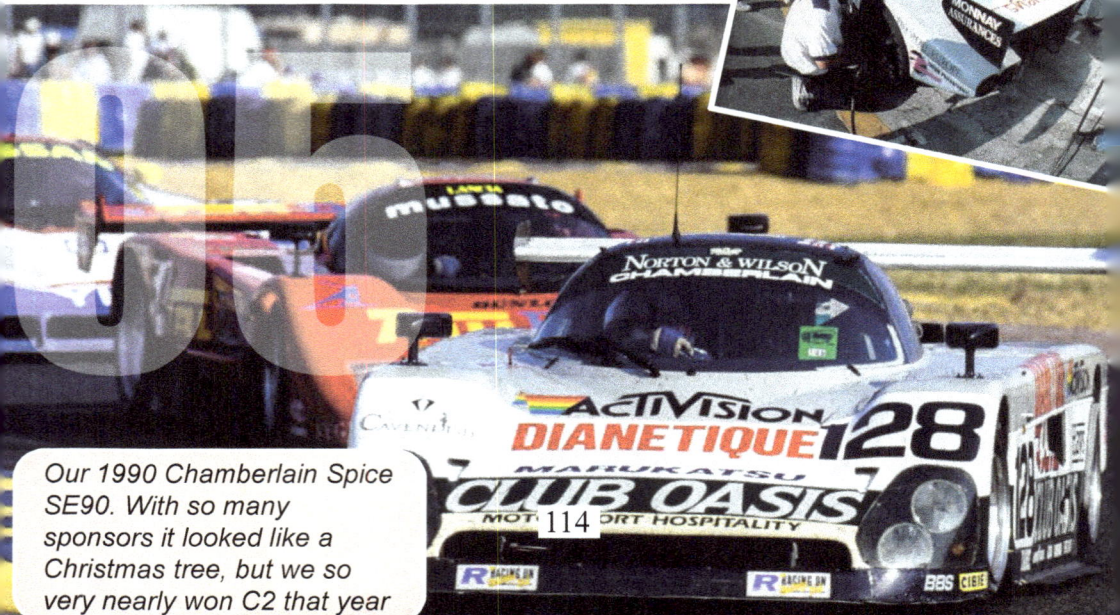

Our 1990 Chamberlain Spice SE90. With so many sponsors it looked like a Christmas tree, but we so very nearly won C2 that year

114

06

1991 Financial Times Chamberlain Spice SE89C with (from left to right) Nick Adams, myself and Richard Jones

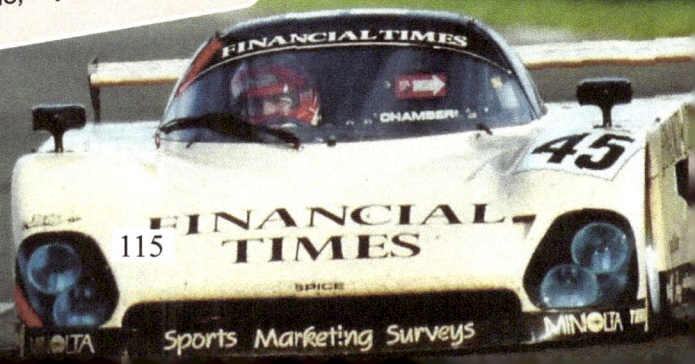

Kremer Racing Le Mans 1992 line up (from left to right): Manuel Reuter, Charles Rickett, me, Almo Coppelli, Giovanni Lavaggi and John Nielsen

Sweaty debriefing with Achim Stroth, Kremer's superb team manager

Below: Being interviewed by revered journalist and motorsport commentator Bob Constanduros

Atrocious rain for much of the time but what a magnificent car the Kremer Porsche 962 CK6 was

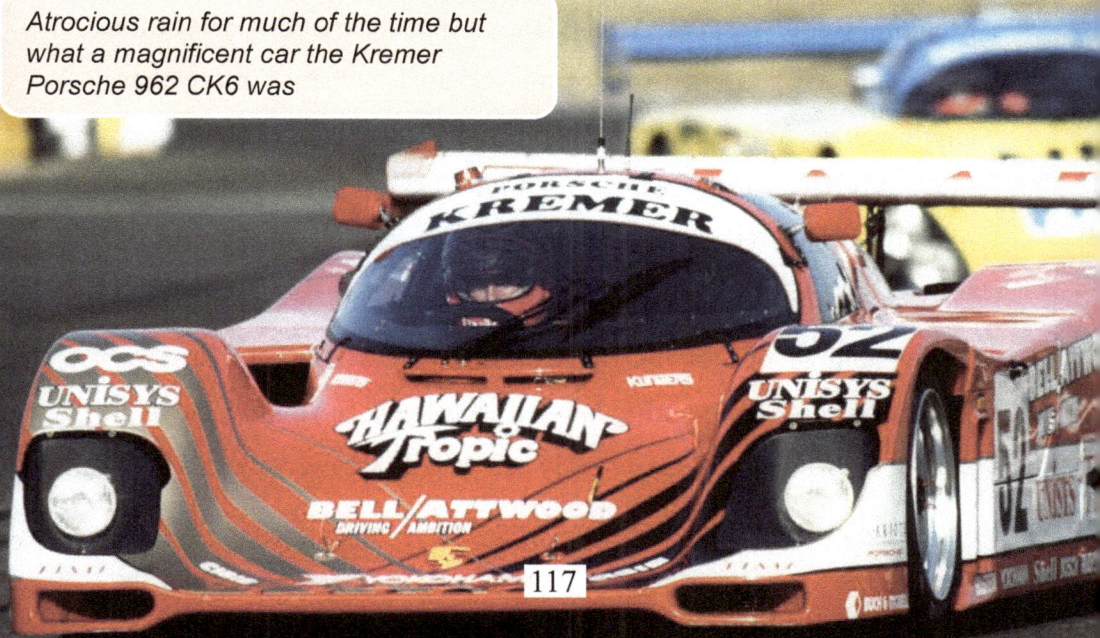

Chapter Twelve
Chequered Challenges

With a few more class wins, I saw out the rest of '86 racing the Blue Hawk Thundersports car. I also participated in selected rounds of the World Endurance Sportscar Championship when commitments and sponsors allowed.

The World Championship rounds always delivered admirable adventures. Despite not being directly linked, one similar one occurred in the final practice for the Spanish round in Jerez due to a differential gearbox failure. We desperately needed a spare output shaft as the big race was the following day. We asked around the paddock after discovering that we didn't have a spare of our own, but the efforts were in vain. The only other choice we had was to somehow bring one out from the UK. Early that Saturday evening, Malcolm Butterworth or 'Mini-Malc', a sponsor friend staying with us, set to work. Here to enjoy the Spanish sunshine more than anything else, Malcolm knew people in the travel industry and, once in the groove, had this madcap idea that one might have customers travelling out to Malaga that night.

Meanwhile, John had also phoned back to the UK and managed to get hold of one of the main players at the Hewland gearbox factory. At home, savouring his weekend break in front of the TV, the poor key holder was eventually persuaded to drive back and open the factory for us. Meanwhile, Malcolm had found another pal to collect the part and whisk it down to Gatwick. Meeting up and delivering a heavy brown paper parcel to two unsuspecting, only very recently briefed, holidaymakers would prove its worth when the part was soon bound for Malaga. That was a major achievement, but now someone had to find a way to get to Malaga Airport in time to intercept the said passengers.

This is where the adventure, headlined in an article that came out in the Motoring News press afterward as 'Bartlett's Spanish Safari', really began. Fortunately, as the race driver, I was ordered to have an early night at the hotel in preparation for the big day ahead. So it was down to John, Dr Clive and another team member, Dave, to jump into the hire car and set off into the night, Malaga bound. These days, your Sat Nav or Google Maps would portray the quickest route to Malaga as being; head south to Gibraltar followed by taking the coastal road east. However, this was the 80s, and the chaps were only armed with a basic map. They headed off in an ever-darkening sky over the mountains in what they thought was the most direct route. In the blackness of the night on an unmarked road, their first setback occurred with the unfamiliar wobble of a front wheel denoting a puncture. All hands to the deck, they were hauling the wheel jack out when John reluctantly remembered the spare tyre was already punctured.

Fooling around on arrival in Jerez four days earlier, he had taken the first tyre out. Finding himself going the wrong way, he had embarked on an ill-planned attempt to change direction by mounting the central kerbing. Of course, moving on, they were now in the middle of nowhere, stranded with three wheels on their wagon.

In the pitch black, Dr Clive made out a sparkle of light in the distance. At low speed with floundering tyre, they tottered their way to the distant glow up ahead. Pulling up at a lone neon sign, they found themselves in the car park of a quiet hilltop guest house. It was obviously locked up for the night. However, they were in luck. After a lot of banging, the front door was unlocked by the sleepy owner having a late nightcap before bed. In John's inimitable style, he declared that they were an international racing team urgently trying to get to Malaga. His assistance in their task would be greatly appreciated. Happily, the owner responded positively to their request and leaving their three-wheeler in the car park, they all hopped into his car and were back on their way, speeding down the mountain to the airport.

On entering, John found the Alamo car hire desk still open awaiting passengers from the last flight of the night as Dr Clive went to meet the disembarked parcel carriers at the arrivals gate. Beaming with relief with a brown paper parcel firmly in hand, Dr Clive made his way back to John who was busy stomping the Alamo car hire desk. He complained the car they originally hired had come without a spare. He demanded they replace it. The manager, eager to get through the car hire passengers queuing up behind him before getting off home, handed a pair of keys to John as he quickly scribbled down his signature on various bits of paper. The show was back on the road.

By now it was the middle of the night as they headed back to Jerez along the same route they came. They again passed the little guest house and bumped their way across numerous half-made roads, missing as many potholes as they could along the way. As day began to break and tired eyelids began to droop, one large unseen pothole shook the car. A pungent smell began to fill the air. Looking at the dashboard the oil pressure light was on, the dial sky high. Shortly afterwards, the engine awkwardly stuttered before seizing to a halt. Stopped in their tracks, they were again left high and dry in the middle of nowhere.

With light beginning to whitewash through the bleak darkness of night, the true panorama of their situation slowly unfolded. Not only was the mountainous trail they were following devoid of tarmac but there was an unseen sheer drop to one side. Thanking the heavens, they had at least not tumbled down to the depths of sea level; they abandoned their second hire car and started on foot. Bereft of any traffic and with not even a farmhouse in sight, the immediate outlook of the car racing that day looked grim.

Then, like Omar Sharif on his camel at the beginning of the Lawrence of Arabia movie, shimmering in the distance was an oncoming bus. Dust trailed as it bumpily got closer. Standing in the middle of the road, arm forcefully stretched out, giving the stop sign, John let the bus screech to a halt before again declaring, 'We're an international racing team on a mission to Jerez, and we need you'. The Spaniard appeared to have no idea what he was talking about but picked up the mention of Jerez. With that, he eagerly nodded and said sí, sí, Jerez, Jerez. With that, the team of three all boarded, optimistically hoping the driver would take them somewhere close. An hour on, and the bus magically parked up right in front of the circuit gates. The bus driver obviously understood more than he was given credit for.

Set in the rolling, sun-baked Andalusian countryside, spectators had already piled into the enclosures and taken their seats for the Jerez 360 km race. With just minutes to spare, crew chief Rex Hart had the new part bolted in the car in record time, which was then hurriedly rolled onto the grid for the start. A start that was to make dubious history as, at the sharp end, Derek Warwick spun his Silk Cut Jaguar on the first corner of the first lap right in front of the other two Silk Cut Jaguars. All three spun off into the gravel traps. Enduring a long pit stop for a major front suspension problem and the boundless searing heat, our team, some more weary than others, looked on as we at least made it to the chequered flag.

It must have been six months later when I happened to be visiting John in his big, converted tithe barn in Sussex. His wife led me to his office, where he was busy on the phone. He was ranting at someone, saying, 'Well, if you don't know where they are, I certainly don't'. As he banged the phone down, I got intrigued. I asked who that was. He said, 'Oh, just Alamo. They still haven't been able to locate their cars.'

The Japanese World Championship was at Fuji International Speedway, set in the foothills of Mount Fuji, which grandly dominated the skyline. But first, we had to get there. Flying into Tokyo, the team was set to take the bullet train to Fuji the following day. My accommodation for that first night was a capsule compartment. Only the size of the bed inside, the compartment had a glass door and a key. It worked in much the same way as a morgue's body storage tray. That was it. Very strange.

Not wanting to stay there any longer than necessary, I was keen to meet up with the rest of the team at 6 pm in a central bar they had suggested. In my eagerness to get away from what can only be called 'claustrophobic' accommodation, I arrived more than an hour early. The bar was very big and empty. Settling down to wait, drink in hand, my attention was drawn as the door opened and the first suited commuter of the day briskly marched in. He found a seat at the very far corner of the bar and placing his briefcase there, went to the bar to order a drink. Some money was exchanged, and he walked back towards his chosen seat with a drink in one hand and a microphone in the other. I was intrigued. What was he going to do next? 80 yards apart, we were still the only two customers in the bar. *En route* to his seat, he dropped some coins into a jukebox I hadn't noticed before. Sitting down, he looked up to a screen that, again, I hadn't noticed before and began to squeakily wail out a Japanese pop song.

Well, what could you say? To an audience of one plus the bartender, this must have been Karaoke in its purest form.

By the time the team strolled in, the commuter had gone. The team had a few drinks but then decided to try to source something a little bit livelier before heading back to their accommodation. Also, the same capsule compartments. With a distinct lack of any English signage and none of us understanding any Japanese, we fell upon a welcoming, neon-signed bar. Warm and relatively cosy inside, it was still rather empty, and a rich, poignant smell of cheap perfume filled the air. But what with the twelve of us plus several very pretty Japanese girls that seemed to appear out of nowhere, it was now more of a party. Seemingly very interested in us, we thought we had lucked in when the bartender said in fractured English, oh just put it on a tab, settle up later.

After a few drinks, my slight alcoholic haze began to dissipate as I slowly started to come to my senses. I asked behind the bar what the bill had come to so far. At first, he didn't want to say, but when pushed, he admitted that the round we had to begin with, was bargain price welcome drinks. The drinks we had since were four times the price apart from the strange, exotic concoctions the girls were on, the price of which was completely off the scale. With not enough yen between us for the week, let alone that evening, I thought I had best retire to the loo for a pee and a think. There I stood, wondering what the inside of a Japanese jail was like, when I noticed above the toilet was a small window. Pushing the latch, this

working gang. A tall, sombre-faced, white South African. Archetypally dressed in black with a matching moustache and cowboy hat, he grimaced before spouting off in that indisputable nasally dialect, 'You just gave that nigger a week's wages.' I was appalled and felt like saying, 'Well, you should pay your men more', even though I knew it would fall on completely deaf ears. It would be another four years before Nelson Mandela was released and yet another three years from there before all the main hurdles to end apartheid had been negotiated.

Come the following practice day, there was a lunchtime break. Unheard of these days, health & safety would never allow back then, John managed to talk the organisers into the idea of taking press for passenger laps in the race car. We promptly put an additional set of safety belts in the so-called passenger seat together with a couple of cushions. Uncomfortable as it must have been with, amongst other things, a big red fire extinguisher between their legs, I took out a selected number of journalists around. Not slowing down happily as it was extra time in the seat familiarising myself with the circuit before the crucial qualifying yet to come the following day.

With ten minutes to spare, it was suggested I take my new girlfriend, Christine out to close the lunch break off. By this stage, brunette Christine, a very special lady with beautiful cat-like eyes and a face to die for, had taken over from Corrine. Through no fault of her own making, Corrine had departed to far more secure pastures anew with my mate, Dr Clive That will be forever a decision I made in haste. That said, I was to spend a loving nine whole years with Christine after that.

Back to the track, and unwillingly, Christine was forced to don a spare helmet before being belted up inside the claustrophobic confines of the small cockpit. As I roared out of the pit lane, I was aware that the agreement was that she would put her hand up if she was afraid or wanted me to slow down. Not something I would even contemplate now, but back then, eager to impress, I ignored her struggling signals as I decided to see just how fast I could go. I thought I must have beaten my quickest practice lap as I thundered down the main straight at over 200mph.

Returning, I switched the engine off on entry to the pit lane and let the car silently roll to a halt. Oops, I thought, maybe I went a little too far. Fortunately for me, Christine was awestruck by her never-to-be-forgotten experience as she clambered out of the car into the inviting arms of the waiting photographers and press.

At the end of that day, after final practice, we all cheerfully fired up a BBQ outside the pit garages. The guys were putting the final touches to the engine they had just changed for qualifying as the chicken and sausages crackled and spat in a keen readiness to be devoured. The evening still glowing with the warmth the day had brought. John loved to make practical jokes and was nearly as practised as Rex, our crew chief. Rex was as lovable as he was wily. With a very dry sense of humour, his actions were often more plentiful than his words. Chewing on a chicken bone, Rex was still on his hands and knees in the pit garage, tightening the last few bolts as John crept out to his crew chief's minibus. Quietly opening the bonnet, he pulled the leads off the distributor cap.

Having had our fill, the pit garage door was finally drawn down before we all climbed aboard our allocated vehicles. Rex and the team in the crew bus, John, Christine, and myself into our car. Chuckling away to himself, John looked on into his rear-view mirror waiting to witness the look on Rex's face on what was about to happen to him. Nothing did. Rex just started his vehicle as normal and drove by us waving with a knowing grin on his face. Ahh, foiled again; you could almost hear John thinking as he turned the keys to start our car. But nothing happened. No response from the engine at all. What could possibly have happened? It was getting dark by now as on further inspection, torch in hand, not only the leads but the entire distributor was missing from our car. It was a long wait for a very expensive cab ride back to the hotel that night.

Although the distributor was magically replaced the next day, nothing more was said on the matter. However, a month or two afterward, long since back in the UK, John endured a terrible smell in his barn for days. He searched the place top and bottom. He started by pulling up floorboards and even had rat control in. He just couldn't find where it came from.

Little did he know, it was right in front of him all the time. Sitting in the corner of his office was John's second briefcase. He always brought two whenever he went away on a big race. His nice one was full of all his day-to-day stuff, the other filled with past travel details relating to the last race. Rex was one of the few who knew that on the return home, he rarely touched this old leather bag until the next time. To John's total shock in nearly every sense he possessed, when the source was finally found, it consisted of the putrid remains of a very old Kyalami BBQ.

With the sun forever beating down and all the massive bright yellow signage from main sponsor Southern Suns Hotels adorning every part of the circuit, the whole feel of the circuit was yellow. After practice, qualifying was surprisingly held over just one televised lap. Coming out of the pit lane you only had the rest of that lap to warm up, followed by one 'balls to the wall' flying lap and one to slow down. It obviously made for good TV, but pretty frightening as I went wide on the last corner, spitting up humongous amounts of dust and dirt before getting it all together enough to head down the main straight to end my qualifying lap.

Come race day, by the end of 500 very sweaty kilometres, we eventually managed to come in 5th. The following day, we ventured out on safari. Leaving straight after breakfast, the 300-mile trip filled with incredible mountain terrain saw us close to arrival as the sun descended over the horizon. Towards the journey's end, sat beside Christine in the back of the minibus, I decided to take a look at the paper. There, headlining on the front page, was a three-column wide picture followed by a big write-up on the both of us. Well, mainly Christine's impromptu escapade. Wow, I thought as, with a big jolt, we began to embark on yet another bumpy, unmade road. We were now on our final few miles toward Sabi River Bungalows. This was another top resort in the heart of Kruger National Park provided by the Sun Hotels chain. Headlights now blazing, as twilight abruptly changed to night, I initially thought a sudden rainstorm had descended upon us. Wipers endeavoured to speed us on our way but struggled to clear what I thought were big heavy raindrops smashing onto the windscreen. It was, in fact, a swarm of locusts making their way past. A somewhat unfamiliar sight in the home counties.

Lions, giraffes, the last of the white rhino, and even crocodiles in our backyard all led to making up a breathtaking experience. Why was it then that, in my mind, the Sun-Times headline, the scary qualifying lap, and a deluge of locusts stood out most?

Chapter Thirteen
The Tortoise and the Hare

Moving further up the ranks with Blue Hawk, come '87, we went up into the 2nd class of Thundersports by taking on a Lester Ray-designed Harrier LR5. Built around an Arrows Formula One chassis, it came together with F1 running gear such as wheels, suspension, steering and brakes before a mighty 3.9 Cosworth engine was bolted into the back.

I won my first time out co-driving with Val Musetti, a cheerful, 'happy-go-lucky' race driver and celebrated stunt man for James Bond movies at the time. The laurels were not so easily forthcoming with Del Bennet, both team patron and driver. Don't get me wrong, Del, who had an issue for the first race and couldn't attend, was a great chap. He just wasn't the most ideal companion for a quick, hard race to the finish. He was more tortoise than hare in his approach. Shall we say he liked to take his time? When the car worked, which was not often, it was like a bullet. The shame was, albeit F1-based, it was not the best-built car in the world.

For example, at Donington Park in practice, I had just rounded the first corner of Redgate and was flat-out accelerating downhill towards the ultra-fast Craner Curves section when the rear bodywork came off. Sean Walker, behind me, said afterwards that he saw the rear wing sky high, at least 40' up in the air. The wing, which gives all the downforce to keep you on the ground, broke away from the rear bodywork, which was following in the same direction. Inside the cockpit, I was reduced to a mere passenger at 150mph as the next turn, the Old Hairpin, approached at lightning speed. Not for the first time in my life, I yet again said my goodbyes. This was not going to end up in a good way. Expecting a hospital visit at best, hardwood fully restricting my elbow space at worst, I careered into the barriers. This was followed by the inevitable big bang and crash. However, within the plumes of dust and flying turf, I eventually came to a stop, unharmed. I just sat there in the remains. There was no front end and no rear end, but hey, I was still breathing.

Back in the pits, I mentioned to Lester Ray, the designer and builder, that next time, it might be a good idea to bolt the rear wing onto the gearbox casing, as everyone else did. The suitcase-sized latches holding both the rear bodywork and all-important wing were not really strong enough.

On another occasion, in the middle of summer back at Brands Hatch, I clashed with Mike Blanchet's Lola going into Druids Hairpin at the start. Maybe he hit me. Maybe I hit him. I'm not sure. What was more of a major concern was forty of my Blue Hawk sponsors and guests had turned up in force for the big, main race of the day. From their start line suite, they all looked across at the panoramic view of the natural amphitheatre Brands Hatch provides. Fattened somewhat by lunch, they were downing copious amounts of wine in eager anticipation for the thunderous rolling start. In full view and within seconds of my first lap, it was all over. I was left, clambering out of the car and in the full knowledge that my next port of call was back to the suite to attempt to somehow silver-line an eager but now very disappointed group. In racing, some you win, some you lose. I think I lost that one.

However, the car was quick, and even with Del co-driving, happy to do the minimum number of laps required, we did win two more races. One at the Snetterton circuit in Norfolk and the last of the series, near Chester at Oulton Park.

Having accomplished my first Le Mans the year before, I was curiously desperate to return. More frightening than any other race I had ever been in before, to me, it was still the ultimate platform, the holy grail of sportscar racing. With little additional sponsorship, I found myself back in the Bardon. This was not ideal as there had been next to no development done on the car. Not only was it overweight, but the promise of a special extra high-powered Saab turbo engine had fallen through. Nevertheless, armed with its ever-faithful Cosworth DFV power plant, at least I had a drive.

Strangely enough, it was not the most memorable of what turned out to be 14 participations. And did it rain! Co-drivers were French Porsche aficionado Raymond Boutinaud and Tim Lee-Davey. Like pop singer Sheena Easton, Tim kicked off his career starring in the BBC series 'The Big Time'. He had moved on swiftly through the categories to get to Le Mans.

One of the main sponsors this time round was Penthouse Magazine. Before the first night's qualifying, I remember a pretty blonde girl in various stages of undress, wriggling around, trying desperately to secure a comfortable position in the restrictive confines of the cockpit. Displaying her splendid bits and bobs to the ever-increasing crowds that suddenly seemed to find themselves squeezing into our small work tent, cameras busily flashed, recording her every pose for the following month's edition.

With all the intermittent rain, qualifying was hard. Even the C2 cars were reaching over 200mph on the bumpy, narrow, and unforgiving Mulsanne Straight. Although the cars were a fraction slower getting up to speed and had to brake a little earlier in the wet, they were still frightfully quick. The big problem was changing lanes. With a C1 car fast approaching from behind, wipers flapping in front of you, headlights blazing in your mirrors, sometimes it was best to not get in their way. They were maybe 20mph quicker, but a small change of direction to the other side of the track was not so easy. Remember, this was usually the main trunk road to Tours. The lumpy painted white lines in the middle of the road were really slippery. Not a problem at 50mph; a major one at 200. You somehow had to slip across them as neatly and carefully as possible while at the time being flat out on the gas. Interesting.

Come race day, maybe I had matured a little, maybe I was a little more in control. The vast crowds at the start were still as I had remembered. The flags were still waving. Autographs were still being enthusiastically signed. The entire event was as big as it ever was, but I felt somewhat detached. Why was I here? What the hell was I doing? I was simply scared. Was I actually brave enough to be doing this sort of thing in the first place? Could I have been thinking back to the tragic events of the year before? Mind games can easily come into play. It has only been Le Mans where I have felt I was really risking my life every time I went out. All other circuits pale into insignificance in comparison. The sheer speeds attained are quite unbelievable. To do this lap after lap, throughout the day and the night, come rain or shine, requires a certain lack of imagination. The dilemma I always had was that I was born an artist. I <u>DID</u> have an imagination.

A small boy distracts me by asking for my autograph. Looking up at all 5'4'' of me, you can see a purposefulness in his eyes. It could be I was doing what he would love to grow up to do. I'm sure many of the spectators would rather be in my shoes. Maybe I should get over myself. Be happy indulging in the aspirations of others. The moment passes. Three minutes later, the pit lane siren sounds. Our car comes to a stop in a cloud of dust and smoke. Quick-lift jacks go up, and wheels are changed. As a mechanic cleans the windscreen, the sweaty driver clambers out as I get in. He helps belt me up. I press the start button. The engine hesitates for an instant and then fires up. Crunching into first gear, I drop the clutch, and I'm off.

Any nerves I had before disappearing as I entered the fray. There is just too much to do. Too much to focus on. Although, in one way, you are a central player in the attention of the crowds watching, you are very much alone. However, I loved that feeling of being in control of my destiny. Just me.

Chapter Fourteen
Smoking the Opposition

The 1988 season had fast approached. I was still hanging onto Blue Hawk sponsorship by my shirt tails, but they were now intent on a change of direction. They wanted to get into the world of touring cars, but the main British Touring Car Championship was proving too much for their budget. As resistant as I was, we settled on the Thundersaloons Series. This was similar to Thundersports, but this time, we would be in the very top class.

We would run the shell and running gear of a Honda Acura Legend with a massive 5.7 litre V8 Chevrolet engine sitting under the bonnet. We were racing against the likes of saloon car legends John Cleland, Dave Brodie, and Rod Birley. Others to join the party were big UK adversaries such as David Leslie, Tony Trimmer, and Tony Lanfranchi.

The car was troublesome, but when it ran well, we did OK in the races these monster, silhouette-style racers produced. I just didn't feel happy; it was both big and cumbersome, with my eyes vibrating along the straights. Heading into corners, such as Paddock Hill Bend, at over 165mph, this thing had a mind of its own. With a mammoth 600bhp at hand, heaving this hefty, front-engine whale through the turns was not fun. I felt I was more of a rodeo cowboy attempting to tame a raging bull. There was no real precision in the car. It lurched from side to side, heavily rolling around on its suspension. I needed to get back into what I saw as a real race car.

Although I was committed to Blue Hawk and their Thundersaloons programme, I found another sponsor. A new I.T. company called Goal Systems. They specifically wanted to do the Le Mans 24 Hours. As well as it being a huge event, the regulations specified there had to be three drivers per car for such a long race. This was good for me because often, many of the teams only ran two drivers for the other World Sportscar events. However, here at Le Mans, another available seat often sprung up into the equation.

I initially found a seat with Charles Ivey's C2 Tiga team, but the deal sadly went south. Instead, I got into the Lucky Strike Argo team at the last minute. This low-slung, lean, and mean-looking machine armed with a 3.3 Ford Cosworth DFL V8, upped to a 3.8 for qualifying, was both run and driven by Martin Schanche. The Lucky Strike Argo JM19C was making quite a name for itself on the international stage, but their star driver, Will Hoy, had previous commitments that year. Therefore, along with Martin, I would partner up with Robin Smith. A pal I had driven within Malaysia.

Moustachioed and Norwegian-born Martin Schanche was known as Mr Rallycross. Already a multiple European Rallycross Championship winner, he was to go on to secure six titles in total. A nice enough chap but outspoken. Ever a cigarette in hand, he was also very, very grumpy. He would complain about everything from the preparation of the car to the catering. The team was sharp, but everyone seemed on edge whenever he was around. They all walked on eggshells and only relaxed when he wasn't there or was out on the track in the car. That at least gave them a little break. We thought part of the reason Martin was even more irritable and grouchy than usual was that he would be missing a big, clashing Rallycross Championship round in Ireland on the Sunday.

I was to never find out why, in his long 25-year career in Rallycross, he also chose to take up competing in thoroughbred race cars. In its time, this car was a state-of-the-art creation. However, each time he came into the pits during practice, it looked as if he'd been rallying it. There was always mud and grass everywhere. Personally, I preferred to keep 200mph plus race cars on the black bit.

Apart from a dramatic multi-spin coming out of Tertre Rouge onto the Mulsanne, my own qualifying in this car was fun and running at 338kph, over 210mph down the Mulsanne, it was one of the quickest C2 cars out there. With all of us safely qualified, we would line up on the grid in the middle of the C2 field.

Come race day, an entire sea of Union Jacks filled the ever-burgeoning grandstands. There was an air of 'Britain Expects' as the British Silk Cut Jaguar was, after four years of trying with previous evolutions, inching ever closer to breaking the all-conquering stranglehold the German works Rothmans Porsche team had here. A massive British contingent of over 100,000 of the near-300,000 crowd had crossed the channel and made their way down to La

Sarthe to witness this true clash of the titans. Porsche 962 v Jaguar XJR-9.

As the flag went down and the mighty 50-car grid thundered past the start line, the factory Porsche team initially led from the first of the Silk Cut Jaguars. However, it was not long before the Jaguar muscled through to the front in the hands of Jan Lammers. A duel that would continue for most of the race. Martin Schanche made a good start in our car, and everyone seemed relieved when he continued to circulate. The year before, in this race, he lasted 4 laps before he crashed out. With both Martin and Robin Smith completing their first stints, all was going to plan until I started to experience clutch problems. Pitting, the entire gearbox had to be removed to repair the clutch. This would take the best part of three hours. By the time it was Martin's turn to go out again, we had tumbled down the field to dead last place. The Argo was fast, but while Porsche and Jaguar were battling it out for the lead, we were fighting against the danger of not being classified at all.

In the cool of the evening air, it was the small WM Peugeot that engineered another milestone for the race. Never to foresee outright victory, their cars were built for speed, not reliability. Their goal is to surpass the 400kph barrier before breaking. This, they did in the hands of Roger Dorchy, who was timed at 405kph (252mph) down the Mulsanne just before the engine inevitably blew itself to pieces. Mission accomplished. They went home happy.

Just before midnight, Martin decided to double stint. So not required for a while, I had enough time to speed down to the Mulsanne and become a spectator for a short time. A team member driving our hire car found the entrance to the Hotel Arbor, the grounds of which directly overlook the flat-out kink two-thirds of the way down the notorious Mulsanne Straight. I stood there, eyes on stalks peeking through the wire fence, totally awestruck. I had never experienced such a dramatic but intimidating sight. In the shadowy darkness, you first heard the thunderous drone of flat-out cars approaching at over 200mph, followed shortly afterward by blazing headlights lighting up the night sky. Then, in an ear-splitting, high-pitched scream, they had flashed past and were gone.

Although this was now my third Le Mans, I had never been out on the track before. The sight that befell me was as frightening as it was exhilarating. Was I really doing this? Why would anyone in their right mind want to? The questions passed as we hastily made our way back to the safety of the paddock and pits. Time to concentrate. My turn next.

Forgetting my traumatic midnight experience, the car felt good, and we were one of the fastest C2 cars down the Mulsanne. However, it seemed that every time Martin got in the car, there was a mystical problem, including two lengthy pit stops of over 30 minutes each with gear selection problems. By very early Sunday morning, he had obviously had enough. He decided, perhaps a lot earlier than any of us knew, that he still had time to compete in the

Irish Rallycross round that day and magically managed to arrange a private flight straight from the airfield next door. Within minutes, he was gone.

For the first time in a week, a big smile broke over the normally stern face of the Team Manager, Gordon Horn. He said, 'Well, we are where we are. Let's just make the best of it, have a good time, and get to the finish. With that, it was as if a giant storm cloud had passed, and beams of sun had shone down on us all inordinately brightly. That lost hour could not be made up, but still, with a third of the race yet to run, everyone now gleefully buckled down to their jobs in hand. Everyone wanted to get to the end.

It was like the good ol' days that I was too young to experience. At the bang of a starter's gun, drivers used to run across the track, fire up their cars, and slither and slide away, trying not to hit any of the other competition, all doing the exact same thing at the same time. It was a time when only two drivers shared the duties as opposed to the compulsory three after the 70's. Now we were two, and it was great. Under pressure, we acted as a team. The car ran well. One Robin in. One Robin out. The pit stops were fast and slick, and we didn't encounter any more problems.

Whipping down the Mulsanne at 200mph in the early morning sunshine was memorising. Someone said, 'speeding with knobs on'. They couldn't have been more correct. Towards the end of each stint, I didn't want to come in. I had got into a groove. I felt at one with the car. And the cherry on top was the fact we had, after that earlier 3-hour pit-stop, worked our way back into classification.

Robin Smith was to do the last 40 minutes while I hung out over the concrete pit wall as far as I dared, waiting, along with the team, to cheer him through at the finish. At the end of the pit lane, the chequered flag was being readied. Above the pits and along the adjacent stands, thousands and thousands of eager fans waved their Union Jacks in anticipation of history being made. So keen were some that they had already scaled the enclosure fences and begun to surge onto the track. Within a minute or two, this had turned into a veritable tsunami.

All the while, out on the circuit, the Silk Cut Jags had all been given orders by their boss, Tom Walkinshaw, by radio from the pits. The leading car, far enough ahead of second place not to worry, was to slow down and wait for the second, 4th place Jaguar. The remaining Jag to speed up to catch up with the others. By the time they entered the Porsche curves finishing the final lap, all three Silk Cut Jaguars were side by side in line together. What a sight. Britain had delivered the crown. And in doing so, had decimated the Porsches' seven-year stranglehold on the race.

As the formation of Jags slowly crossed the line to a vigorously waved chequered flag thirty years on from their last win, an immense roar came out from the stands. The circuit was already heaving with well-wishers as massive Union Jacks were manhandled down from the enclosures to greet their heroes. As the flags ebbed and flowed and air horns sounded off all around, drifts of red, white, and blue-coloured smoke bombs filled the air.

The crowds now on the track were so huge that there was no chance that any of the remaining race cars could pave a way through the throng to do their traditional slowing down lap. All cars were left marooned amongst the masses on the grid as we jumped over the pit wall onto the track to join Robin as he crawled out of a now very dirty and tired Argo. The Lucky Strike, a cigarette-sponsored car, had followed in not far behind. Within this sea of noise, colour, and jubilation, the winning drivers, Andy Wallace, Jan Lammers, and my old sparring partner Johnny Dumfries, had not even managed to get to the podium yet. The Brits sure knew how to party, and the celebrations were already well underway. Hot and sweaty and as drained as we now felt, we were just happy to be a part of this historical event as we looked on to hail the winners when they finally stepped up onto the podium.

I finally did get to drive for Tiga C2 for Charles Ivey in the 1000km World Sportscar round at Brands Hatch later on in the year. Co-drivers were Tim Harvey, who would soon become British Touring Car Champion in 1992, and Chris Hodgetts, who had already taken the outright title twice. Esteemed company for sure.

Chapter Fifteen
Total Gridlock

With all the initial enthusiasm and effort that went into the start of the 1989 season, it really did prove to be the pits in every way. Try as might, with the means at hand, there was no room to make headway in any direction. Whichever way I turned; I met a total impasse.

With Blue Hawk's support, we made ambitious plans to step up into the British Touring Car Championship. To become known throughout the world as the most successful production-based race car ever, our mount would be the iconic Ford Sierra Cosworth RS500. As a snarling, fire-breathing monster, this 500bhp+ turbocharged beast of a machine would become synonymous with the Group A era. Sadly, just not in the hands of us!

The championship had become so successful that every round was now being televised. As a result, big money came in. Up against the likes of the Rouse-prepared Kaliber and Labatt's-sponsored RS500s and the similar NEC Cartel-sponsored, Dick Johnson-built, Trackstar models, our small budget petered into insignificance. All the touring car big names were there including Andy Rouse, Guy Edwards, and Tim Harvey. Chris Hodgetts, Will Hoy, and Robb Gravett and half of the 30 cars in the championship were RS500s. Our team would enter three cars. One for my race-winning '85

Thundersports partner Mike O'Brien, one for Touring Car guru Dave Pinkney, and another for myself. Run by Terry Drury Racing, who did a good job preparing Tim Harvey's car the year before, we initially thought we would be there or thereabouts. However, with the relatively microscopic budget, the lack of power from the engine supplier, and the general unreliability of the cars, we were to flounder against the big boys.

Nevertheless, we persevered whilst I was also competing in selected rounds of the BRDC British C2 Championship. This championship was for Le Mans-type C2 sportscars. Dominated by the Spice and Tiga chassis, our sportscar season fared little better with an underperforming Lester Ray-built Harrier powered by a big 5-litre Chevrolet engine.

May arrived with a clash of interests. Johnny Johnson, a former F3 driver, was a keen enthusiast whose company, JJ Properties, sponsored both my BTCC and British C2 efforts. Based in Kent, he had guests in a hospitality suite I had at Brands Hatch for the C2 round. This was held on the same day as the long-distance, two-driver British Touring car round at Donington Park in Leicestershire. My priority was still with the BTCC, but I figured with a little bit of lateral thinking, maybe I could do both. Timing was touch-and-go, but in theory, with the help of a pal who owned a helicopter company, I could do both rounds. Without the travel funds, I negotiated a deal that included Starline Helicopters emblazoned on both the C2 car and the Touring Car.

So, there it was. I started the C2 race at Brands Hatch, doing the minimum number of laps allowed, and passed over the rest of the driving duties to my co-driver. I then ran over to the helipad with Johnny, and within minutes, we were up in the air, flying to Donington. I would like to say the flight was uneventful, but I was a little troubled by the pilot. As if struggling with the navigation to find Donington, he seemed to follow all the main motorways. Much of the time was spent above the M1. Maybe it was my imagination, but the pilot seemed to only lower the aircraft to read the motorway signs. Eventually, he turned left at Junction 23A and set down two minutes later at Donington.

With helmet in hand and only armed in the sweaty overalls I was wearing; I ran down to the pits. I was just in time for the pit stop that would see my co-driver Mike out of the car and me in. And boy, we were doing quite well. This was with other acclaimed drivers joining in the only two-driver BTCC event of the year, including Damon Hill, Tiff Needell, Johnny Dumfries, and Wyn Percy. Could we finish pretty well in this one? Not a chance. With a handful of laps to go, the brakes failed, and we were out again. Flying back to Brands Hatch, along the same route of motorways with a few railway lines thrown in, we eventually landed back safe and sound. Job done – albeit with no result.

Having at least finished in the top ten at Thruxton, all eyes were then focused on the British Grand Prix support race at Silverstone. Of course, all my Blue Hawk sponsor guests were there in force. Of all the races in the entire season, this was the one to do well in. Not to my surprise, the turbo again blew within five laps. Icon motorsport broadcaster Murray Walker was frantically commentating as I nursed the car back to the start/finish line straight, where I found the main straight BBC camera. Coming to a very smoky halt right in its pathway, I planted the car in full view. My thinking was, if it could not finish at least their logo would be seen every lap to the chequered flag. Indeed, it worked. I was happy, and Blue Hawk gave me the impression that they were, too. That said, after that abysmal season, they never sponsored me again.

Le Mans did not fare much better. I found a drive in the works factory Tiga C2 car. Co-drivers would be John Sheldon and Max Olivar. Even back then, John was a championship winner as well as being an all-round gentleman and nice guy. He would go on to even greater things later. John had a massive 200mph accident on the Mulsanne Straight at Le Mans in 1984 in a works Aston Martin. The car blew up, and the fire lit up the forest. Suffering severe, life-threatening burns, he was unbelievably back at Le Mans the next year for his fifth of twelve Le Mans, which he accomplished. Frenchman Max was revered in Morocco, his lifelong country of residence, as the greatest driver they ever produced. Again, a lovely chap, Nineteen eighty-nine, would see him start his 16th of an incredible 21 participations in the 24 Hours. He was one of the guys in the sister Kremer Porsche that was called in by the team when Jo Gartner was killed in a Kremer Porsche in 1986.

A great team, but nothing really went our way. As the sun was beginning to set, I remember exiting Mulsanne Corner and pushing hard toward the first flat-out kink when I saw smoke. Rounding the first kink, the white smoke became immense; it covered the entire track and billowed skyward towards the heavens. Burning debris was scattered all over, and there was no way you could see the road ahead. Was I to brake hard at approaching 200mph and risk going off or carry on through? What could be on the other side? Could I hit an unseen car or cars lying broadside in the middle of the track? In that split second, all I could do was lift and hope for the best. I held my breath, and within the blink of an eye, I was through this complete white blanket unharmed. Whew, I thought. What happened there?

Every time you go out on a racetrack, things happen. You can have any one of a number of dramas in one outing, so it wasn't as if I even asked the question when my stint was over. As it happened, it was an American driver, Dominic Dobson, in a Takefuji Porsche 962 whose turbo had caused the fire. Burning through the brake lines and sitting in a ball of flames, his only choice was to slow the car down by edging it toward and running it along the Armco barriers. Finally bringing it to a halt, he got out in the nick of time before the fire fully engulfed the cockpit.

When the car was on song, I always felt a defiant, scary delight running at Le Mans. Especially profound in the middle of the night. There is always that intense, heart-stopping feeling rushing down the Mulsanne Straight at some stupidly unbelievable speed. And as an artist at heart, I loved ploughing into corners such as Mulsanne Corner. Entering behind a gaggle of cars, in that split second, you could see the flicker of flames bursting out of the turbos in front of you. Each car delivers contrasting colours as they all desperately down-changed. The varying sounds of their different engines and the sight of their rear lights dreamily pass your vision. I have forever wished that I could paint a sound and light picture that could capture that experience. Put it in a bottle or place it on a wall.

However, with incessant starter motor problems that handicapped us throughout, our poor old Tiga finally ground to a halt just after 3 in the morning out on the track. Max, in the seat at the time, had to thumb a marshal's long lift back along the unmade forest roads of the circuit's interior.

At least we could say we were in esteemed company. 36 other cars followed us into retirement, including both of Richard Lloyd's Porsche 962s Derek Bell in one, Damon Hill in the other, two of the three Silk Cut Jags were out with, amongst others, the previous year's winners, Jan Lammers and Andy Wallace gone, as were a host of others. Only 19 would make the end of the race.

At the sharp end, come 4 pm, it was Sauber Mercedes in their mighty 5-litre C9 who would take overall honours. And unknown at the time, this would be the last Le Mans race, in which its most legendary of all straights, would be free of chicanes.

In an obstacle-ridden season where nothing much could be achieved; you sometimes just have to take the good with the bad. Much more upsetting was the news that I received on my Birthday, 18th December. Word filtered through that the Starline Bell Jet Ranger helicopter and pilot I had flown with back in May had gone down just leaving Biggin Hill. It soon became known that the relatively new pilot didn't have an instrument rating on his licence and had no actual instrument flying experience, had got spatially disorientated in a heavy cloud and he and his four passengers were all lost.

Chapter Sixteen
Spice World

The following year looked bleak. After their grim intro to the British Touring Car Championship, the top echelons on the British Gypsum board changed direction and their time as a Blue Hawk sponsor was up. As a jobbing race driver, I took drives as and when I could. It was a year that the UK went into recession, Maggie left office, and my company was one of many in crisis. Suffice to call it a lean year for me, but one that introduced me to two great, larger-than-life characters.

The first was Stuart Radnofsky, a very clever, if somewhat over the top, expat American with boundless enthusiasm. With a background in marketing, he was a marketing operations manager for two Polaroid divisions before becoming marketing manager for Benetton Formula One, Stuart was keen to start his own company. He is a fairly big chap compared to my small stature. Where he wore a suit, I did not. Stuart liked to talk endlessly on the phone. I did not. Enviously, he could play guitar, piano, and trumpet. Sadly, I couldn't. Indeed, talking about Yin and Yang, we were polar opposites. There was practically nothing we had in common apart from a love of all things motorsport. Within no time, we had built up a solid relationship of sorts, and amazingly, he brought a group of his long-time business pals together to meet each week to discuss how they could get me in a better car. For all intents and purposes and want of a better word, Stuart became my manager. We became good friends, and although we don't see as much of each other as we did, I would like to think we always will be.

Anyway, through Stuart or one of his pals, I was introduced to the delights of a certain Hugh Chamberlain. Ultimately winning a brace of FIA endurance sports car world titles, the vibrant 'Churchillian' personality of Hugh, would give him folklore status to all those in the motorsport industry. A wonderfully personable chap who epitomised the great British bulldog spirit at its very best.

Well-versed and extremely passionate, Hugh's company, Chamberlain Engineering, ran Spice C2 cars in the World Sportscar Championship, where they were reigning C2 World Champions. The Spice, at the time, was the car to have, and if I could get my bum into one of his seats, it would certainly be a step up. Strolling around the picturesque gardens of his beautiful, listed cottage in the depths of East Hertfordshire, we came to a deal for Le Mans. Now, all I had to do was find the additional sponsorship monies to compete.

Stuart and I would spend hours at his kitchen table trying to work out how we could progress things. Amongst the cornflakes and his two young kids' demands, we worked out a plan. Like 'Rogers & Hammerstein' he would type up the next lead to follow, and I would draw the presentational pictures. It was all a bit of a mish-mash of small sponsors, often on contra-deals, but we got there in the end.

Once the marching bands have beaten their last drum, they, along with the press, celebrities, and bikini-clad promotional girls, are hurriedly cleared from the grid. You're then just left with the cars and their appointed start driver. Well over 30,000 brake horsepower, waiting to be unleashed, just quietly sitting there waiting for the sign. An electric silence descends as the marshals get ready. Official flags wave, and sixty engines crackle and burst into life. The cars then move off following the pace car. The time is 3.48 pm. Keeping grid position, they slowly wind their way around the circuit, weaving from side to side, warming up cold tyres. With less than 30 seconds to go, they come round again. The pace car peels into the pit lane as the field approaches the red start/finish line lights. As the clock strikes four, the lights turn to green, and with a thunderous explosion of noise and dust, 60 cars pedal to the metal and flash past flat out. The race is on.

While the pole-setting Nissan was taking on the might of the Silk Cut Jags, known as the Silk Cats, as well as a burgeoning group of Porsche 962 machinery, we fought out our own battle in the C2 ranks. Against us, we had the likes of the ADA, ALD, and Tiga chassis, as well as a raft of Spice cars. The top French Spice teams, Graff and Lombardi, opposing the comparable UK-based Spice teams such as GP Motorsport, Mako, and PC Automotive.

After six hours in, with a quarter of the race run, we were keeping to an even pace. A pace that kept us in the mix but one that didn't seriously compromise the gearbox or brakes. However, like the tortoise and the hare, the French Spices had scorched off into the distance, a full 5 laps ahead, as we closed in on the battle for fourth.

The gearbox was getting a little rough and sticky, but Hugh was looking on the bright side as he spoke to one of the TV commentators. He said the brakes were fine, and the engine was running like a song. Fuel was a bit of an issue as the drivers were starting to go too quickly, and he couldn't slow them down. He also whispered that we were all behaving remarkably well. Above the roar of the passing traffic, he also added, 'It's all very worrying'.

With a few imperfections, such as the gearbox, the race was mainly running to plan. Mostly with quick driver and tyre changes, refuelling, and the odd brake pad change. I did have one trouble when the seat broke loose and had to finish my stint, hanging onto the steering wheel for dear life, but hey, that was a minor inconvenience compared to some of the other teams' problems. As darkness descended, the French hares broke. We were elevated to third and then secured second.

We were now firmly in contention, albeit adrift by four laps from the leading PC Automotive car. Driving the race of our lives, by early Sunday morning, we had forced the gap down to two laps. I must say that I put in an impressive double stint during this period, and by the time the next bulletin was posted, we were just 90 seconds behind. After nearly half the race had run its course, we took the lead. Sadly, it wasn't to last as 4 hours later, Philippe sailed into the pit with a bunch of neutrals. The gearbox had finally given up the ghost.

As with so many other times at Le Mans, when you're ready to pull the garage doors down and lock up, the team is there, ready to throw themselves wholeheartedly at the unenviable task of replacing all the bits and pieces. I was always in awe at the speed and motivation behind their dedication. After thrashing about in an undecipherable busyness, unpicking the mess and bolting in new parts administered in a host of profanities, 50 minutes later, we were out on the track again.

With the attrition of other cars, we were still far enough ahead to claim second, although the leaders had a massive 10-lap advantage by then. However, we now had the bit between our teeth, and we were each gaining an unheard-of 10 seconds a lap. By breakfast time, we were 7 laps behind when the gods turned in our favour, and it was the turn of the leading PC Spice to pit to replace a broken rear rocker arm. With the PC car soon out again, the gap was now three laps, but we were still gaining time hand over fist.

As the gap forever went down, I could now see the smoking and equally battered PC Automotive car in the distance on the Mulsanne. Each time I went around, I got closer and closer. Hugh had worked out that all things remaining the same, we would take the lead back again by mid-day. When they then risked everything and upped their times, we extended this closer to 1 pm. Was it possible that we would take the C2 win in the most legendary races in the world?

Stand on the top of that revered podium and, as well as the cup, be able hold my very own Le Mans legacy forever, that no one could take away. Hard to fathom, but we were clearly on course. Our hopes only mounted as we closed in on our prey. Like the car ahead, we were running purely on adrenalin and not much else at this stage. As the clock ticked down, we were still on schedule. A slow, wry grin was beginning to formulate on Hugh's face as Phillipe took the wheel and scorched out of the pit lane after a routine stop. All we had to do was hold it together for the final laps, and the top-step laurels would be ours.

As we stood there in the pits, readying ourselves for the ultimate glory of the podium ceremony, the call came through from the signallers at Mulsanne Corner, our car was parked down there. The engine had blown. I looked at Hugh. He at me. More of a wriggled 'snoopy' smile befell Hugh's face. Suddenly, it was all over. However, with head held high, and dignity fully intact, he marched into the post-race press conference to announce in true British bulldog fashion, 'Well, we nearly won it though, didn't we? We went out having a go!' In the silence of the next day, bags packed, and last tool trolleys placed back on the transporter, I could only look back at what might have been.

The Silk Cats had won the C1 division the day before. What was to become a seven-time world F1 champion, a certain Michael Schumacher, came home 5th in a Sauber Mercedes C11. We all then went our separate ways.

Chapter Seventeen
Pretty in Pink

Over the years, during the off-season period, we used to hold the occasional karting evening. Smaller sponsors, potential sponsors and friends were all warmly invited. They would pay a small fee that covered the costs. We used a great little indoor circuit in Uxbridge known as Trak 1. The circuit had this very high-banked hairpin that I think only the careless or the stupid could take flat out. I always did. The problem was I always knew I stood a 50% chance of cracking a rib. Nevertheless, it was a risk I had to take as the star race driver to make sure I was always the quickest. The rib always took around a month to mend.

One of these events was around Christmas time. Stuart, as always, was also having a go. Within the confines of the indoor venue, all you could really hear was the tinny sound of 2-stroke engines and the little kart tyres skidding and squealing around the tight bends on the shiny, painted concrete floor surface. On one such bend, Stuart tried to go into the corner far too quickly.

The circuit Trak 1 rented took up half of a giant warehouse, the other part half was divided off by a large plasterboard wall. Stuart missed the entry to the corner and continued straight on. With a huge ca-thump, he shot clean through the plasterboard, leaving a perfect silhouette of a 'Stuart in kart' shape. You had to laugh. Particularly when the black hole left started to crack around the edges. For those old enough to remember, a true Looney Tunes 'Road Runner' cartoon moment. Long afterwards, my ribs hurt each time I chuckled over that evening, and it had nothing to do with the hairpin!

On a more serious note, after taking stock, Stuart and I worked ourselves to the bone to return to Le Mans the following year. A sponsorship scheme was devised where we would secure, at no cost, expensive full-page ad spaces in the Financial Times. We would then sell these pages on to partners who had never before been involved with the esteemed newspaper at a discount price. Everyone would also get space on a pink Financial Times car running in the fabled Le Mans race at no extra cost. A win, win situation. Surprisingly, through the penning of Stuart's eloquent writings and my pink 'magic marker' pictures, we pulled it all together.

We lined up on the grid the following year with a pink Financial Times car plastered with decals from the likes of Bang & Olufsen, Atari and Minolta. All new to the iconic pink pages of the world-renowned business newspaper. However, as I couldn't see myself marching around the paddock in pink, my only request was that the driver overalls be black, with a pink band for the crucial Financial Times logo. I thought I had to draw the line somewhere.

The car, in all its resplendent livery, was prepared before arrival. Not as had been the case with my other five participations, where stickers were hurriedly placed on the car before qualifying. The driving partners this time around were the same as my very first:

Nick Adams and Richard Jones. On arrival, the car looked amazing, but would it do the job?

Obviously not. A far cry from the year before, nothing went right. From our fifth-row grid position, we just seemed to go backwards. With an underperforming engine, we struggled around as best we could, but after three battery changes and having to replace the clutch, alternator and starter motor along the way, the car finally ground to a halt at 5.30 am with electrical gremlins. A sad end to my time with Spice, the marque which I had gotten so desperately got close to winning in the year before.

The actual race would see Japan winning their first Le Mans with the deafening rotary-powered Mazda 787B. By far the loudest car ever to compete at Le Mans it was a complete nightmare for all those drivers, like me, sleeping in paddock motorhomes back then. Trying to grab a little shut-eye when not behind the wheel was rendered virtually impossible. And Johnny Herbert, taking the chequered flag, had put in so much effort into his final stint that he collapsed before the podium ceremony. Standing on the top step, Mazda co drivers Volker Weidler and Bertrand Gachot had to spray the champagne to the awaiting crowd without him.

Miserably driving home in the Golf GTi I had borrowed from a sponsor, as I had had to sell my beloved BMW to pay the company bills, all I could do was concentrate on the next race. This was the Willhire 24 Hours, back at the Norfolk circuit of Snetterton. Open to Group N production touring cars, a large, mostly local crowd had descended upon this East Anglian venue for one of their most established annual races of the year.

The team, sponsored by Sky TV, was running a Sierra Cosworth in the top class. The driver lineup was me, John Bartlett, one-time British Touring car racer Angus MacKay and World Sportscar competitor David Mercer. The team manager was the revered Malcolm Swetnam. A master of his trade if ever there was one. Like Le Mans on a much smaller scale, the venue had its own all-night funfair, thousands of campers settling in for the entire weekend, and numerous sweet-smelling BBQs snapping and crackling all around the circuit. After two days of qualifying, the entire show was somewhat dampened as big black clouds rolled in for Saturday's 4 pm kick-off.

In torrential rain, I took the start for what would be a very wet race. The car had qualified at the sharp end of the burgeoning 50-car grid, so I was up to third within no time at all. With slick, Malcom Swetnam-managed pit stops and driver changes, we were looking good as nighttime fell and the rain continued to tip down. Then things took a turn for the worse. For some reason still unknown to this day, Dave Mercer finished his stint, walked to his road car, and proceeded to drive home to Kent.

Out on the track, Angus MacKay experienced the fire extinguisher accidentally going off inside the cockpit. Inhaling the contents made him hallucinate to the extent that after somehow managing to get the car back to the pits, an ambulance had to rush him straight to the hospital. Completely away with the fairies, the TV broadcaster at the time said Dave's last bewildered mutterings as he left were all to do with pink elephants and rhinos. In the space of an hour, we had lost two drivers and had tumbled all the way down to last position.

However, as far down as we were, I must admit I enjoyed the climb back up the field. Without a break in the rain, wipers constantly swiping across the windscreen in what seemed a forever desperate urge to dispel the onslaught, all I could do was relish being in one of the quickest cars out there. In the murk and darkness of the night interspersed with the odd hazy light from a camping van and the surreal blurred glow of the still busy pit lane as I swept past every couple of minutes, I was making good progress. As I made light shrift of the lower-class competitors, I felt like I was racing in a Silk Cat at Le Mans, busily eating up the lesser opposition that dared to swing in my path. I was having fun in what was fairly easy in comparison to a full, out-and-out sports racing car.

Double stinting, John and I made it through the night and as dawn broke, so did the rain. John, out at the time, radioed in to say he was being held up and thought he could easily take second place. Malcolm told him to closely follow but not overtake. I think John grimaced, but there was method in Malcolm's madness. Standing in the pitlane, he turned to me and said, watch, that second-place car will come in within the next few laps, mark my words. With almost psychic accuracy, a couple of laps later, it came hammering into the into the pits in great clouds of smoke. The brakes totally shot. The driver had completely overworked them in his attempt to keep John at bay. Game over for him. Malcolm gave out a wry, knowing grin.

With a good 22 hours of the race run, it was again my turn to get the car to the line. It had run like a train, but like many, trying to get a war-beaten Group N car, not as strong as a pukka, Touring Car, to the finish of 24 Hours was still an unenviable task. By then, the clutch was slipping, and the brakes had all but faded out. I radioed to Malcolm that the brakes were really shot. The radio crackled back through with his usual message: stay out.

We were catching the leader, hand over fist. On lap times, we could still catch and pass, but they were more than a couple of laps further ahead on the overall leaderboard. With no brakes left to speak of, it was more a case of just nursing the car home. With great relief, the chequered flag finally fell. We had won our class and come second overall, even after our lowly nighttime position of dead last. Just as I thought the drama had finally abated, I could hardly get round the next corner on the slowing-down lap. My braking foot went right down to the floor. Whew, I thought, but then Malcolm, of course, knew that. He had timed everything to the last degree.

Ray Bellm, Will Hoy and Kurt Luby won overall in their Class B BMW, but as class winners we came in a proud second place. John and I afforded a good slap on the back each for that. After the champagne ceremonies I nervously, quite sleepily drove home that night. In my road car, I couldn't help wondering why I had not chosen an easier route. Compared to the ultra-fast, fire-breathing monsters in international sportscar racing, I could have so easily made my mark on the British Club scene first. Instead, I chose to jump into the big ones as soon as I could. Perhaps a bad mistake, but by then, there was no going back.

Chapter Eighteen
Stepping Up

Eager as always, Stuart told me I should step up. Why not try the really big boys, he said. How about talking to Kremer for Le Mans?

Well, I couldn't take him seriously, to begin with. Kremer was in a different class on at least a billion major levels. Firstly, they were in C1, the very top division. Secondly, they were one of the most admired private Sportscar teams on the planet. Aside from the works Porsche team, they were one of Germany's big three, the other two being Joest and Obermaier. Kremer Racing, very much run by Erwin Kremer, always fronting for his much quieter brother Manfred, had won Le Mans outright. Celebrated Formula World Champions Mario Andretti, Keke Rosberg and Alan Jones had all run under their banner. What was I to do, just swan up and ask them for a drive?

Why not, said Stu, if you don't ask, you don't get. Maybe Stuart saw something in me that I didn't see myself but 'hey ho' I thought, you get the meeting, I'll come along for the ride. True to form, after a multitude of persuasive phone calls, Stuart announced we had our meeting. 3 pm Thursday afternoon in their offices in Cologne. I felt sick, I felt elated. Hell, I didn't know what to think or what to feel. What on earth were we expected to achieve?

With no Eurotunnel for another two years, we took the late-night ferry to Calais and set off for the long drive to Cologne on a horrible day. The rain poured throughout, and we only arrived just on time. We were met by Achim Stroth, team director and acting secretary to the great Erwin Kremer. Achim invited us in. Seated in a reception area, coffee was served amongst the glittering silverware, intimidatingly looking down upon us from every available windowsill. I felt very out of place as I hesitantly nibbled on a biscuit.

The next half an hour was spent with Achim, who went through my CV with a fine-tooth comb. With great zeal, Stuart explained how we would finance the second car and bring in other competent drivers to fill the remaining seats. Shuffling up his notes, Achim stood up. Thinking this was the end of the meeting, we both stood up to shake his hand, but he said to hang on. With that, he disappeared up the central staircase to what we could only assume was the main office. We both nervously waited another 15 minutes when the great man, Erwin Kremer, marched down the steps, Achim following close behind.

With his Teutonic demeanour, Erwin briefly shook our hands, hardly making eye contact as he sat down. Very soberly, he looked through my CV laying on the table whilst Achim spoke to him in German. Every so often he would ask a question, the answers to which Achim duly translated. After another 15 minutes had passed, the austere lines on Erwin's face fell aside to reveal a robust grin. Then, in perfect English, he said welcome to the Kremer family and invited us to tour the workshops. I can only assume he wanted to firmly check us out before his sudden and total grasp of English became apparent. Such a lovely man. From that initial scare, he would become almost a father figure to me. Particularly over the next three years.

Back in the UK, I off-handedly mentioned to my dad I had driven all the way to Cologne and signed for the revered Kremer Porsche Racing team. He gruffly replied, 'Oh, I used to go there all the time'. Suddenly coming to my senses and remembering his particularly antagonistic dealings with Germans in the past, I said, 'Sorry, I thought you had a bother with the Hun. You always used to throw them out of your pub'. He came back with, 'Well, I remember going to Cologne regularly in the old days. We used to turn left at the Cathedral and bomb the railway station'. Conversation over.

Having signed with Kremer, it was again down to Rogers & Hammerstein to come up with the goods. With grand aplomb, Stuart went about the task in hand with great gusto. Again, with me illustrating many of the presentations, it wasn't too long before we matched up Unisys with Time Magazine on a deal that would replicate that first done with the Financial Times. The new Bell Atwood Driving Centre helped, as did my local Tom Walkinshaw-owned Porsche dealership, Chariots.

Perry Robb was the dealer principal of Chariots. I remember first visiting him before my first Le Mans. He was very keen at the time until I had to share with him the fact that it would be Ford Cosworth-powered. He said, 'Come back to me when you're driving a

170

Porsche'. It was a full seven years until I would proudly march into his offices again. In later years, Perry was to move on to H.R. Owen Porsche and then to Porsche GB Centre in Hatfield. Whenever I drove a Porsche, Perry's support was always there.

For co-drivers, we had the Italian stallion Almo Coppelli. Known for his double stints, he was a true rock of a driver and a former C2 World Champion. We also had Charles Rickett. An old Stoic, Charles had won the National division of the British Formula Three championship a couple of years before. Both would bring talent and additional budget to the party.

All set, we arrived at Le Mans in good time on the Saturday, a full week before the race. Many of the teams had already arrived, as there was a lot to do. There would be scrutineering in the town centre Monday and Tuesday, followed by qualifying Wednesday and Thursday. Friday would be the day the drivers had off whilst engines were changed and the cars prepared before the big race. As the start of Le Mans week, Saturday and Sunday came and went with no sign of Kremer, we started to get worried.

All the other teams had parked up their huge transporters behind the pits. Already unloaded, teams were busily fettling their cars in the garages. Mobile phones were not in general use, and we were finding it hard to get hold of Kremer. Our own scrutineering slot wasn't until Tuesday, but by Monday, we were beside ourselves. As Monday slowly ticked by, we thought they must have a problem. Come tea-time Monday, we were giving up all hope.

As we were about to leave the track for a spot of dinner and work out what the hell we were to do next, the two pristine Kremer transporters arrived. They were both as clean as a whistle and immaculately presented, all branded up with the Kremer Racing logos, the sponsors and even the driver names. With all the other transporters already in place, unperturbed they must have both done fifteen-point turns to position themselves in their allocated spots behind the garages.

With a quiet whirr of the tail lift motors, the cars were quickly rolled out into the pit garages. There were three. Two for racing and one as a spare. They were all exquisite. It was our first chance to see that the pit had already been pre-prepared. Everything from the pit flooring to the tyres to the toolboxes were already in place. And with that, they pulled down the garage doors and left for dinner. No last-minute fettling required. All that had been done. The German way and professionalism at its very best. Wow, we thought. We really have joined the big boys.

The next day, I drove into town. All the race cars' technical checks were ceremoniously carried out in a large, picturesque car park next to the Place des Jacobins, a central square that sat next to the historic cathedral. As is still the tradition, the transporters would have to give up their hard-fought circuit slots to journey downtown to unload their gleaming contents to the awaiting crowds. Colourful gazebo tents with ramps were allocated for each stage of the proceedings. Overseen by official scrutineers, everything from ride heights to bodywork was finely measured to ensure the cars were both safe and in compliance with a huge book of regulations.

The carnival atmosphere carried on throughout the two scrutineering days as ongoing driver interviews were held on a large central stage for the fans. Along with all the other drivers, I signed on and presented my overalls and helmet for safety checks. When the car had received its last check and awarded a pass, the engineers placed the permit decals on the roof, and the car was rolled into position for the official team photograph with all the mechanics and management standing in position behind the car, the drivers taking pride of place in the foreground. While we then busily signed autographs, the pictures would be sent on to the press office for the local evening newspaper edition.

Arriving back at the circuit, Achim presented all the drivers who had never driven a Porsche 962 before with two sheets of A4 paper sellotaped down the middle. Littered with knobs and dials, the illustration we held in our hands was of the dashboard inside the cockpit of a Porsche 962, which looked more like that of a fighter jet. Our homework, we were told, was to learn every button and switch by heart. He would test us the following day. His request was not without substance and true to form; test us he did.

At least this kept my mind somewhat away from the terrible nerves I was feeling. Tomorrow, I would drive a Porsche 962. A lethal weapon in the wrong hands, the 962 was and still is iconic. One of, if not the, most revered Le Mans cars ever. The 956 and its derivative, the 962, had previously taken outright laurels an incredible six times in the Le Mans 24 Hours. Before the chicanes, its top speed on the Mulsanne was over 245mph. Weighing no more than a small Ford Fiesta, albeit twice the size, this full ground-effect beast had 1000bhp on tap with the turbos turned up to maximum. This was going to be a whole new experience. I just hoped I was up to it.

Qualifying finally arrived and all went much to plan. That was, once you were attuned to the power at your disposal. This had to be administered with respect. In the No. 1 car, Giovanni Lavaggi stamped on the accelerator pedal with full force, leaving the pits, and with 800bhp going through the driveshafts, he promptly drove this very expensive bit of kit into the wall before he even managed to get out of the pit lane. Whew, I thought, good job, it was him and not me.

But with both cars running again, Kremer was busily preparing the spare. What was that all about, I wondered. Apparently, the No. 1 car was radioing in what was wrong with the car. Instead of making a lengthy, unscheduled pit stop, the team would just prepare their cloned spare. The driver would just come in, swap cars and be out again. Something you could lawfully do back in the day. They had the lighter, all-singing-all-dancing chassis, whereas we had the old aluminium-based version. However, pretty cool stuff, all the same, I thought.

And cool stuff, it really was. Feeling a little out of place, we had the great Norbert Singer overlooking our progress throughout. Norbert, being the factory Porsches' revered top racing engineer who, was instrumental in the design of the legendary Porsche 956/962 and the seven outright Le Mans winning titles it claimed during the 80's and 90's.

On that first day, I was finding my feet with the power and the speed, but I wasn't taking full advantage of the extreme ground effect the car was blessed with. Enter John Nielsen, outright 1990 Silk Cut Jaguar Le Mans winner and No. 1 car team-mate. John was built like an ox, and I was expecting any word to come out of such a frame as being deep and growly. He was looking at the telemetry monitors and caringly advised me, in a surprisingly high-pitched squeaky voice, he said I was doing OK, but I was getting the very fast and sweeping right-hander 'Indianapolis' all wrong.

On the speed trap, I was approaching Indianapolis at 220mph. The approach has a tunnel effect on you. The track is very narrow there; the huge pine trees on either side seem to wrap around you. With no run-off area in those days and with the entry of the bend hidden by trees, you're racing directly towards the forest dead ahead of you. My first time out, I was braking and shifting one gear down from top. John told me I had to keep the faith. You had to believe 100% in the full force of the ground effect. He said all you do approaching Indianapolis in the top is to give yourself a tiny confidence lift. This will balance the car and bring the nose down a touch. Then, you power through on full throttle. The ground effect will keep you sucked to the tarmac. He expanded that if I did this right, other corners, such as the very fast and sweeping Porsche Curves, a little further on, would be a doddle. Mmm, I thought. Easier said than done.

The next time out, I found myself braking for Mulsanne Corner at the end of the long straight when John's advisory words came back to niggle me. Blasting out of the corner, all the time shifting up through the gears, engine screaming as it reached peak revs, the straight that followed had two flat-out blind curves before you again approached Indianapolis. On another day, this is a nice country road that pleasurably takes you from the village of Mulsanne to Arnage. In a race car, this entire section is over within a matter of seconds.

Within no time, the 200-then 100-metre boards signalled the approach. I metaphorically closed my eyes as I slightly lifted in top and, with little more than blind faith, put my foot straight back on the gas. Holding my head up against the G forces, in a split second, I was through and was busily scrambling down through the gearbox for the next tight left-hander. I very much appreciated John's advice, but more than that just felt happy to still be alive. The ground effect obviously worked. It got easier after that first experience.

Come final qualifying day, I climbed up into one of the massive transporters Kremer had brought to change into my race gear, and to pop in my contact lenses. The shape of my eyeballs must have been going through a change, and I needed them for long sight. I felt a little self-conscious as I didn't think this was very racing driver-like. I was joined by Manuel Reuter and John Nielsen. To my delight, they were doing the exact same thing. It made me feel a whole lot better.

I then strode over the pits. I remember bumping into my co-driver, Almo Coppelli, who was just sliding on his helmet as he was the first out for the session just about to start. I just couldn't help myself. I thought back to the classic Le Mans movie. The scene where Steve McQueen grittily approaches his co-driver at the back of the old pits. Tapping Almo on the shoulder, I sternly said, as McQueen had done in the movie, 'Be careful out there'. It sounded so out of place. He, too, recollected the scene, and we both cackled. Movies remind us that they sometimes bear little resemblance to real life.

My own qualifying time was ok but could have been better had I turned the turbo up. I thought it was something you did stationary, but the request was radioed into me as I was whistling down the Mulsanne. The dial was to the left on the dash, but at well over 200mph, I failed to turn it as, after trying a couple of times, I preferred keeping both hands firmly on the steering wheel. In this instance, choosing discretion to be the better part of valour.

With the introduction of the new, naturally aspirated 3.5 engine regulations in the World Championship, the older C1 cars were given special dispensation to start and would run in their own class. Behind the even more powerful 3.5 litre marques of Toyota, Peugeot, Mazda, and Lola we would line up on the ninth row of the grid next to Derek Bell, his son Justin and Tiff Needell in a similar Porsche 962.

Race day was upon us. The No. 1 car was that of the Kenwood-sponsored Kremer Porsche, to be driven by esteemed pilotes Manuel Reuter, outright Le Mans' winner in 1989, John Nielsen, outright Le Mans winner in 1990 and Giovanni Lavaggi, who was to go on to Formula One, three years later. However, it was our No. 2 car, sponsored by Unisys and Time Magazine, with a prominently displayed Hawaiian Tropic sponsor that grabbed all the press. The bikini-clad Hawaiian Tropic girls seductively smothered the entire car on the grid for the pre-race photographs. You must remember, this was back in the day when this sort of activity was not so frowned upon.

As a side note, the Hawaiian Tropic brand was to sponsor me on and off, when their image allowed, for eight years at Le Mans. It was a different place in time. For the first year, I was the man. Arm around their waists. I began as a central figure to the start-line pictures taken with the girls as a heaving gang of press photographers would bunch around behind our roped-off area, fighting for position. The girls, all in their skimpy bikinis, were of course, always turned out unbelievably tanned and totally delectable.

They were all winners of various state Miss Hawaiian Tropic pageants. Miss California, Miss Arizona, Miss Florida, etc. Their prize was some cash, a trip to Paris, FRANCE (a big deal), with a tiny diversification to Le Mans for the Saturday race start. By teatime, they were all gone, back to Paris. Although I was always under contract to at least join them for a short while, it did not take me long to feel more at home chatting with the engineers in the back of the pit garages.

Back to the race and under ever-darkening and murky skies, the thunderous pack lit up the tarmac as the lights turned to green. It was going to be a wet one. It wasn't long before the track was awash as we tried to get into some form of routine. Mere feet apart at over 200mph shooting down the Mulsanne, the spray was so bad sometimes, you could only pick out the rear wing of the car in front of you.

On Charles's second stint, all appeared to be going well, but as he exited Dunlop Chicane, he put the power on too early and had the almightiest spin all the way down the track towards the Esses. We watched on the TV monitors in the pits, hearts in mouths, as he nearly hit everything but didn't. Erwin Kremer looked on without expression as his pride and joy was so nearly destroyed up against the barriers. The team pit-signaller readied the inboard, but Erwin quietly demanded no, keep him out. At the end of his scheduled stint, Charles came in.

The car went up on its quick-lift jacks; I got in as Charles got out. Belts were fastened, checks were made. A new set of tyres went on as the windscreen was wiped. The engine burst into life, and I was off again down the pit lane. From time to time, Charles would ready himself when he thought he was due for his next stint, but it never came. Rightly or wrongly, Erwin had decided that Almo and I would try a shot of going the rest of the duration alone.

Deep into the middle of the night, it was only after the rain had subsided for a while that blankets of heavy fog came down to envelop the circuit. It was particularly bad on the Mulsanne. Not long after I radioed in, the teams IN-board came out. This was an unscheduled stop, so I wondered what the problem was. As soon as I reached the pit, the team surrounded the rear end of the car. The rear bodywork was off in a flash as Achim, with his Germanic tinge, kept shouting, 'Vot is wrong with 5th gear, vot is wrong with 5th gear'. Nothing is wrong with 5th gear, I replied. All I radioed in to say, 'It was foggy out here'. With that, he curtly suggested I message only when in trouble and that he had no interest in the general weather forecast. Obviously, my observation, however inconsequential to the job at hand, got lost in translation. However, although we had lost a few minutes, I was soon back out on the track again.

Through the rain and fog, Almo and I soldiered on throughout the night. By now, the car was running in the top ten and as the light broke over the horizon and the skies cleared, we found ourselves in a battle of the Porsches. The No1 Kremer was a couple of places higher as we were sandwiched between the Porsche 962s of the Obermaier car of Yver, Altenbach and Lässig and the ADA version driven by the two Bells & Needell.

I must say this is the time when it's good to be alive and doing this. As the campsites were busily frying up their bacon, sausage and eggs, the action out on the track had become calmer. There were now fewer cars as many had retired in the night through technical failures or the inevitable accident. The engine still felt strong, and it was just a delight driving around this legendary of all circuits. I felt at one with this car. For once, I was very much at home. Often with a clear view in front of me, there was a feeling of time on your hands as I mastered every braking area and bend with far more ease than the busy, fractured night of before. From that small boy with very little confidence, I was coming into my own.

Gear changes were much more precise, although my right hand, by this time, was always a bit of a mess. In those days of H-box gear shifting, the constant effort took a toll on your gear change hand. Blister upon blister would appear, and I had to wrap my hand in Gaffa tape or bandages before putting on my fireproof Nomex gloves. It usually took a couple of weeks to heal after Le Mans.

It might sound strange, but out there on that day, it later occurred to me that I must have been in a similar zone as my Mum was in her 20s. A long time past now, she was once a ballerina. For that job, the qualities required were strength, stamina, balance and control. You also had to be precise and forceful, as well as being highly delicate and completely at one with your partner. On my side, my partner was my car.

With 20 hours run, the suspense was kept up as we chopped and changed places with the Obermaier entered Primagaz car. Running well to our fuel allocation, Erwin Kremer came up with what he thought was a cunning plan. We could run to the finish, but it would be very tight on the Obermaier Primagaz car. Kremer ordered that the signallers post a pit board saying IN. FUEL. We were all told to ignore the board in the hope that the Obermaier team, stationed in a nearby pit, would see it. Perhaps they would be fooled into thinking they had a short amount of time on their hands and bring the car in for a 'splash and dash'.

The term for a quick top-up. We, of course, planned to carry on and get ahead. Sadly, it didn't work with the Obermaier car, but the ADA 962 saw we were coming in and, gasping for fuel themselves, roared into the pits for a quick drink. So, in the end, the status remained the same for the final laps of the race. We took the chequered flag just behind the Obermaier car but ahead of Derek Bell & Co. in the ADA Porsche.

Kremer immediately pulled the pit garage doors down as the onslaught of fans was, as always massive, descending from the stands in their thousands to run up to the podium. On their way, they would pull down the big team signs above the garages as souvenirs and anything else they could get their hands on. The team just rallied in the pits as if it were in an air raid shelter, hiding. We all shook hands and slapped each other's backs. We had overcome the incredible demands the 24 hours brought to finish in the most celebrated endurance race in the world.

It brought tears to my eyes, thinking how close we had all become during one small week of the year. It amazed me that the mechanics all lined up to ask for my autograph. It was touching but uncalled for. They were the true stars of the day. With their far superior knowledge of all things mechanical, they were the ones that kept the car going through thick and thin. Through night and day, they were the ones who jumped upon the car with such gusto every time we had a problem.

Maybe this had something to do with Erwin Kremer. Maybe he had influenced them in some way. Frightening to some, Erwin and I always got on well. We just bonded from that first day after he decided to speak English. That was even when, like a naughty schoolboy, he caught me smoking in the garage WC. Unlike some of the superstars that had signed for him in the past, I know he liked the way I came with no airs and graces. No provisos or special requests. I was quick and just got in and did the job.

While Peugeot celebrated the outright win up on the podium at the other end of the pitlane, we popped open the champagne, happy to celebrate our third in class within the dark confines of our pit garage. Tomorrow, we would leave. Never perhaps to ever be as close as we had been that very small week away in La Sarthe.

Chapter Nineteen
Deux Chevaux Odyssey

Back in the UK, my pal Eugene O' Brien contacted me. Eugene was the similarly talented younger brother of Mike O Brien, the chap I had raced with in Thundersports. He said how about I drive with him in a big race he was doing in Ireland? What could it be, I thought. As far as I knew, there were not any big, international sportscar races in Ireland at the time. He said, no, no, this was for the 24 Hours of Mondello Park. I was still none the wiser. Mm, ok I said hesitantly. What kind of cars are we talking about here? Well, Citroen 2CV's, of course, he replied.

In a mixed season that had me driving in big 200mph Group C sportscars and a similar American IMSA version both in Europe and the States, I had never contemplated racing a tiny 2CV. A little dumbfounded, I mentioned how bizarre the suggestion was. No, not all. It'll be really good fun. You'll have a laugh. I promise. Well, not doing anything that weekend and having never been to Ireland, to hell with it, why not, I thought.

Less than an hour's drive from Dublin, Mondello Park is a picturesque circuit set in County Kildare. Their mid-summer 24-Hour 2CV event attracts a huge contingent of racers from far and wide. Normally, three or four drivers per car, their skill sets ranged significantly. There were fully fledged, professional British Touring Car drivers to downright amateurs just feeling their way into the sport. In this particular year, we had Irish star David Kennedy competing. Not only was he a former Formula One grand prix driver, but had won the GTP class at Le Mans three times. We also had a group of senior Girl Scouts who managed to get themselves a racing licence and bought a 2CV between them for £400.

In the space of three weeks, I had swapped a twin-turbo, 1000bhp Porsche 962 capable of speeds approaching 240mph for a mighty 600cc, 45bhp 2CV that maxed out at 75mph. I'm sure that was downhill with the wind behind it and with the car lightened by taking out all the seats and every bit of the limited trim the original had to offer. A simple roll cage made sure you wouldn't be squished if it went on its roof. Not until the race was I to see how many that would be.

Thoroughly welcomed by the Irish, a warm and light-hearted atmosphere prevailed throughout the proceedings. Run by 2CV expert Scotsman Norry Taylor, our two-car 'Le Shark' entry, together with fearsome-looking shark teeth painted over the grills, were amongst the frontrunners. I was to be part of a four-man team in one, Eugene the same in the other. Our progress in qualifying was somewhat diminished by our perceived indestructible engine packing up. No problem said, Big Jim. Jim was an integral member of the team. A giant of a man whose beard and tattoos were nearly as colossal as his muscles.

There are only a couple of major bolts that keep a 2CV engine in place, and with all the bits undone, big Jim lifted it out in one swift, back-breaking heave. I can't remember exactly where we started on the mighty 50-car grid that stretched the length of the main straight. What I do remember, was sitting behind the wheel as we lined up on the start. In front of me was a simple speedo, and that was about it. Gone were all the high-tech digital readouts of the Le Mans Porsche. I asked how long I should stay out. Well, about 2 hours should do, Norry replied. But how do I know when two hours is up?

Throwing his eyes into the back of his head, Norry took his wristwatch off and Sellotaped it to the dash. Happy now, he said. I could see this being a journey into a whole new low-tech world as, just before 2 pm, we set off on our rolling lap. The narrow tyres squealed as much as the soft, gloopy suspension rolled as we all tried to keep in formation. Next time round, the green light was on, the starter's flag had fallen, and we were all off.

From that moment on, this surreal experience I had brought entirely unto myself just became more bizarre and funnier by the minute. Wailing in tears of laughter, I had to try sticking my fingers through the opening on my full-face helmet to wipe my eyes dry whilst still holding onto the steering wheel. Although the tears subsided after a few laps, I did spend much of my first stint, indeed stints to follow, lightly chuckling away to myself. At a snail's pace, the only way of passing a car running to similar lap times was patience. I would have to slipstream for three or four laps, watching out for any weaknesses. Perhaps where they braked too early or took the wrong line into a corner.

If they didn't show any weak areas, I just had to wait behind and be ready to pounce when they made a mistake. I started to think just how good the cars would be summoned to work in a race school.

The skills and disciplines a rookie racer could learn first racing bumper to bumper at a non-distracting speed. How, without the fear element, you had time to carefully think your next manoeuvre through.

As the race progressed, we slowly climbed up the leaderboard from our lowly grid position caused by our time-consuming engine change during qualifying. All the cars would bob and bounce around on their pram-like suspension, and on occasion, one would topple over onto its roof. At Le Mans the race would be effectively neutralised with safety cars released to dramatically slow down the pace until the incident was cleared. Here at Mondello, with the pace already slow, we all just raced on. All that happened was marshals would wave a yellow flag in one hand and a white flag in the other. The yellow was to say, caution ahead, slow down, no over-taking, the white to advise an alien vehicle was on the track. This was usually a digger. That, with a couple of hefty helpers, was enough to push the 2CV back on its wheels. Job done.

Beset by the odd problem along the way, by the mid-morning, we had, quite literally, crawled our way to 4th overall. The podium is just out of our reach. And that is where we stayed as the chequered flag fell. With that, after surrounding the podium for the winning ceremonies, we all adjourned to the circuit bar for a well-earned drink. The Guinness flowed, and the diddly dee band played the night away. Within the warm, welcoming, and light-hearted atmosphere afforded by our new Irish friends, I found it hard to leave the shores of the Emerald Isle. Whether we had come 4th, 14th or 44th, the whole jolly experience had been a lot of fun. A truly wonderful encounter, never to be forgotten. Thanks Eugene.

Chapter Twenty
Win Some, Lose Some.

Flying back, I sauntered into the office with a big smile, hard to wipe off my face. That didn't last long after Stuart picked up the phone. It was urgent and he immediately passed the phone over to me. It was a Stateside Doctor working at Springfield Hospital, Massachusetts. He told me that my Dad had been admitted after collapsing in a restaurant. Dad was in intensive care, and the prognosis was not good. It was 50/50 whether he would react to treatment. If I wanted to see him, he suggested coming now. Within minutes, I was out the door. Stuart was organising a flight for me as I dropped home to pick up my passport. Parking directly outside the entrance to Heathrow, I was met by BA staff who comfortingly shuffled me through security with great tempo, and I was off. I can't remember what happened to my car, but this was long before the days of 9/11.

I was headed to New York because flights to Boston didn't match my crucial time frame. That was ok as I knew JFK pretty well and where Alamo car hire was. Before long, I was flat out heading north on Route 91. Going as fast as my little hire car would carry me through Connecticut, I saw flashing lights in my mirror. I was being pulled over. For f…ks sake, I thought. I had no time for this.

Stepping out of the car, I was immediately hurled up against the car roof, arms splayed, guns pointing at me. Blimey, I thought, this was just like the movies. I had no idea that removing myself from the car was seen as an act of aggression and certainly the wrong thing to do. Explaining my dilemma, depicted in the best possible English accent I could muster, they soon placed their guns back in their holsters. Then, amazed as I was, they told me to follow them. They could take me as far as the Connecticut border with Massachusetts.

Afterwards, I would have to keep my speed down if I wasn't to invite further interest by the cops in my further progress. Foot down, following the flashing lights, the border was reached in no time. They then pulled up and, with a quick 'good luck' flash of their headlights, turned around and headed home.

At the hospital, I found my dad all wired up with tubes seeming to come out from everywhere. He was, however, responding and I was told to stay in touch and come back in a couple of days. Feeling guilty learning how to water ski on the Quaboag with pals I had in North Brookfield, I awaited news. A few days later, it came, and I rushed back to the hospital. Dad was ok. The worst was over. He was sitting up in bed in high spirits, surrounded by glamorous nurses.

It seemed as if I spent quite a long time that summer crossing the Atlantic. I raced at Lime Rock in a Porsche 966. This open-top car was the owner's own derivative of the Porsche 962 and had all to do with a deal we were compiling for the following year. The team was Gunnar Racing owned by Kevin Jeanette. Laid back and amiable, Kevin was an absolute master of his craft. First run in the Daytona 24 Hours, I took his lithe version of the 962 to an easy win in the July 4th Independence Day meeting they had there. Second place went to well-known ex-pat Brian Redman in an older Porsche. On a later visit, I caught up with Dawn, a very special friend who lived in Buffalo.

We had met in the States some years before. As warm and funny as she was beautiful, I immediately fell for her with a total passion. I really did think she was the one. We had occasionally met up both in the UK and America, but sadly, what with the racing kicking off and the big gulf commonly known as the North Atlantic was a step too far at the time. On this trip, Dawn invited me down the Finger Lakes with her new boyfriend, Pete. A really nice chap, Pete was a skydiver, and he treated me to a tandem jump over the lakes. We circulated up into the skies in this battered old plane.

Reaching 10,000 feet, I was asked to sit in his lap. Belting me up, he quipped that of all the skydivers present. I was to be the only one jumping out without a parachute. Kind words, I thought. As it happened, I took the 5,000ft free fall that followed in my stride. Compared to spearing down the Mulsanne Straight at 200mph+ in the rain and the fog, this was nothing. In fact, I remember the amusement I felt as my mouth reached Wallace [as in Wallace and

Gromit] proportions on the way down. My mouth wriggling uncontrollably.

At 5,000ft, the parachute opened, and we floated safely to the ground. Looking a little upset that I found the experience more amusing than terrifying, he looked a bit glum as he unbelted me. Perhaps the new boyfriend didn't like our past history. But this was only conjecture. Both Pete and Dawn remain very happy together to this day.

The next time I went, it was to escort my dad back. He had run out of the additional medical insurance he took out for the trip to see his greatest friend, some eight weeks before. However, he was in good form based on the remnants of the party he had with the nurses the day before. Party balloons and well-wishing cards still littered his private room. I thought he was in for a big surprise taking him on to the NHS of the time back at home, as all the nurses turned out again to kiss him goodbye.

The next time I was to see Kevin's Porsche 966 was back in Kent at Brands Hatch. John Bartlett had done this ultra-complicated prize indemnity scheme where he talked his sponsor into putting up the premium for a two-race deal. Either he or I would have to secure the car finished in the top five in at least one of two European races. The prize being $250,000. Prize indemnity was famous in the early 90's for providing a hole-in-one in golf. The unsuspecting winner receiving a brand-new Jaguar or similar. Insurance companies extended this to anything where the odds on winning were very unlikely. Against the burgeoning numbers of Porsche 962s competing at the time, John still thought this a risk worth taking. The idea being that if we won the prize, we would buy Kevin Jeanette's car.

Kevin duly had his car flown over from his base in Palm Beach, Florida. Kremer was there with their own open-top version. With both Kevin Jeanette and Erwin Kremer standing up in their individual cockpits, shaking hands, photographs of their 962 derivatives were taken as they sat there, side by side in the pit lane.

The race was a European Interserie event. I attempted to qualify first, with the exact same result as Giovanni Lavaggi had experienced at Le Mans. Without carefully feeding in the huge amount of power it had, I went straight into the wall before I got out of the pit lane. Silly me. I had destroyed the special, Gunnar-prepared U.S. nose box as well as a few more parts we could not replace closer to home. Kevin went into scramble mode and had to draft over the most important part from the USA. The next morning, a bleary-eyed young chap arrived armed with the massive front end. He had a passport he'd never used previously. In his twenty years on the planet, he had hardly left his county, let alone the State before, and here he was, over 4,500 miles from home.

John decided I couldn't be trusted and raced the car himself. A good enough show saw him finish 9th. Sadly, not enough to claim the big prize. The open-top Kremer, driven by my Le Mans No. 1 car team companion, Manuel Reuter, won. All eyes turned to the next round at Zolder. It was here that 10 years before, adulated Ferrari superstar Gilles Villeneuve had lost his life during qualifying for the Belgium Grand Prix. I would take the wheel for this event so I could feel all those eyes boring into the back of my head.

Like the Interserie round at Brands Hatch, there would be two races. Visiting the weeds a couple of times in practice, I eventually qualified 7th and lined up next to Otto Altenbach in a Kremer CK7 for Race 1. Otto, one of the drivers in the Obermaier car at Le Mans that year, was now racing for Kremer.

As the lights turned to green, we scorched off, only for a front wheel to come loose soon into the race. It was hardly diagnosable, to begin with, but as the laps went down and I wasn't making any headway, the wobble became far more acute. After pitting and a new wheel firmly bolted on, I had lost a crucial couple of minutes. By the time I blasted out of the pits exit with over half the race run, I was dead last. This was not good for the $250,000 that was riding on the result! By the time the chequered flag fell, a lowly 12th position was all I could deliver. And even to get there was hard work.

As the Race 1 result determined where I would start for Race 2, things were looking bleak as I took my grid position back on the sixth row. All I could do was keep my head down, embrace the race and see where it led. A frenetic race ensued. With three laps to go, I was up to 8th place and on the next lap, I made a dramatic lunge for 7th. I had scrambled my way up close to the sharp end of the field, but with less than two laps to go, I would need an act of God to get any further. Then it happened. Just around the corner, two of the leading contenders clashed.

Through the dust and debris, I flashed past. But where was I? Had they spun round and managed to carry on, or were they behind me? Passing the chequered flag, I experienced an uneasy slowing down lap. John had rushed up to the press office to get the official results as I peeled into the pit lane. Exhausted and disillusioned, I unstrapped my belts and climbed out of the 800bhp monster that had been my office for the afternoon. The team looked as bewildered as I was. The premium-paying sponsor just painfully solemn. Then, a stoney-faced John, clutching the result sheet came across. He kept the act up as long as he could before a big grin began to beam across his face. We had secured 5th by just over a second. The prize was ours!

Suffice to say, gluttonous amounts of champagne were consumed before the beers were liberally issued to all and sundry. A good day in the office. What followed was yet another trip to the States, where John decided not to take the 966 deal and duly paid Kevin off. Eventually, going for two ex-Granatelli Lola Indy cars, complete with Indianapolis 500 scrutineering labels still stuck to the inside cockpit walls, that we raced in the Interserie Championship the following year.

Back in the UK, Sadly, in November, I received the call I had been dreading. My Dad was back in hospital and unlikely to make it through the night. I dropped everything, but after the two-hour trip down to the south coast, he had already passed. My father always had a sharp sense of humour, so it was no surprise when the vicar turned up 20 minutes late for his cremation. In a cloud of dust, he parked up in a gleaming red, open-top sports car. Tellingly, the registration plate was VIC 1. Yet again, Dad had the last laugh.

For the wake that followed, we partied in a pub now owned by one of his former barmaids to way after closing time. After my Dad's colourful stories were retold, we danced the night away, just as he would have wanted. And as a side note, two funny things occurred around four years later. I was going to the States and thought it would be a good idea to scatter Dad's ashes onto his beloved Quabaog. This was the lake he loved, where he would sip gin, watching the blood-red sunset with a bag of pretzels in hand. The same place I learned to sail.

My brother Simon agreed, but we couldn't find him. We had both forgotten which undertakers we had used. It took a couple of weeks of detective work, but we finally found his urn on a dusty shelf, along with his name tag hanging from it. At the 11th hour, my brother decided he would like to say his final goodbyes with me at the lake. The Boston flight was from Gatwick, so I spent the night beforehand at his house close by in Sussex. Pride of place, Dad's urn was positioned on Simon's mantelpiece above the fireplace in the lounge, awaiting an early departure the next day.

Now, Dad could be grumpy. I could see him being especially upset, being left on some back-room shelf for years on end. In full view of both my brother and me, the urn moved five feet from one side of the mantelpiece to the other. We both just stood there aghast. Not believing in the supernatural, I immediately took a coin out of my pocket and placed it on its side where the urn had been. Unbelievably, it didn't move. The mantelpiece was completely level. That was funny, peculiar. What happened early the following morning was more funny, funny.

My brother and I were standing around in his kitchen, having a slice of toast before heading for the airport. We decided to carry on dad's urn to place him more conveniently in one of the overhead compartments. We popped his urn in a plastic bag, which I was holding as Muffey, Simon's Springer Spaniel, got involved. With front legs down on haunches, rear legs up in the air, Muffey grabbed the bottom of the bag. Then, with a fun-filled growl, he shook his head from side to side. The harder I pulled, the harder he held the bag. Oh my god, I yelled to Simon. I was thinking that if he doesn't let go, the lid of the urn will pop off, and in a cloud of dust, the furthest Dad is going to get is the kitchen floor. We'll have to hoover him up. Fortunately, with some strict orders from Simon, the wrestling stopped, and Muffey released the precious package. Disaster avoided.

Back on the all-important Le Mans trail for our 1993 campaign, Stuart was talking to American global adventurer Steve Fossett. A

Colorado-based self-made billionaire, Fossett gave up his business pursuits to concentrate full-time on setting records. Although he was to go on to set many more, he had already secured records in ballooning, gliding, sailing, swimming, and mountaineering. As an all-round action-man and sometime IMSA racer, he dreamt of competing in the Le Mans 24 Hours. At the time, in the UK a race driver had to be in possession of a super-licence to drive world championship races. All it seemed you required in the States at the time was a driving licence, a pulse, and a wad of cash. Stuart was only happy to help him spend it.

I was over the moon as we were to join the celebrated Kremer team again. We would be running in one of three Porsche 962s they entered that year. The No. 1 car, a special carbon fibre version, would be driven by Italian Giovani Lavaggi again. He was partnered by South African superstar Wayne Taylor and 12 x Le Mans veteran Jürgen Lässig from Germany. The second car would be seen running in the capable hands of battle-aged pro-Francois Migault. As well as fitting in three seasons in Formula 1, this would be the Frenchman's 21st appearance at Le Mans. His hot-shoe partners would be American IMSA pilot Andy Evans and Kremer regular Thomas Saldana from Spain. For our car, we had my favourite Italian ox driving again, Almo Coppelli, as well as Mr Fossett.

In qualifying the Peugeots and Toyota prototypes were in a class of their own, followed by a deluge of Porsche 962's and Courage C30's. Although mid-pack of the sharp end, we qualified ahead of

197

the other two Kremer cars thanks to Almo. Steve was a little off, but that was expected, especially going into his first Le Mans. In fact, Steve was off in several ways. He was nice enough but always appeared a little aloof. I think he just felt he was on a separate planet from the rest of us. It was nothing personal. Very much focused in his own thoughts, maybe he was. What did become blatantly apparent was he didn't like driving in the dark. A small problem for a 24-hour race.

Before the 4 pm start, we all lined up on the grid for the traditional pre-race fanfare and festivities. Again, Hawaiian Tropic was emblazoned on the front of the No 3 Kremer Porsche. So even the crowds around the pole-sitter bore little resemblance to the mass attack of press and photographers eagerly vying for position of a clear shot of the girls around ours. Horns sounded, the grid was cleared of people, and within minutes, we were yet again on another magical mystery tour into the great unknown.

After brake and oil leak problems slowed us down with unscheduled pit stops to begin with, we started to make headway. The progress continued. We were clearly on track to push ourselves into the top ten overall before nightfall. A now-bespectacled Steve spent most of his non-driving time off reading a book in the back of the pits. Not so unusual to some perhaps, but I had never seen anyone, let alone a driver, find this the time or the place for such leisure activities.

Closing the book, he took off his glasses and casually announced he was off to bed. Give us a call in the morning, he said as he left. Memories of '92 came flooding back. We were now the 'Almo and Robin' show yet again. To be honest, although we could only pass a hurried word or two as Almo clambered into the cockpit as I got out, I think we were both pretty pleased. We could now both double-stint at a higher speed. The night was ours. Without outward expression, Erwin Kremer just looked on.

Unlike the year before, the night was beautifully clear. Apart from the odd minor mishap, the car was on song. All was going to plan. With the fuel allowance we had back then, a normal stint lasted around an hour. I would still have to pit and refuel, but doubling up the stints meant there was less time wasted changing drivers all the time. The car would roar in and instantly go up on air jacks. I just sat there, trance-like, as 80 litres of high-octane fuel was pumped in, and tyres were changed.

Staring straight ahead, with the busyness of the pit stop going on all around me, everything seemed removed, sounds deadened. The banging sounds of the newly-tyred wheels being hastily rammed on and the clatter of the pneumatic wheel guns driving them safely home were all estranged and muffled. With my mind still travelling at 200mph, I only had my heavy breath and the sticky feeling of my own hot sweat chilling to distract me.

Through the cockpit window, I could see the warm glow of the pit lane lights and the flashes of the press cameras. Achim, headphones on, striding around in the foreground, mechanics busily working on the rear tyres in my mirrors. With the windscreen wiped off a billion dead bugs, engine fired up, our signaller would raise the out sign. Crunching into first gear, I would roll out of the pit lane, then carefully floor it as I hit the pit exit line. The torque of 800bhp would then thrust me out into the darkness again.

Light blankets of early morning fog would lay in parallel strips on the Mulsanne. At 200 mph, I would thump through each floating blanket in a split second. It gave the effect of driving over a bumpy road. The lighter sky gave the first welcoming signs of dawn approaching. Don't get me wrong, I loved driving at night. With headlights blazing all around, I could see where everyone was. I could easily position the car, something harder during the day. But dawn meant we had made it through the night and were that much closer to our goal. With that, the team agreed it was a good time to rally up a sleepy Mr Fossett. A good call, we thought, as both Almo and I were both pretty knackered by then. As the early morning sun began to steadily rise over the grandstands, Steve took over from Almo.

At the time, we were squeezing in an extra lap every stint by flicking the reserve switch on as we passed the pits for the last time. This was helping us slowly creep up the leaderboard. With radio contact kept largely restricted, this was usually communicated by a pit signal, although by the time the board was seen, we had normally flicked the switch already. Steve was well briefed to do the same.

Just after 7 am, word came through that Steve had stopped a mere 200 metres from the pit lane entry. He was out of fuel. He had completed his stint, forgot to flick on the reserve switch and missed the pit board. We all rushed down the pit lane. We could see him just metres away. Kremer radioed to him to try to move the car on the starter button. He edged closer but not close enough. The marshals strictly adhered to the rules, and with all the help of the pit crew ready and eager a short walk away, Steve and our healthy '93 challenger was condemned. So near, yet so far.

We were all speechless as Steve wandered back to the pit garage. After apologising profusely, he invited us to dinner that evening. We can choose the restaurant, he added. Peugeot would again take the overall win, and both the other two Kremer cars would finish respectably. After the podium ceremonies were over, we quietly waited in the traffic to leave the circuit. Destination, the very best restaurant in town.

At least we would see the day out with the entire Kremer crew for the feast. I sat next to Almo; Stuart sat the other side whilst Steve placed himself at the head of the table. For once, we felt we had no reason to look at the menu prices first as the pricy wine liberally flowed. At the end of the evening, we were all in higher spirits as the head waiter duly delivered the bill to Steve. He immediately pulled out his wallet.

Quickly doing the maths in his head, he laid down enough notes on the table to cover himself before announcing it would appear we each owed 'X' amount each. It was only then that it became apparent that his kind invitation did not extend to anything other than that. After I and a few others scrambled to borrow funds, the bill was paid, and we wished Billionaire Steve Fossett, a good night.

Before leaving Le Mans, Stuart and I went to the circuit the following morning to say goodbye to the Kremer team. They were busy loading the transporters for the long haul back to Cologne. The last car to go on the tail lift was Kremer's CK7. This was the open-top version of the 962 that the team were cleaning up with in the Interserie Sportscar Series. At the time, open-top cars in the top classes were not eligible for Le Mans or the World Championship. Erwin, passionate about his new creation, had the car on static display all week in an attempt to lobby the ACO [the governing body of Le Mans] into changing their rules. Little did I know at the time, but this car would play a significant role in my life for 1994 and that of the Le Mans 24 Hour race as a whole in future years.

Towards the end of that '93 season, the Indy cars I jointly owned with John were impounded. John, who had this adept ability of playing three-dimensional chess, had fallen foul of the authorities. They blasted him on his genuine prize indemnity scheme, but I believe his downfall was more to do with his other multiple insurance plans he had in place. So ultra-complicated, it would take me another book to even attempt to explain, even if I could. Suffice to say, in the years that followed, he would eventually write his own non-factual, award-winning Amazon book that, from his perspective, accounted for it all.

On 3 September 2007, Steve Fossett took off in a single-engine Champion 8KCAB Super Decathlon light aircraft from a private airstrip in Nevada. He went missing, and a massive search and rescue operation, the largest effort ever conducted for one person within the U.S., was instigated. It would take nearly a month before personal items were recovered high in the Sierra Nevada mountains by a hitchhiker. The aircraft wreckage was found a day or so later. It would take another month before two bones found at the scene were confirmed as being a DNA match to Steve. In July 2009, The National Transportation Safety Board declared that the probable cause of the crash was the pilot's inadvertent encounter with downdrafts exceeding the climb capability of the aeroplane.

Chapter Twenty-One
The Return of a Legend

With the Indy cars now a hazy memory, I was stuck competing in the one-make Dunlop Rover Turbo Cup Series. Blue Hawk had returned, but not being able to afford the British Touring Car Championship, they considered this the best alternative. I agreed but hated it. Sealed engines are delivered to the teams with the cars at the start of the season. With one make you either receive a good engine or a bad one. I had a bad one.

I had to focus on the bigger stuff if I was to make any significant headway. For Le Mans, Stuart and I had a few things tentatively in place. The main national weekly magazine Autosport was hanging on with the promise of supporting another Le Mans campaign, along with their sister publication Classic & Sportscar. We had pledges from the likes of Autoglym, Unisys, Polaroid and the John Watson Performance Driving Centre at Silverstone, and we were beginning to make small inroads with Porsche GB. What we really needed was some magic, 'big sponsor' glue to stick all these pieces together.

Over a two-week period, I became a hermit in my own house. I didn't go out. I spent the entire time muddling through the sponsors we already had and the potential partners that could lend a hand given due cause. From a long list, I then went through who could be pulled into this mix in a bigger way. With a bunch of magic markers to hand and an A2,-sized drawing pad, I began sketching out various scenarios. I was particularly proud of one image created. That of a Gulf Oil-sponsored Porsche. The car really stood out on the page emblazoned in the company's iconic powder blue and orange colour scheme.

The Gulf Oil colours were almost as famous as the 24-hour race itself. The brand's livery broke cover for the first time with the Gulf-JW Automotive team, which, between 1967 and 1975, transformed every Ford GT40, Porsche 917 and Mirage race cars in its colours into legends.

Gulf-backed cars achieved victory at Le Mans in 1968, 1969 and 1975, as well as taking World Championship Sportscar honours. Their feat was immortalised by the 1970 movie "Le Mans" with Steve McQueen playing the role of Michael Delaney, and with it, a Gulf-style icon was born.

Legendary drivers such as Jacky Ickx, Jackie Oliver, Pedro Rodríguez, Richard Attwood, Herbert Mueller, Peter Revson, David Hobbs, Brian Redman and Lucien Bianchi all combined to rack up victories relentlessly over that period.

Winning Le Mans in 1968 with Rodriguez and Bianchi and a year later with Ickx and Oliver was a highlight that emphatically put the Gulf Porsche combo on the map, entrenching the pairing in the mainstream forever. Six years later, Jackie Ickx and Derek Bell would take victory at the 1975 Le Mans in a Gulf-liveried Mirage-GR8.

Gulf had not been seen on the international sportscar racing stage for nearly twenty years since. Maybe it was time for a grand return. With my visuals done and the hankering idea, however unlikely, that my childhood hero and British Le Mans legend Derek Bell might be induced into playing a starring role, I took my findings to Stuart.

True to form, Stuart jumped on the idea straight away. There was no stopping him. Burning through call after call, it was not long before we had our meeting all set at the Gulf Oil UK headquarters in Cheltenham. On a cold winter's day, we headed west armed with our presentation and practically a library full of old Le Mans books. The books were to become a handy addition as the relatively young marketing team had no real understanding of their illustrious motor sport history. Fortunately for us, we could not have timed our marketing attack better.

Gulf were just about to launch a revised livery that would brand every one of their 500 service stations. In would come the same bright orange set against a deeper, slightly metallic blue. Out would go the fabled powder blue. After a sweaty hour or two, we came out with a firm 'yes.' More intricate details to be gone into at a follow-up meeting. Uncontrollably smirking, we high-fived each other in the lift from the board office back down to reception.

Next stop was the Racing Car Show. Derek, who now lived in Florida much of the time, would be there. After his Gulf-sponsored first of five Le Mans wins, Derek was keen. Before his first Le Mans win, he had also raced the 250mph Gulf Porsche 917 and became a pal of Steve McQueen as one of the star professional drivers involved in making the movie.

Although warm enough to the concept, Derek had two main concerns. One was an issue with Kremer Racing. Of the top three Porsche teams it was Kremer who liked to creatively explore the boundaries with revisions not altogether approved by the factory. Like Colin Chapman before in Formula One, Erwin's cars were fast but fragile. F1 driver Manfred Winkelhock had died in a Kremer Porsche at Mosport in Canada in 1985, and Jo Gartner a year later at Le Mans. His second concern related to the third driver. Happy enough with my somewhat haphazard development up into the higher ranks, this was the biggest international race on the sportscar calendar. Derek still wanted full assurance that anyone joining us would be a driver of good standing.

Like a couple of politicians caught on the back foot, Stuart and I set about justifying our case. In this year of change, we said, the ACO have considerably reworked the regulations. At the sharp end you would have the slightly earlier 90's prototypes competing on a level pegging with the newly introduced top category GT cars. Should the new GT's not get their act together quickly enough, we stood a very good chance of competitively competing for the overall win.

We added that the Kremer Racing Porsche CK7, which had won almost every race in the last two years in the Interserie

Championship, was going to be replaced with a stunning brand-new K8 version. The ACO had finally come round to Erwin's way of thinking, and it would be built exactly to their latest open-top prototype regulations.

On the driver front, we proposed Jürgen Lässig. A veteran of twelve Le Mans, eleven of those in Porsche 596 and 962s. He had already taken a 2nd and a 3rd overall, and to top it off, he would bring substantial funds to the party.

That was enough to sway Derek. It was worth the risk. Having agreed his fee, we shook hands on the deal there and then. As we all stood up, a multitude of admirers, politely standing by for the appropriate moment, descended upon him for autographs. Blimey, I thought. I'm to drive with an international legend.

Since the very dawn of Kremer Racing, the team had only run Porsches, but now they were being heavily romanced by Honda to prepare and run a three-car team. This giant manufacturer wanted to make a big statement at Le Mans in the LMGT2 class, and the promise of a large cheque was compromising the Kremer brothers. Erwin's very special baby was being built, but they were getting embroiled in an offer they were finding very hard to refuse.

After what must have been a massive deliberation with his own ego, Erwin finally and reluctantly announced his decision. He said that however much he wanted to run his new Porsche Kremer K8 at Le Mans that year, he couldn't. He would loan the car to us for someone else to run. With that, Stuart set to work. With the full support of Gulf, Gulf Oil Racing was born. Highly experienced New Zealander Graham Lorimer would be team manager. He would draft up loyal mechanics from his past exploits that would work to the calibre required. Everything began falling nicely into place.

Service stations were being fully rebranded, and Gulf, in the meantime, launched a nationwide 'Win a Porsche' competition in the press, including pages in the magazine titles we had on board as sponsors. A brand-new Porsche provided courtesy of Porsche Cars GB. The John Watson Performance Driving Centre at Silverstone provided a second prize.

All suited up in our new Gulf Oil racewear, Derek, Jürgen, and I duly attended the 'Return of a Legend' launch of the K8 and Gulf Oil's major involvement at the Dorchester Hotel to the awaiting press. A far cry from the Bardon launch at the same venue eight years before, this was a professionally choreographed and glitzy affair. A vast number of specifically invited guests from the mainstream press, as well as the specialist motorsport publications, all came. After being treated to copious amounts of the best champagne and canapes in the house, the room fell into darkness.

A mix of carefully combined slides and video footage projected from a large screen encapsulated the history of Gulf at Le Mans. It finished with the words 'Return of a Legend'. As that part of the presentation finished, in the darkness, the car, hiding behind curtains, was silently slipped onto the stage under cover of dry ice.

As the mist subsided and to tremendous applause, spotlights slowly came up to reveal the new Le Mans challenger in all its glory.

As the lights came up, we took our seats on the panel for the press conference along with Stuart, Erwin and our new team manager, Graham Lorimer. We were individually and most eloquently introduced by refined orator Brian Jones. After a Q&A session, cameras flashed as photographers surrounded the Porsche. After posing with the car, we retired to the bar to supp up the further available fizz. Job done. Next time out, we would hear the silent lion roar.

Testing couldn't come fast enough. We had to wait on Kremer as there was still a lot to do to get the new car race ready and the team's Honda commitments had distracted them. Scarily, our shake-down test didn't come until 2 or 3 weeks before Le Mans. This was held at the Autódromo de Most circuit in the Czech Republic. Quite a way to go for a test, but outside Le Mans, it was the home to the longest straight in Europe. Now that the Mulsanne had been dissected by two chicanes, one a third of the way down, the second equidistant to the first, the Most straight was much the same distance from start to either chicane. We could get a good idea of top speed, gear ratios, etc.

As I was familiar with the circuit, having raced there the year before in the Indy Car, for me it was more about learning how the car handled. This was a different beast to the 962. The power had been trimmed a little, but with it the ACO regulations had reduced the downforce by 50%. We now had to run with what's called a flat bottom. Gone were the big venturis (which channelled air under the car) that gave us so much more downforce before. Still wrestling with a huge amount of power being fed through my right foot, the car was more skittish in the corners. Nevertheless, the car behaved, and I got to grips with it as best I could. Derek did the same, but his vast experience shone through as the test ended. If he was happy, I was happy.

With time to spare before we caught our evening flight home, I suggested Derek follow me into Prague. Again, I knew the city quite well. Parked up, we were soon looking on at the stunning Gothic and Baroque architecture and magical pulsing atmosphere of the insanely beautiful old town square. Sat outside one of the many street cafes that line it, we ordered and an ice-cold Czech beer and a sandwich. Casually chatting for longer than we should, long early summer shadows reminded us it was now late afternoon. We had better head for the airport. See you at Le Mans, I said, as the plane touched down. See you at Le Mans he replied.

I was in high spirits as I swung into the entry of the traditional downtown scrutineering venue at Le Mans moments after Derek Bell had arrived. I parked up next to him. We both had virtually identical road-going Porsches. No doubt he owned his, but at least mine was brand spanking new, having just come out of my sponsors 'Chariots Porsche' showroom the day before. Other than a quick hello, Derek, I said nothing. A pretty cool start, I quietly thought as we walked down to the signing-on office.

Back at the circuit in our fully branded Gulf hospitality unit, staff sporting uniformed Gulf-branded sportswear were busily preparing supper. But the branding did not stop at the unit, the race team, or the support crew. Gulf had been promoting their new leisure wear department to coincide with the 'Win a Porsche' competition and their imminent assault on Le Mans. There were also shops in the circuit trade village now selling Gulf products. They were leaving the store shelves as quickly as UK trucks were coming in with replacements. As the week progressed, I could see the amount of support we were enjoying as nearly every Brit in the paddock, stands, and enclosures began wearing blue shirts sporting the iconic Gulf emblem.

I must admit, I was beginning to enjoy the ride. As we started moving up the leader board in qualifying, I was suddenly catapulted into the big league. Massive crowds surrounded the pit lane garage. I was encompassed by fans requesting autographs every time I journeyed out beyond the confines and safety of the pits. The 30-second walk to the hospitality unit would now take me 20 minutes. That is if I wasn't hounded down by the press for an interview. They hardly spoke to me driving an old Cosworth-powered C2 car just a short few years ago, but now they wanted to hear and write down everything short of my inside leg measurement. Television crews would follow me everywhere, tricky sometimes when I only ventured out of the garage doors to head to the nearby loo for a pee.

Derek Bell was getting an even bigger slice of the media cake. In his early 50s, this was to be his swansong of an awesome career that had seen him on the top step at Le Mans an incredible five times. Winning his first Le Mans as a Gulf driver, he would end as he began, in their iconic colours. The press couldn't get enough of him.

Among other things, Tuesday was spent making a special baby seat for me. At a towering 5'4, I was a fair few inches shorter than Derek. The position of the safety belts also proved a problem. The engineers eventually chose to bolt in two separate sets. Blue for me, Red for Derek and Jürgen.

Aside from a few niggling, new-car problems, Wednesday practice went mostly to plan, with all of us getting to grips with the new regulation changes. With a big push to allow production-based GT cars to compete on level terms with the larger prototypes for the outright win, the changes to our category included engine air-inlet restrictors, smaller fuel tanks and a heavier minimum weight. From a driver's point of view, the hardest addition to come to terms with was the regulation change from full ground effect to flat under-floors. All the grip we were used to for the past few years had now magically disappeared, so it felt a little bit like roller skating on ice to begin with.

Thursday and final qualifying duly came around again. In the pits, Erwin whispered to Derek to turn the turbos up to full capacity and with that, he blasted out of the pitlane like a scalded cat. The result of his astonishing efforts? A front-row position on the grid alongside pole-sitter Alain Ferte in the Courage C32LM. Wow, this was really big-time stuff!

My own final qualifying went without any significant problems. In comparison to many of the other cars I had driven, and as one of the quickest cars out there, this was simply superb. Derek was to set the qualifying time, so without having to push to the absolute extreme, my times still matched Jürgen's; a full-time Porsche 956 aficionado and our other co-driver Derek so eagerly wanted. In a strange way, I almost felt a little depressed at how relatively easy it was with the right machinery to hand. How hard it was, and the additional risks I had taken all those times without this luxury.

One remarkable manifestation I experienced was just how much I could take in travelling at lightning speed. For example, I saw my girlfriend Christine earlier that day at the circuit. Unknown to me she had gone back to the house we stayed in at the side of the track. It is positioned halfway up the ultra-fast stretch between Mulsanne Corner and Indianapolis. Flat out having already snatched top gear, I not only saw her standing there watching at the entrance gate that was now covered by an Armco barrier, but I noticed she had changed clothes. I mentioned this to her later, and she was simply gobsmacked. How could I have noticed such an inconsequential detail?

Our downtime Friday came and went in a blur of photographers, press and TV descending on our garage. Although I went to bed early that night, the significance of what had been achieved engulfed me, and it was hard to secure any substantial shut-eye. Tomorrow, our Gulf-sponsored car would stand proudly on the front row of the most famous and mythical sportscar race in the world. A legend of Le Mans, former winner in a Gulf car, and team mate to little me, would start. Just like Steve McQueen in the now classic movie 'Le Mans', I would be in a Gulf Porsche racing at Le Mans. The only difference being I would be driving for real.

Moreover, we stood an outside chance of actually winning the world's greatest sportscar race. This was a world apart from banging wheels in Formula Ford and beyond any real expectation I had or thought I deserved. Sleep finally came, but boy, was it intermittent.

The big day arrived. In those days, we had a parade in open-top cars right along the start line. The crowds, looking down from the stands, all brandishing their Gulf shirts and waving their Gulf flags, blended into a beautiful sea of blue. As I waved back, the empowerment I felt was all-embracing. Hey, even if it was just for one day, I could believe I was Mr Steve McQueen.

When the lights turned to green and the starter flag dropped, Derek thrust the K8 ahead into the first corner. All the photographs of that '94 start have our Gulf Porsche firmly in the lead. For that small moment in time, we were ahead of the pole-sitting Courage shared by pole-setter Alain Ferte, French legend and 3 x Le Mans winner Henri Pescarolo, and Frank Lagorce; the works factory Dauer Porsches, Eddie Irvine's factory Toyota. Everyone.

Sadly, it wasn't going to last long, and as Derek turned the turbos down, we fell back. However, 24 Hours is a long time and still firmly in the front-end mix, we settled down into our own routine. For what was effectively a new team, we worked in perfect harmony. Pit stops were slick and efficient, but our progress was hindered by a set of niggling 'new car' maladies, mostly small and annoying bodywork problems, and illumination issues – including the headlights going out at 200mph on the Mulsanne in the middle of the night. Thankfully, this was on Derek's watch.

However, I always enjoyed racing at night, and this was an extraordinary night. The warmth of the day, followed by a stunning sunset, had led into a beautifully fresh and clear night. And although everything is happening at a million miles an hour, I tend to go into my own little world when half the rest of it are asleep. With one of the quickest cars out there, for that short time I felt special in so many ways. I was thundering past more slower cars than I had ever done before. I was top of my game in the most famous sportscar race in the world and carrying a legendary sponsor to boot.

As pit signals came out and short bursts of radio messages came in, I had been made aware that Eddie Irvine in the Toyota had come out for his next stint and was hot on my heels. Eddie was to later become a teammate at Ferrari to seven times F1 World Champion Michael Schumacher. However, at the time, I was unconcerned. In the crispness of that night, I felt untouchable. One lap, he would gain a second or two on me, the next lap, I would gain the same on him. We carried on in this status quo for what seemed an age. That was until my bladder suddenly announced I needed a pee urgently.

My bladder had never caused a problem before. The change came from the fact I had never trained as hard as I had for this race. As well as going to the gym, I was running seven miles a day, sometimes twice a day. Come the big day, I was fitter than I had ever been. In those days, we just drank what seemed like gallons of water to keep hydrated. We didn't have the dedicated fitness gurus they have now, looking after your diet and handing out electrolyte and carbohydrate fluid mixes. I was still drinking as much as I always did, but I wasn't dehydrating as much.

Oh no, I thought, things could become difficult. I radioed to the team that I was desperate to go and could I come in four laps earlier than scheduled. Graham, our team manager, came back with a fck' off NO type of answer. The somewhat terse response he gave was backed up by another burst on the radio - 'pee in your pants'. Well, that's all very good, I thought. Plenty have done the same in the past, but Derek was the next driver in. How could I possibly leave a puddle in the bottom of the seat for a living legend to sit in. Mighty busy in the cockpit for the remaining part of that lap, I left radioing the team again until I was back on the Mulsanne.

Pressing the radio button on the steering wheel, I made one last 200mph plea for help. I am really, really busting, I shouted out. Not quite as abrupt as the first response, Graham explained that because of maximum fuel loads, coming in early would throw their schedule completely out. Pee or bear it. Unlike an average race circuit lap, four laps of Le Mans is over a quarter of an hour. However, peeing in my pants was not an option. Suffice to say, those last three or four laps were some of the quickest I had ever done.

Storming into the pits, all I had to do when the car stopped was jump out and help Derek with his belts. As I did so, his hand pushed down on my arm as he complimented me on my stint. As he fired up the car, I had already run out of the pits past the awaiting debriefing management team and charged through the doors of the long-awaited and welcoming loo. As the overwhelming relief of the last 15 minutes splashed down over the porcelain, I chuckled to myself. As surprisingly complimentary as his words were, little did he know the full story, I thought.

A few more petty problems curtailed our progress further. All silly, new-car syndrome stuff. Issues like doors coming loose and engine cover not attaching properly. Nothing big or dramatic like the clutch needing replacing or a driveshaft failure. That said, it still meant that we totalled a full 45 minutes in the pits over and above our scheduled stops.

As night turned into another heat-blistering day, our chances of a podium finish had evaporated, but we were still running strongly in the top ten. All we needed was a clean run to the finish. With everything hanging together pretty well, we reverted back to single stints. My penultimate stint finished at 2 pm. It was then Bell, then Lässig and I was down to do the last short stint to the 4 pm finish.

With Jürgen Lässig completing his last turn in the car and I was busy readying myself for mine, team manager Graham Lorimer took me aside. He explained that in view of the fact that this was supposed to be Derek Bell's last ever Le Mans before retiring, would it not be a good move to have Derek finish. He mentioned the vast blue and orange bedecked crowd facing us in the grandstands opposite. Frantically waving their flags and banners, Graham reminded me they were here to support Derek as much as Gulf. However much I wanted to finish, I could not have agreed more.

Just before Derek got into the car for the very last time, he waved to his army of followers. His gesture was rewarded by a huge roar that sounded out from the masses. The team rushed over to the pit wall to see the final countdown to the chequered flag. As every lap passed, we all witnessed in awe this sea of blue and orange urging him on. They were everywhere. Opposite us in the burgeoning grandstands, above us, looking down and as far as the eye could see into the first corner.

As the clock turned to four, the flag finally fell on the winning works factory, Dauer Porsche. Taking a strong 6th place overall, Derek came through amidst a battle for 2nd between the sister works Porsche and Eddie Irvine in the factory Toyota. As they all crossed the line virtually together, it was Eddie who snatched 2nd. I thought that was pretty cool as Toyota had chosen to keep the name of

Roland Ratzenburger, scheduled to drive the Toyota that year, above the names of Martini, Krosnoff and Irvine as a tribute. Ratzenberger having been killed at the San Marino Grand Prix the day before Ayrton Senna just a few weeks previously.

As Derek climbed out of the Gulf Porsche, he waved at the crowds again. The roar from the crowds was even more tumultuous than it was when he got in. And 'hey', we had all done a good job. After a gruelling 24 hours, we had brought the new car home. We were the first-placed privateer against the might of the factory efforts from Porsche, Toyota, and Nissan. Gulf were beyond happy, and we were guaranteed a great season with them for 1995. What more could we have wished for?

1923-1993 (70)
24 HEURES DU MANS
19-20 JUIN 1993

*1993: The three car Kremer Racing team at Le Mans.
From left to right: Jürgen Lässig Giovanni Lavaggi,
Wayne Taylor, Almo Coppelli, myself, Steve Fossett,
Andy Evans, Thomas Saldana and Francois Migault.*

08

221

AUTOSPORT
Le Mans Yearbook 1993

1994: The Return of a Legend. The launch of the Gulf Oil Kremer Porsche K8 at the Dorchester Hotel in Mayfair.

And along with Derek Bell and Jürgen Lässig, me being Steve McQueen for the week

Gulf NEWS

A legend i bac

222

Leading the start of the most legendary sports car race in the world in the hands of Derek Bell

96 Club INTERNATIONAL

🇬🇧 DEREK BELL
🇩🇪 JÜRGEN LÄSSIG
🇬🇧 ROBIN DONOVAN

SPORT MAGAZINE

Gulf

5

Living the dream

My girlfriend Christine sat to the left of Gulf marketing guru Martin Allerton in the centre

THE RETURN OF A LEGEND

THE GULF PREMIER PORSCHE
LE MANS 1994

🇬🇧 DEREK BELL
🇬🇧 ROBIN DONOV
🇩🇪 JÜRGEN LÄS

Gulf-Porsche

223

1995: The Agusta Calloway Corvette Racing Team.

Front left to right: Rocky Agusta, Eugene O'Brien, and me.

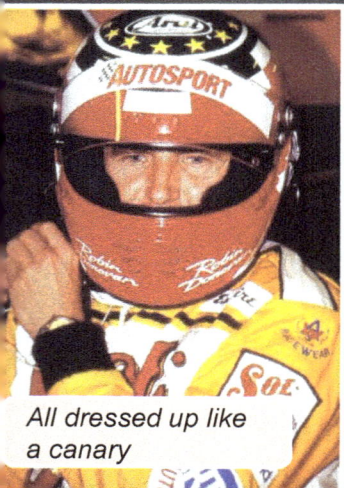

All dressed up like a canary

The pit-wall celebrations

Just before the start of the 1996 Le Mans 24 Hours

Arty shot but you can just make out the damage caused to the right rear end

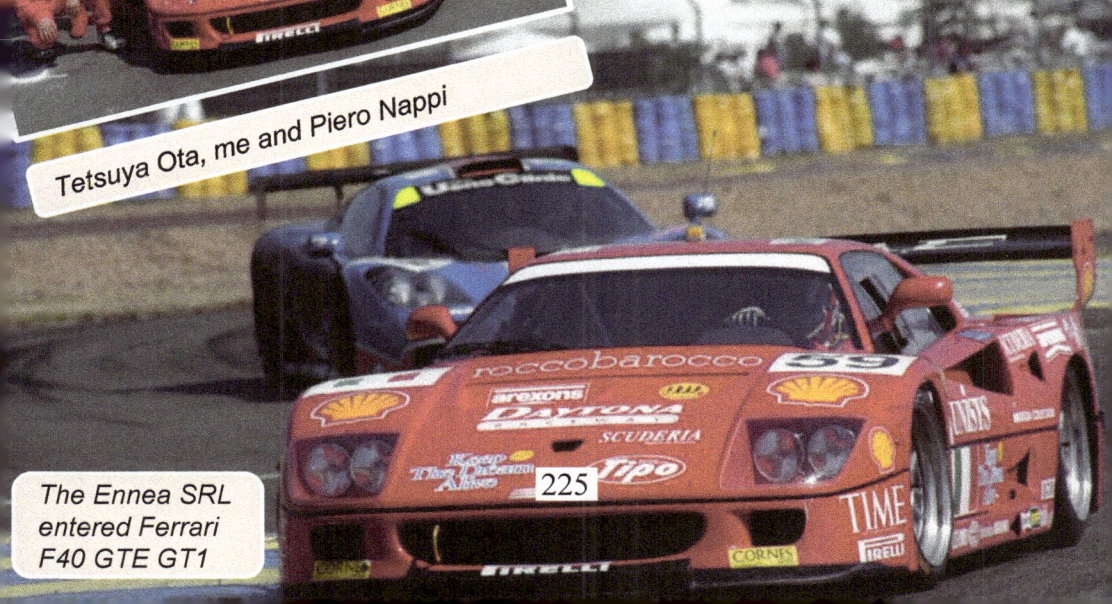

Tetsuya Ota, me and Piero Nappi

The Ennea SRL entered Ferrari F40 GTE GT1

Winning in Jarama, Spain and Paul Ricard in the South of France with Arturo Merzario

Monza 1000 kms, Italy

Le Mansbilar i ANDERSTO 15–16 augusti

International Sports Racing Series

Toppstallen och toppförarna i mästerskapet för de supersnabba sportbilarna kör 4:e deltävlingen på Scandinavian Raceway.

Scandinavian Raceway

1998: The Elf Team Centenari line up in Misano, Italy with (left to right), Jacques Villeneuve, Xavier Pompidou, me, Beppe Gabbiani, Filipe Ortiz, Fulvio Ballabio, João Barbosa, 'Rael' and Loic Depailler

226

Le Mans podium:
Joao Barbosa, me and
Xavier Pompidou

Misano pit-stop

Brno podium

Marlboro sponsored Alfa Romeo Centenari
M1 SR2 enroute to Jarama race win

The pre-race launch at Sony in Paris

1998: With Larbre Competition: All dressed up and ready to go

Me, Carl Rosenblad and Jean-Pierre Jarier with Emma seated in the front

13

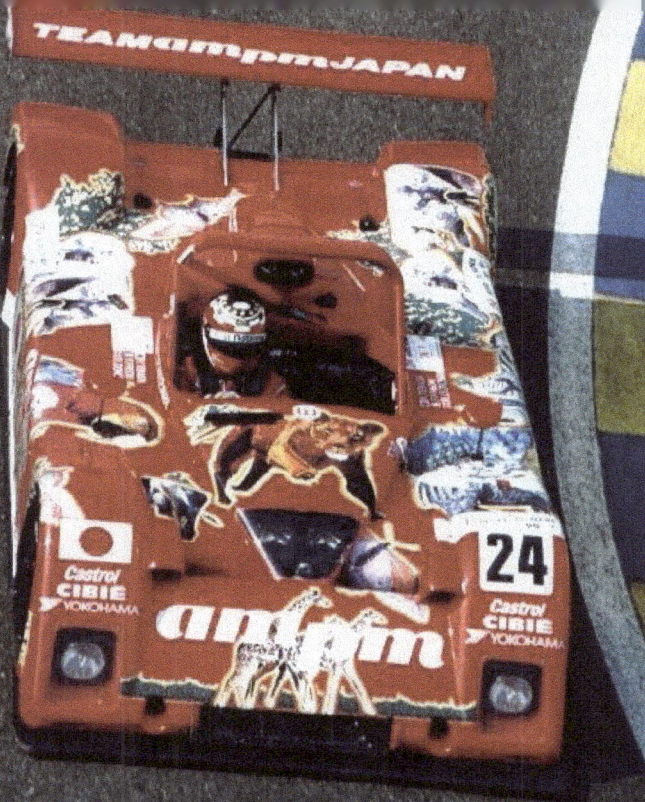

1999: Yojiro Terada's owner/driver AutoExe Le Mans 24 Hours team with Frank Freon and me

Racing Engineering team photo at my last Le Mans 24 Hour race competing in 2001

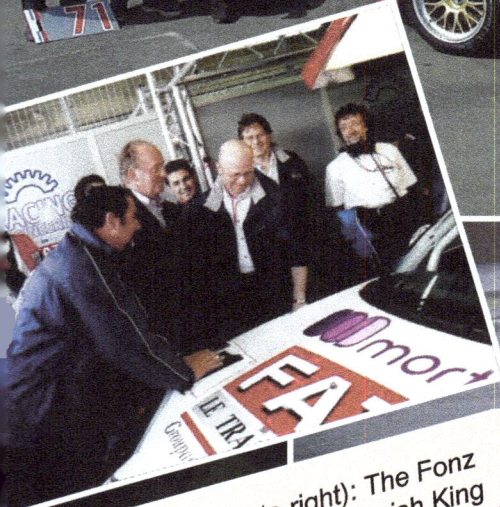

Left insert (from left to right): The Fonz with hand on the bonnet, Spanish King Juan Carlos, Driver Terry Linger, Stuart Radnofsky and Dr Clive

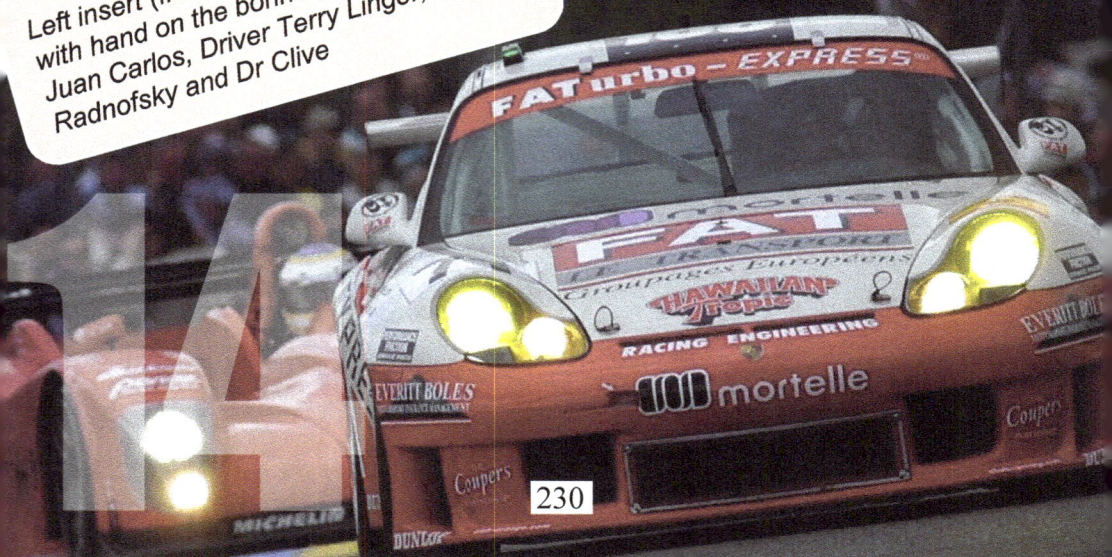

230

Me in the Porsche RSR GT2 during qualifying before race-days total downpour above

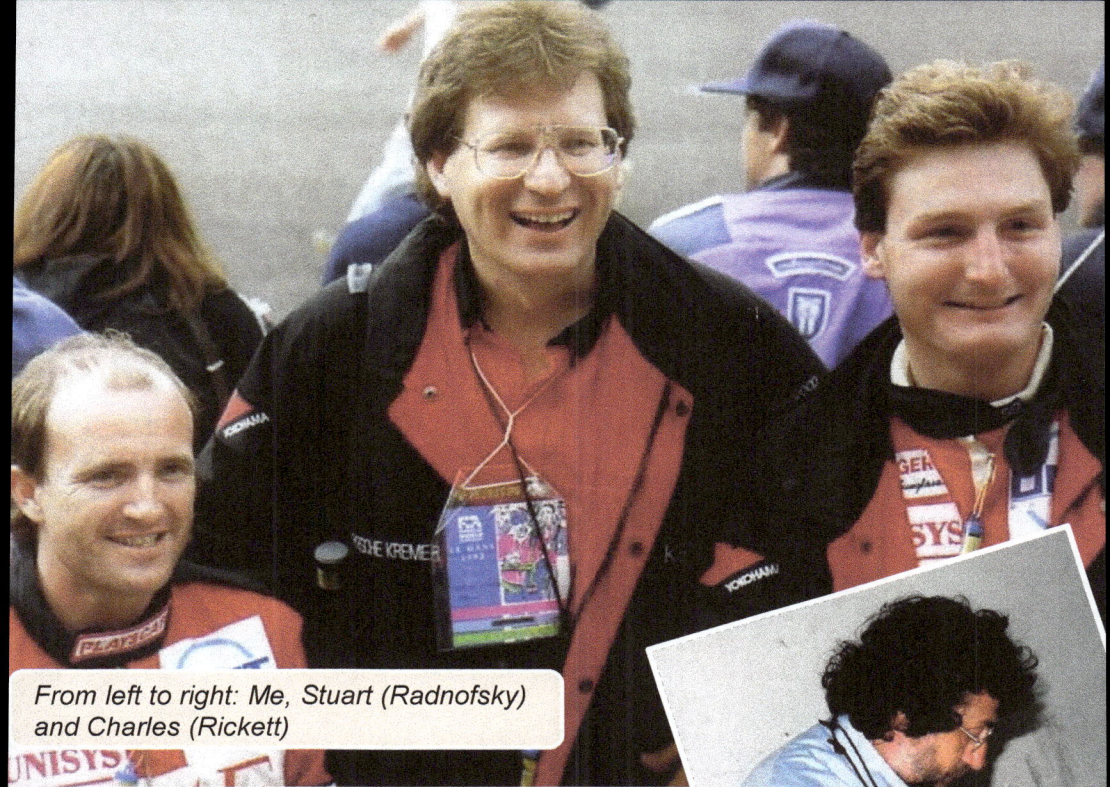

From left to right: Me, Stuart (Radnofsky) and Charles (Rickett)

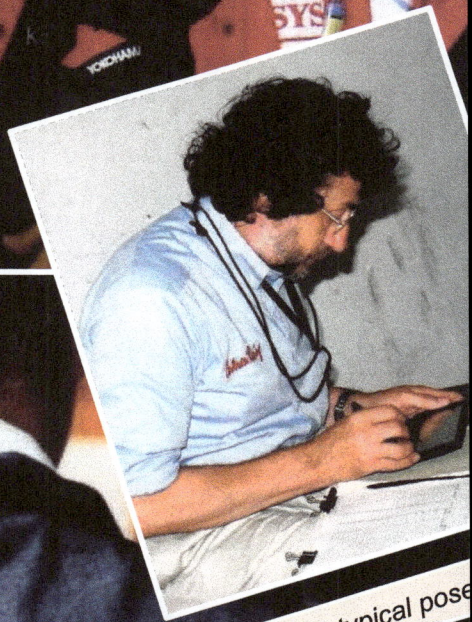

Dr Clive in typical pose

LIFE
BEGINS
AT
200
M.P.H

YOU' LL NEVER KNOW

HOW MANY FRIENDS YOU HAVE,

TILL YOU SPONSOR CAR-RACING

The back of our sponsor Helmet Schwingen, President of F.A.T. Le Transport

And, as well as World Sportscars, we had:

Le Mans Classic: Dodge Hemi Charger

Barcelona 6 Hours: ITTC BMW M3

Vallelunga 6 Hours: ITTC BMW M3

Lime Rock: IMSA Porsche 966 Spyder

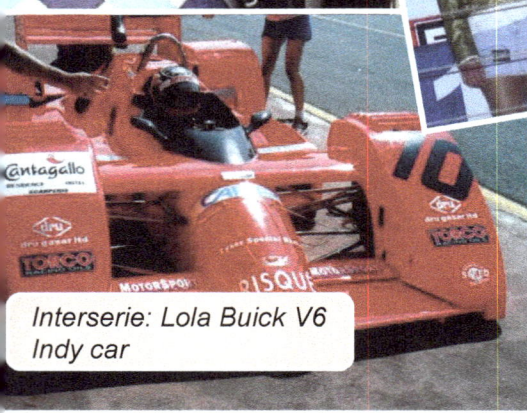

Interserie: Lola Buick V6 Indy car

Thundersaloons: Class 1 Honda Legend Acura 5.7 V8 Chevrolet

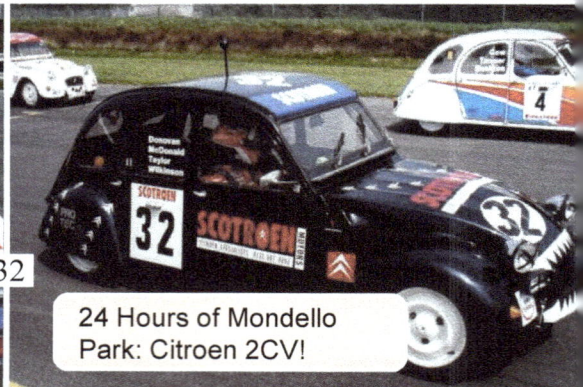

24 Hours of Mondello Park: Citroen 2CV!

Just about summitting my first Himalayan peak

At Everest Base Camp: 5,364m / 17,598 ft

CONGRATULATIONS!
YOU ARE NOW AT

UHURU PEAK, TANZANIA, 5895M. AMSL

AFRICA'S HIGHEST POINT
WORLD'S HIGHEST FREE-STANDING MOUNTAIN

ONE OF WORLD'S LARGEST VOLCANOES.
WELCOME

The top of Kilimanjaro: 5,895m/19,340 ft

234

Yep, I managed to do more than alright in the end.

Chapter Twenty-Two
Singin' in the Rain

OK, so all my aspirations didn't exactly go to plan for the 1995 season. I thought I was peaking. I was virtually at the top of my game. After all those years, I had finally got close to where I wanted to be. And now, almost for the first time, I understood how important it was to be in one of the best cars out there. Indeed, how much easier it was. Gulf had said in no uncertain terms, do well at Le Mans, and they would be with us. What could possibly go wrong? Stuart and I set out our plans for carrying on with the new Kremer Porsche K8 for the following season. They were all keen, contracts nearly signed, and then it all went pear-shaped.

Ray Bellm, wealthy beyond belief but a good chap and a great racer, approached Gulf. He said he would invest, run, and race in a new two-car McLaren GT1 team. He proposed that in their first year, the cars could run in the colours of Gulf virtually for free based on a commitment that if they did well, Gulf would sign up for further years. We had no way of competing, and armed with a number of professional co-drivers, Ray did massively well in 1995 and brought the championship honours home the following year. That was whilst we were firmly relegated right back to square one...

One off-season winter's day, drowning my sorrows in my local watering hole, by chance, an old Kiwi pal from my distant past walked through the door. Ewan Warrender was a freelance marketing man, and as I nattered on to him about recent dilemmas, he said he knew the very person I should meet. In what seemed like no time at all we had struck a deal with Sol Beer to run at least 'something' in the Global Endurance GT Championship.

Stuart and I immediately set to work on trying to find a suitable team and car to run with. We heard that my pal and Kremer co-driver at Le Mans Almo was now running the race shop of the newly formed Agusta Racing team. The team was owned by Count 'Rocky' Agusta, heir to the fortune amassed by the family's celebrated aviation and motorbike companies. In his mid-forties, Riccardo, aka "Rocky", was a true gentleman. Always gracious and cordial, he could still come across as a little aloof. Rocky would arrive at the European races in his chauffer driven Bentley but then, dressed in jeans and polos, much the same as the rest of us, would knuckle down to the job in hand. However, with that cool Italian, aristocratic edge, I always felt I should know my place in his presence.

Agusta Racing were taking possession of two brand-new Callaway Corvette racing cars. Powered by monster 6.3-litre Chevrolet engines, these beasts were a force to be reckoned within the burgeoning GT2 class.

And while expat Italian Almo, based just outside Silverstone, was the ideal man to pull everything together in the workshop in between his racing duties, the team manager's job fell into the capable hands of Keith Greene. Keith, a marvellously entertaining raconteur, was a former Formula One driver who went on to enjoy a lively team management career both in F1 and sports cars.

Although we were moving down into the GT class, this was certainly panning out to be a great team in the making. With the Sol Beer funds we had been promised, we just needed another driver with a half-decent budget aboard to guarantee safe procurement of the second car for the season. A call to Eugene provided the last piece to the jigsaw puzzle. Eugene O Brien was brother to Mike, the chap I raced with in Thundersports. Hot off a two-year programme driving the works Peugeot in the British Touring Car Championship, Eugene was keen to prove his worth on an international stage. Still having the support of his long-time sponsor 'Auto Windscreens' he happily went along on the wave created.

I had a soft spot for Eugene. Far less fiery than his brother, arguably the polar opposite, he had this way of taking things very seriously when required but loved to fool around in equal measure. If it was not work, it was playtime. He always had this kind of reserved smile on his face that timidly and respectfully lent into a delightful way of allowing his strong sense of humour to slowly filter through.

We had a mixed set of results leading up to Le Mans. The prequel to the big one at the celebrated Nurburgring being the most memorable. Here, we only entered one car as Rocky was away on business. Halfway through the race, before the end of my allocated stint, I had to pit as I was chocking. The cockpit was full of smoke, and I was gagging as I tumbled out of the fume-ridden cockpit blue-faced. The carbon fibre undertray was positioned too close to the red-hot exhaust. The team tried to patch up the problem as best they could, but I thought the car would be retired on the spot. Almo, our trusty Italian rock ape and boss without the presence of Rocky, was having none of it.

We stood aghast as he belted up for the next stint and thundered back down the pit lane and onto the track. His inconsistent times fluctuated as the last laps of the race ran its course. Indeed, we thought he had gone missing on his last lap, but with us all hanging over the pit wall, we cheered as he eventually came into sight. As the chequered flag fell, the car rumbled to an eventual stop in the middle of the track.

A great plume of locked-in smoke and fumes escaped from the car as we rushed over and opened the door. Almo just lay there, eyes closed with head over the steering wheel. Completely away with the fairies. We pulled him out and laid him up against the track side of the pit wall, where the paramedics took over. Releasing him after an hour or two, he was as right as rain, but he did give everyone a scare. That said, it was a true testament to Almo's 'never say die' spirit of character, even if he nearly did.

A couple of weeks later, now with the Corvettes fully race-prepared for Le Mans, including the fixing of the dastardly exhaust problem, we optimistically headed for the great race. And if not, this time going out for the outright win, 'oh', what fun we still had all the same.

I think it must have started with Eugene's entry onto the then-new channel tunnel car carrier. With me sat in the passenger seat, he let the car ahead of us on then sat there and waited, holding up the queue behind him. Letting the burning clutch up, he floored the pedal only for the car to rocket down the bumpy confines of the empty train. We just about stopped before hitting the parked car ahead at the end of the carriage.

On arrival at the circuit, even at the beginning of the week, there were plenty of the eager public taking pictures and videos as well as the official TV crews keen to secure early footage. Eugene chose to film them filming us, which, as they say, is one for the book. Indeed, he kept up his video-making right up until the race six days later.

Friday, being a supposed day off for the drivers, all of us attended the downtown drivers' parade around the city centre.

In car number 75, we had Eugene, team boss Rocky and me. In number 76 was Almo, Frenchman Patrick Bourdais and Dane, Thorkild Thyrring. To a certain extent I guess that having me in one car and Almo in the other equalised the team strength.

This was my first experience with a front-engine car, so pre-qualifying for me was all about seeing over the giant six-plus-litre power plant entrapped under a bulging bonnet straight ahead of me. Hard enough for a taller driver, I stood no chance. A baby seat had to be made for me to fill the size of Nebraska. Basically, you hold yourself up in the cockpit while a black bin liner is positioned underneath. Two cans of liquid chemicals are poured. Reacting together, they change into a foam. When the liner heats up, you slightly lower yourself into position. A strange, all-encompassing, toasty experience feeling creeps up through your lower regions as you try to hold yourself steady. Within a minute or two, the foam hardens to your body shape. Job done. Ready to go.

First, all the drivers and team management had to attend the ACO race briefing. Held in vast room high up in what we call 'Gods Country', it is way above the pits where the normally, prohibited offices of the organisers and race officials reside. Anyone who fails to attend is heavily fined. It's all a bit silly really, as in those days the entire briefing, however serious, is delivered by an aged, blue blazered ACO director, solely in French. For the strong international contingent present, this largely tends to fall on deaf ears. Without any translation we all had to either muster up what French we might know or gather information from those in the audience who would. The idea is to emphasise the rules we should already know, and expand on new ones introduced. In dangerously heavy traffic, what side is it best to overtake or be overtaken. What coloured warning lights each car category should carry. Pit-lane speed restrictions, warning flags and lights etc.

At this particular briefing I was late. Only one seat towards the front was left available. I rushed to grab it and sit down there.

Looking up I immediately saw I was sitting next to Mario Andretti. In my eyes, a huge star. The only driver to have ever won the Indianapolis 500, the Daytona 500 and the F1 World Drivers Championship in one lifetime. I felt like a small schoolboy again. My immediate thought was to hunt around for a pen to ask for his autograph before quickly coming to my senses. What am I doing? He is a fellow competitor racing in the same event. My schoolboy dilemma quickly subsided when he turned and sighed, and in his strong North American drawl casually asked, 'do you understand what this guy is talking about'? I gave a blank, unknowing shrug. We then both smiled and happy to be on the same page, sat back in mutual bewilderment to the end of the briefing.

Back to the track and fortunately, the cars were quick. At the end of two days' qualifying, Almo, in the #76 car, was quickest in the GT2 class. This was ahead of the Porsche, Nissan, Toyota, Honda and Marcos' entries in the same category. I was quickest in our #75 car, a few rows down. That said, both Eugene and I were quicker than both of Almo's co-drivers, so our hopes were up for the 4 pm start on Saturday.

With the massive crowds looking on, the usual fanfare began. Marching bands, air displays and fireworks led to a second drivers' parade, precariously sat on the back bonnet of open-top cars on the start line. We again waved at the crowds to a multitude of cheers from fans before the cars were placed on the grid. After photo calls with the Hawaiian Tropic girls, Hawaiian Tropic continued to be a supporting sponsor, and the inevitable autograph sessions, it was time to take my position on the grid.

As the lead qualifying driver in this car, you cannot help feeling the inevitable butterflies. They tend to muddle your brain as well as your stomach as you're belted up and the mechanics close the door down on you. With all the noise around you, everything beyond the cockpit seems silent. All you hear is your own inhalation filtering through the confines of your fireproof balaclava and helmet. The unknown is imminently out there. It's up to you whether you're up to discovering it, but really too late to turn back.

To distract myself, I thought of my relatively new girlfriend, Emma. For the next 24 hours, she would have even more fun now. Emma was very pretty, young, outgoing and slightly crazy. Although gifted with Meg Ryan looks, she was much more happy mucking out at the local stables back in the UK. With a figure to die for, she used to get all the fellas going just strutting into our regular bar at home in body-hugging jodhpurs and boots. Full of character and popular with the boys, they didn't seem to care that this attire always came with a very dirty, straw-scattered, fleece smelling of horse.

With me now effectively out of the way for hopefully the next 24 Hours, she would have more time to flirt with the mechanics. This was more a pastime than anything more serious. The funny (peculiar) thing was she could see me racing at 200mph and not worry. Whereas I would watch her compete in the county shows and have kittens. My whole being would be on edge, particularly when she took on much bigger horses in the high jump competition known as puissance.

I was brought back to the here and now when the five-minute siren rang out. This denoted that that anyone left on the grid, get off. A few minutes later, the pace car in front of the huge grid moved forward as we all took our initial rolling lap. We all swerve back and forth in places like the Mulsanne at 100mph to warm up our tyres. As I get to the start line again, the red lights on the gantry are out. The green now shined brightly. The race is on.

All goes well on my first stint, and I enjoy a very quick changeover to Eugene. Rocky will follow, but not before it starts to rain. And does it rain. In what would become one of the wettest Le Mans races on record, the heavens opened, and it pours.

Because of the heavy cloud cover it is near enough dark when I take over from Rocky. As the light faded, the torrent went on. I was travelling at break-neck speed and trying to miss the inevitable spins in front of me as a multitude of cars skated off in the deluge. Eyes on stalks, attempting to keep a careful eye on the dark, rain-swept road ahead, I also had to flick attention over to the rear-view mirrors to snatch the glare of any fast-approaching cars suddenly appearing out of the gloom. At over 180mph, my cramped office was busy enough, so not expecting what was to happen next.

Suddenly, the windscreen wipers that were frantically swiping from side to side to allow some small form of coherence as to what was occurring outside the cockpit of my projectile stopped. At that moment, a GT1 car flashed past, throwing up a huge plume of spray. The windscreen was totally awash and taking a lifetime to clear. All I could do was take my foot off the throttle and hope not to hit anything. I then slowly crept my way back to the pits in the murk.

Back in the pits, the mechanics hectically went about finding the problem. I sat there and waited. It wasn't until the lead engineer told me the motor had packed up and couldn't be replaced, I unbelted. It was all over, forced into retirement by something as simple as a windscreen wiper motor. I was halfway out of the car when I was pushed back in. Where do you think you're going, Keith, the team manager said. With that, they sprayed the windscreen with the rain-repellent Rain-X. Not convinced, I pressed the starter button and the massive Chevrolet engine burst into life and skated out of the pitlane into the unknown.

Beyond belief, it worked. The natural airflow of the car dispersed the worst. With no let-up in the biblical weather, the only time I had a problem was on the Mulsanne. When a quicker car kicked up a cascade of spray as it passed it would take two or three seconds to clear. That doesn't sound a lot, but is forever and a day when you are covering around 300 feet a second.

As I have always enjoyed racing in the rain, I quickly fell into a groove and began to feel at home. The engine was strong; the car was quick. Even with the unscheduled pit stop, we were still right up there. I even began to enjoy a trick I discovered blasting out of the famous bend 'Tertre Rouge', leading onto the notorious Mulsanne Straight. Here, the flooding led to streams of water running across the track from left to right. It caught me out at first which led to a frightening, lurid opposite lock movement I had to make on the steering wheel to correct the rear end. Tertre Rouge is very important as the quicker you can carry your speed through the corner, the faster you will be onto the Mulsanne. This could amount to another 10-15mph halfway down. I found that if I turned the wheel slightly left a millisecond before I hit the shine of the streaming water, the car would straighten itself up without having to lift.

I was oddly enjoying myself while the incessant rain was causing havoc all around. No end of incidents included racing legend Mario Andretti crashing out, having tangled with a Kremer Porsche in the Porsche Curves, *regenmeister* Hans Stuck throwing his Kremer Porsche into the wall at the first chicane, and pole setter Patrick Gonin in his WR Peugeot going off at frightening speed on the Mulsanne. Aquaplaning before somersaulting into the barriers, Gonin was taken to hospital with multiple fractures, and the safety car had to be brought out for nearly 40 minutes whilst circuit personnel rebuilt the Armco.

All of this was happening as, bit by bit, we edged ever closer to our prize. I had squeezed the car up to second by the time I finished another double stint and handed over the reins to Eugene. Eugene, also double stinting, kept the pressure on to naturally bring the car up to first. Our frustration came on the few occasions Rocky, our ultimate boss, got behind the wheel for the odd single stint. In the closely matched GT2 class and lacking the outright speed, we would tumble back to third or fourth, only to have to work ourselves up through the field again.

Delighted Eugene was now leading, I was in the back of the pits, lightly nibbling away at some cold pizza, when news filtered through that our sister car had had an accident. Like Hans Stuck earlier, Thorkild Thyrring in car number 76 had also crashed going into the First Chicane on the Mulsanne. It was now 1 am, and up until then, Almo's mount had been running in a strong third place. Apart from Thorkild's pride, no irreparable damage was done. However, it was only after the race was over, I heard that a marshal had witnessed a couple of spectators walking off with the abandoned car's bonnet. I found it funny to think some souvenir hunter would have about 11,000€ worth of bonnet to prop up in their garage or taking up a large proportion of their bedroom space somewhere.

As dawn broke, the unabated barrage of water that had been the blight of our lives all night began to dissipate. It was first replaced by lighter rain before drifting into an uneasy set of intermittent showers. Worn out by the intense pressure and immense concentration required to get through the night, I now had to be master of another challenge. Wets or slicks. The scary wet sheen was transforming into a dull two-tone grey. The fast, draining, but still slippery tarmac was beginning to dry in places.

Taking over for my last double stint, I took the chance. With the car raised on jacks and the mechanics busily refuelling and wiping down the dirty windscreen, I suggested we go for slicks. It was a dangerous risk, but we were now back down, battling for third place. If I could keep the car on the black stuff, I could run faster on the dry bits and attempt to tiptoe over the wet bits. I never felt as good, almost superhuman, as I roared out of the pit lane. Running to plan, I had the bit between my teeth as I quickly moved into third place. On a roll, I caught up and passed the American entered works factory Callaway Corvette. Now in second place, I slowly began to catch up with the leader, the Japanese Honda NSX GT V6. Nothing could stop me now.

Having to pit for a quick splash and dash refuel, as most cars would have to do, I still felt the big prize was ours for the taking. With less than an hour to go, I hurriedly made my way down the pitlane and just sat in the car, eyes firmly fixed on Keith, the team manager in front of me. He would be the one to give the pit out sign as soon as the last drop of fuel went in.

Instead, eyes nervously twitching, he told me to get out. Rocky was going to do what remained of the last stint. I could not believe what I was hearing. We had the best chance ever to take the GT honours and Keith was effectively asking me to give it all up. In what must have been a split second but felt like an age, I duly got out and reluctantly helped Rocky belt up.

As Rocky headed out for the last time, Keith took me aside. He explained that at the end of the day, we are all hired guns, he is beholden to Rocky as much as I am. As the outright owner of Agusta Racing, and whilst thankful for all the work we had put in, Rocky wanted to take the finish. It was his right. Keith couldn't stop him, and neither could I.

As the chequered flag fell 40 minutes later, we had inevitably fallen back down to third. Still, a good result in most people's books, albeit I think we all knew it could have been so much more. *C'est la vie*. What more could you say? That's life, and as such, the party must go on. And so it did, until the wee small hours of the following morning.

Chapter Twenty-Three
Dangerous Liaisons

Apart from some one-off European Touring car races the next couple of years were fairly bleak on the racing side of things. Quite a few of my sponsors had moved on and I had stupidly been lax in replacing them. As ever, I was keen to do Le Mans, and in true Rogers & Hammerstein style, Stuart and I had put forward a presentation to the famous fuel and oil additive company STP. Stuart looking after the copywriting while I did the conceptual illustrations. The plan was to procure the last available seat in the Kremer-run Porsche K8.

As things progressed, we found ourselves falling short on full funding for the effort. Step forward Stuart's global adventurer friend, billionaire Steve Fossett. He was keen to take another at crack at Le Mans. Perhaps wanting to make amends for the fairly disastrous efforts of three years before. Ironically, the additional funding he brought left me with no place to go, and I had to sadly step down.

Stuart did not leave me in the lurch for long, and with a lot of ringing around, true to form, he came up with a plan B for me. I was to join the three-car Ennea SLR Ferrari team. Resplendent in striking blue and yellow livery, Ennea ran two identical IGOL oil-sponsored Ferrari F40 GT1s in the main global GT championship, but for Le Mans, they would enter three. This late third F40 entry, my office for Le Mans race week, would run in Ferrari red. Okay, so I wasn't to get a drive in my beloved Kremer Porsche team, but to drive a Ferrari at Le Mans, indeed a red Ferrari had to be a very good second best. My co-drivers would be Italian star Piero Nappi and Japanese Ferrari specialist Tetsuya Ota. Our main backing came from Shell and Time Magazine with a mishmash of smaller support sponsors brought in by the three of us.

What I never expected was the out-and-out adoration the Ferrari crowds gave us throughout the week. Passionate to the point of being fanatical, the *Tifosi* arrived in their thousands to support their beloved brand, and our car, being red, was the cherry on the top. In our red racing overalls, sporting the legendary black and yellow prancing horse logo, we could not go anywhere without Italian TV crews or autograph hunters trailing our every move. During qualifying and the race, massive Ferrari banners and flags would be waved every time we appeared in sight. I wondered what it must be like for a Formula One Ferrari driver.

The power from this iconic, if, brutal Ferrari F40 LM GTE, delivering a mighty 720bhp to your right foot, was immense. A beautifully raw scream would blissfully ring out of its Tipo 3 Litre engine as it would clear 100kpm in under 3 seconds from a standing start. I could not fail to fall in love with the world of Ferrari as indeed all their many supporters had done.

Chief engineer on the car at the time was Amato Ferrari. No relation to Enzo. He would go on to set up the famed A.F. Corse team. Never running anything else other than Ferrari's, A.F. Corse would go on to win numerous team and driver championships on their way to becoming one of the most acclaimed GT teams in the world. Moving the clocks even further forward, A.F. Corse were tasked with running the new works factory Ferrari 499P in the centenary edition of the Le Mans 24 Hours race in 2023. Here, they came home with a spectacular, history-making win, half a century on from the factory's last foray into the top class of the world's most famous endurance race.

Against the might of the dominant McLaren F1 GTR monsters and a host of other marques in our class, ranging from Dodge Vipers to Porsches, we unsurprisingly qualified in the middle of the mix. And after the normal ceremonious splendour that surrounds the carnival of the downtown drivers parade on Friday and all the many on-track pre-race celebrations that lead up the 4 pm start on Saturday afternoon, yet another Le Mans 24 Hours thundered off in a theatre of noise, smoke, and dust.

On the first lap of my second stint, approaching the very fast entry to Indianapolis, I saw the remains of the STP Kremer Porsche I was going to drive smashed up against the barriers. There was little left of the rear end of the car and the hole on the remaining half of the gearbox was flush with wood. I heard later that 1989 Le Mans winner Stanley Dickens had a huge accident on this, one of the fastest parts of the track, cris-crossing the track twice and obviously getting airborne enough to collect a tree enroute.

The approach to Indianapolis is disconcerting enough at the best of times, let alone with the constant reminder left by the STP car that was not to be moved away by marshals until many laps further on. Once you navigate your way around the tricky Mulsanne corner, you shift quickly up through the gears, flat out, pedal to metal, all the way to Indianapolis. At least a mile done in a matter of seconds. On the way, you endure two flat-out curves to the right. The second is on a slight crest. This is nothing in a hire car, but in a race car, the rigid suspension goes wickedly light. So much so it feels as if you will take off. Going over the crest at near 200mph or more, I always have to make a split-second correction to the steering wheel. I envisage it's a bit like landing an aeroplane in a crosswind. All your instincts tell you to lift, but of course, you can't. The once-every-lap circumstance would often lead me to utter a guttural shriek into the confines of my sweaty helmet to help me on my way.

Long dark shadows intermingled with the last of the sunshine produced a surreal atmosphere in the cockpit. The light was beginning to fade, but, on some stretches, intermittent bright rays could almost blind you. Strange how I can recall the metal dust created by quick shifting through the solid; some would suggest agricultural Ferrari H box. As I changed gear, these microns would float around like minuscule fairies dancing around, undecided of their destination. What a strange thing to remember I thought in the middle of competing in a 200mph racing car.

As the warm colours of dusk faded into the harshness of night, everything still felt good. Taking on my first graveyard shift, the weather was clear, the car was well-balanced, and the beautiful-sounding engine remained crisp and sharp. That could not be said of the other GT Ferrari's. They were all out, including the two IGOL-sponsored Ennea sister cars and a sole-entered PILOT-sponsored F40 LM for Michel Ferte. In GT1, our car was the only Ferrari left running. If it wasn't for a sole remaining Ferrari 333 SP in the WSC division, the only other having crashed out early, the weight of *Tifosi's* expectations would have been resting on our shoulders alone.

A swift pit stop halfway through a double stint for fuel and new tyres helped send me on a charge. I loved racing at this time of night and particularly recall a memorable moment teetering past a Gulf McLaren F1 on the outside of Dunlop Bend. Side by side at 140mph, with the bend ever tightening up before, the Dunlop Chicane keeps you very much awake.

After the chicane, you plummet down a fast section into the acclaimed Esses. Tip-toing with the power so as not to get the tail out too much, there is only one corner to go before the notorious Mulsanne Straight: Tertre Rouge. Getting this corner right is critical. Too much power in will see you sideways and losing time, straightening yourself up, coming out. Not enough, and you will be slow all the way down the straight. If possible, I try to enter a gear higher than usually expected and carry the speed through. You must be clean and precise and use every bit of the curb on both sides that are not too high. Use the higher bits, and at best, you will unsettle the car and, at worst, break it.

Blasting out of Tertre Rouge, you quickly pump up through the gears onto the Mulsanne and head for the first chicane. The speed is tremendous as the trees and the buildings flash past you in a millisecond. The strong headlights pick up the white line. As the regular public Le Mans to Tours main road, normally filled with commuters and trucks, these are broken, overtaking lines in the middle of the road. At nearly 200mph, they are just one white line. The headlights also pick up the marshalling lights that appear across the track from dark, mysteriously hidden gantries. The choice of colours blazing out similarly mimics the marshals' flags waved during the daytime. Yellow for take care, no overtaking. Blue for pass, etc. Other than that, the only other thing you will see of any significance is the countdown braking signs: 300m, 200m and 100m.

Here, towards the end of my double stint, at around 3 am, all hell broke out. One of those moments when you think the end is imminently nigh. Flat out at around 200mph, I had passed the famous 'Auberge des Hunaudieres' restaurant and was lining myself up on the far-left-hand side of the straight, ready to brake heavily before the right-hander chicane. Suddenly, there was an almighty bang, and the Ferrari dramatically lurched right at an uncontrollable angle. After kissing the barrier, it went into a series of high-speed spins. Precariously going round and round, mostly off the ground, the F40 collected everything in its path. Taking out a few tyre walls and splashing through the gravel trap with kitty litter raining down on the windscreen, it eventually came to a halt on the far side of the chicane.

Furiously waving flags, marshals swiftly ran to the scene as I sat breathing heavily into my helmet. Blankly staring ahead, I had to spend a few seconds gathering my thoughts. Everything fell silent during the chaos of the situation as I ignored the glare of all the headlights and the noise of the cars thundering by. Relief. I was all in one piece.

All the marshals could do was move the car to the side of the track, out of harm's way of the oncoming traffic. They could do no more, as to help further would place the car into instant retirement. Shouting across to me, they explained I had endured a left rear wheel blowout, and the car was in a bit of a mess. It was only a fair bit later it occurred to me that had it been the right tyre that blew, I could have been minced meat. The car would have violently turned left over the barriers into the trees.

Quickly getting my thoughts back together, I radioed back to the pits, sharing the marshals' observations. Amato came on and asked if I could get it back to the pits. I said I could try, but I think we're out. He insisted I attempt getting it back if at all possible. I got the marshals to take a quick look, and they advised that I should be ok if I went very slowly. With that, I fired up the engine, and set to on the long way back. Six miles at twenty miles an hour seemed to take an age. All the while trying to keep the car in a straight line as it bumped around on three tyres and the remains of a flailing fourth, engine temperatures shooting up ever skyward.

Finally, I got back to the pit entry, switching off the engine halfway down the pit lane. The Ennea mechanics then pushed the car back to the pit garage. The damage was there for all to see. This massive blow-out, maybe caused by some other car's debris left on the track, had taken out the rear wing and a large part of the rear bodywork and undertray.

In theory, these could be replaced, but not so the engine. Unknowingly, the attack on the chicane had smashed a hole in the oil sump. By the time I had got back to the pits, this wonderful Ferrari engine was in total meltdown and once cooled down, it was found to be completely seized. With an engine only good for a skip or a coffee table, we all shook hands, patted each other on the back and left. By the time the garage doors came down and the pit locked up, dawn had long since broken. Le Mans was now left to others to race on for another eight hours. In basic terms, just the length of five back-to-back Grand Prix races.

Still wired, I was about to head back to the house we rented when I had a change of mind. I remembered that 1990 pole sitter Mark Blundell had gone to the circuit funfair after his car retired. Why not do the same, I thought? It would be a way to wind down. Also, the house we had rented for the race sat next to one of the fastest parts of the track. It wasn't as if I could get any sleep there anyway. So, in the early morning, I strolled across the Dunlop Bridge to the funfair. I milled around the surprisingly still busy crowds.

I ate a hot dog, watched a spectator lose his pants on a bungy jump, and ended up on a contraption I have no idea of the name of. Buckled into a chair, it went high in the air and swirled around. As it went up, I could look down and see the cars still blitzing past. As the swirls seemed to speed up, so did my stomach. Urgh, I felt so ill. My god, I thought. A couple of hours ago, I was out there mixing it with the best. Taking full control of the massive G-Forces racing a 200mph projectile. Now, in civvies, just looking on, I had a tummy to match.

It was a couple of years later I heard that my Japanese co-driver, Tetsuya Ota, was involved in a life-changing, catastrophic accident racing a Ferrari back home in Japan at Fuji Speedway. In torrential rain, a safety car was instrumental in causing a multi-car pileup. In the melee, Ota's car was rammed and immediately exploded into a violent fireball on impact.

Poor Ota was trapped inside, exposing him to 800-degree temperatures for nearly two minutes. Eventually dragged out by a safety marshal, it was found that his helmet visor had melted into his face. After a long spell in hospital, undergoing numerous plastic surgery procedures, he then had to endure many months of rehabilitation.

As a result, Ota filed a damages suit in 1999 for 290M Yen. It was not until 2003 that the court found responsible parties, including the race organisers, guilty of gross negligence. They were ordered to pay 90M Yen (around $800,000) compensation for the pain and suffering he had to endure.

Chapter Twenty-Four
Over but Not Out

I found myself in a year of change come 1997. I still had that desperate urge to race, but the drives were not forthcoming. I had got to a stage where I didn't want to get myself behind the wheel of anything. With more time on my hands, I tried to concentrate more on the sponsorship and events business I had first formed a few years back. This time around, I was working side by side with Stuart, my one and only racing manager. In our separate lives, we were like chalk and cheese, but Stuart remained close to my heart with anything race-car related.

As Le Mans began to approach, that burning old itch to compete kicked in, but nothing was readily available. Stuart had made contact with the Belgian driver, Bernard de Dryver, a one-time F1 driver and a veteran of Le Mans. He was attempting to run a new Nissan-powered prototype he was involved in called the Matrix MXP-1. I knew his name alright, but I was far from being convinced about the car. However, as he had put my name down as one of the drivers, I thought I should attend the Le Mans pre-qualifying test, held in those days the month before.

I made my way down through France with my old pal, Doctor Clive. The one who involuntary gave me an entrée into the world of top level sportscar racing world, a decade or more before. Listening on the car radio, we chuckled enroute as John Major quietly muttered in monotone, 'Well, we lost', as Labour gained a resounding, landslide victory. Tony Blair winning by the largest majority since 1945.

Arriving at the track, Bernard came across as a nice chap, which is more than can be said of his car. It looked the part, but soon into pre-qualifying, we all knew it wasn't going to make the grade. As fast as it may sound, with a quickest lap of 4.05 minutes for the 8.5-mile circuit, the Matrix was out.

Pre-qualifying was over for him before the afternoon session even started. Not overly surprised with the efforts of the Matrix and not even being given the chance to slip into my racing overalls, Clive and I decided to go for something to eat. Just as we were unlocking the car, we noticed an immense plume of black smoke filling the sky.

At first, we thought the smoke could be a local farmer burning a mega bonfire, but we soon came to the conclusion this could be something more sinister. The track was still not open to the public, but as pass-holders, we could access the circuit. Quickly following the now dissipating plume coming from a South Easterly direction, we found the source. To the right, on the very fast approach to the Porsche Curves, we noticed the soaking wet trees still smokily smouldering as the last of the fire trucks left the scene.

We hesitantly approached, not wanting to show any signs of any morbid curiosity. But parking up on the grass verge, I saw that numerous drivers were there, even Derek Bell, who was not competing that year. They were not there for any other reason than to, as much as possible, download what had just happened. Every time they go out, all race drivers take a calculated risk. They were all there to try and find out and understand what had happened and why. No other reason.

What we eventually found out was that the young French, up-and-coming driver, Sebastian Enjolras, had been a victim of a major car bodywork fault. The WR Peugeot's one-piece shell had broken away from the chassis. With no ground effect to keep the car on the ground, it launched into the air. Going up and over the guardrail, it continued flying upside down into the trees. The ensuing fire set the pine forest alight. Sadly, Sebastian was killed instantly.

Three weeks later, I had to again return to Le Mans in civvies for the race itself. This would be the first time I had not competed after eleven consecutive years. I ended up working as a pundit for journalist Andrew Marriot in the press office, broadcasting live on radio. Having perhaps had that one too many beers on Saturday race night, I arrived with no time to spare Sunday morning. Without any briefing, he just shoved a set of headphones on my head as soon as I walked in. We were squeezed into just one of an entire row of tiny soundproof cubicles. Each press box could seat no more than two at best but did offer a superb panoramic view of the pits and start line straight. Within 20 seconds of being there, Andrew announced I was now live on air to South Africa. It was a fun experience but commentating on the real thing is not the same thing as <u>doing</u> the real thing.

In a quiet year, Stuart and I still kept lots of irons in the fire, but it wasn't until the end of the year elements started to come together. I'm not sure if it was through an Italian contact made when I was with Ferrari, but a phone call came into the office from Italy. In broken English, the girl at the other end of the phone said her father, a Giovanni Centenari, who owned and ran a Milan-based sports prototype racing team, had heard I was looking for a drive. They told me their number one driver was the acclaimed Italian veteran Arturo Merzario. He was looking for a good co-driver.

I had never met Arturo but knew all about him. He had served seven years as a Grand Prix Formula One driver, including a stint with Ferrari. He was instrumental in saving the life of Niki Lauda after his horrifying accident in the 1976 German Grand Prix. Arturo had jumped into the fire and pulled him out of the wreckage. On the international sports car scene, he was also a very big player. He had won both the formidable Targa Florio and the Spa 1000kms outright and had come second at Le Mans and in the Nürburgring 1000kms.

With contact details close to hand, I immediately sent my CV and was surprised when they got back so quickly. Oddly, I thought, this time, they wanted to know how tall I was. Well, if you are as short as me, 5'4' and a tea leaf, it's not something you can keep quiet for long. After hesitating, I just had to tell the truth. Almost crunching the phone handle with apprehension, I both closed my eyes and bit my lip, thinking I should have said 6'4. Their response was, you're in; details to follow; see you at the last round of the year in Jarama, Spain. Don't be late or forget your helmet and licence.

Later they explained this Centenari SR2 car was built and developed around Arturo Merzario. They further explained that, like me, he was vertically challenged. OK, so that made some sense, and I flew with Dr Clive to Madrid with high hopes. We made our way to the circuit a day before race practice began and found Alfonso, a casual race driver friend of mine, in the clubhouse bar. Affectionately known as 'The Fonz' by racers, Alfonso is nephew to what would become the former King of Spain, Juan Carlos. The official title of 'The Fonz' is, in fact, Don Alfonso de Orleans-Borbón y Ferrara-Pignatelli, 7th Duke of Galliera. To me he was just an aristocratic playboy pal I had ambiguously got to know who liked and raced fast cars and always had an eye for the ladies.

Showing off to his friends and drowning what had to be at least his fourth glass of Rioja, The Fonz was brandishing the keys to a brand-new Ferrari 355 he had just purchased. Indeed, it shimmered in the Spanish sun just outside. After a while I happened to mention I had never competed at Jarama before. With that, he just threw the keys over to me. Have a little play, go, and learn, he said.

Taking full advantage of his perhaps slightly tipsy generosity, I must have got at least fifteen exploratory laps in. A good grounding for the following days' open practice. That evening the Fonz invited us to his favourite Sushi bar hidden in the depths of downtown

Madrid. Not knowing the area, I suggested I follow him in my hire car. Looking back on the experience now, I was being a tad over-optimistic. Planting his foot firmly to the floor as soon as he was out of the circuit gates, his brand-new Ferrari made a growling rasp and tore off into the distance. It was tough enough to keep him in view, let alone keep up with him.

As we ventured further downtown into the busy streets of the city, I occasionally caught the odd glimpse of him, but whenever I got close, he would, with wheels spinning, forever jump all the red lights. I sat there with Dr Clive completely lost. All we had was the name of the restaurant but asking a Spaniard for directions was nigh on impossible. And remember, mobile phones were in their infancy. It wasn't as if I could Google map the venue on my Nokia. Finally, we found an English-speaking local who drew a map for me.

We probably arrived a good half hour later, where we found the Fonz and his cronies again, partying at the restaurant's bar. I happened to mention that I had tried to keep up with him, but he drove through all the red lights. "How did you get away with that?" I asked. "What's going to happen' he confidently replied. "My uncle's the King of Spain".

Open practice day arrived, and frustratingly, the bright sunshine of the day before was replaced by dark, threatening skies for my trial run in the new race car. I guessed that Arturo would drive first, but there was no sign of him. His flight was delayed coming back from Miami.

Looking glorious in its smart red and white Marlboro livery, courtesy of Arturo's long-time relationship with the cigarette manufacturer, this 3-litre V6 Alfa Romeo-powered Centenari SR2 car was magnificent. Something I really started to appreciate as I took my first exploratory laps. The car literally begged you to go faster, and within no time, I was right up to speed. As the lap times fell significantly, so then did the rain. Caught halfway through a fast corner, on slicks in a sudden downpour, the car swapped ends. Looking intently into my mirrors, I rapidly headed backwards into the gravel trap. Fortunately, I came to an undignified stop just before I hit the barriers in a shower of stones. Oh boy, I thought. What a way to impress my new team.

Practice stopped; the car was hauled back to the pits on a trailer. The team busily went to work, hoovering out 5 inches of kitty litter from every orifice before the second practice begun. Please don't turn up now, I mused as a short chap with a massive, signature white cowboy hat strode in. Arturo looked at the car and then glared at me. Don't tell me he is my new co-driver he said to Giovanni, the team owner, without taking his eyes off me. I'm no Sherlock but I deduced he was not overly impressed.

However, things got a little better after there were no upsets in qualifying and we were almost on speaking terms come race day. I had this last chance to impress in the final championship race of the year if I stood any chance of being a part of the team for the following season.

On paper, against the might of the top category Kremer and Courage Porsche and Ferrari 333 teams, we were on a hiding to nothing. However, this little class 2 car was quick. Very quick. With Arturo taking the start, he battled through the field until we were right up there playing with the front runners. As the car roared into the pits, I clambered into the confined cockpit, just praying I was not about to let the side down. With my hands held high in the air, Arturo belted me up and then brusquely thumped me on the top of my helmet. "Be quick, don't crash", he severely threatened loudly above the noise.

With that, I let the clutch up, and I was gone. Letting loose of the highly revving engine and with tyres squealing, I had entered my first and only race of the year. Concentrating as if my life depended on it, I was happy to not let the side down. Taking the chequered flag, we had won our class and taken an amazing second overall position. Pictures of us on the podium have us both swinging our big, shiny cups. If you were to look down on the same pictures, you would see the remains of Arturo's half-smoked Marlboro, still snugly held between his fingers.

In the evening, we all celebrated in a nearby restaurant. Giovanni and his troop were great, but they only spoke Italian. We only spoke English. How were we to communicate better? Team owner Giovanni had the answer. He grabbed two forks from the table and ordered two cocktail sticks. The trick he accomplished by holding up two precariously balanced cocktail sticks tip to tip and then raising two alarmingly adjoined forks into the air was nothing short of magic. The bonding was done, and we were all set for the next season.

I spent the off-season securing the odd sponsor to at least get me up and running with the team and refining that dastardly intricate trick.

Chapter Twenty-Five
Alien Endeavours

For 1998, I was about to embark on a lively season that included everything from high-profile sponsors to spacemen and everything in between. It was one of those years you just could not make up, so although I have been trying to keep to mostly Le Mans stories, this is just another tale I could not leave out.

Sporting a new Elf Oil livery the season kicked off at the holy grail of Italian motor racing, Monza. The race was the celebrated Monza 1000km. This magnificent circuit, renown as the Temple of Speed, is one of only a few classic tracks that still remain on the Grand Prix calendar. Flat out on full throttle for no less than three-quarters of the circuit, the sheer speed attained here is simply breathtaking. I loved it.

As well as being the cardinal home to the fanatical *Tifosi,* it was practically on the doorstep of the Milan-based Centenari Team. They entered two cars. One for me, Arturo and a highly personable chap called Fulvio Ballabio. Born next door in Milan, Fulvio had risen through the ranks to competing in Indy Cars. The second car was all set for Loic Depailler, son of French Formula One hero Patrick Depailler, and Italians Giovanna Amati and Marco Lucchinelli. Giovanna was not only famous for being the most recent female to secure a seat in F1 but earlier for being kidnapped.

Her wealthy parents having to pay out 800M Lire, around $1M, for her safe return two months later. Marco was a former Grand Prix motorbike racer who had won the world championship in 1981. He was now trying his hand at car racing.

So, with an Alfa Romeo team mostly full of Italians, it was a delight to hang out. And Arturo was a god at Monza. Strutting up and down the pits in his famous Marlboro cowboy hat, hordes of eager fans would follow his every move. When he was not in the car, he was autographing programmes, tickets, tee-shirts, and more.

He beckoned me to one pit garage where his compatriots Giovanni, Fulvio and Marco had converged to pay homage to the great Ferrari F1 driver Clay Regazzoni. Sat there in a wheelchair, disabled since his major accident in the United States Grand Prix back in 1980, he was still ever the gentleman. In awe, I shook the hand of one of my all-time heroes. Daunted just by his presence, he wished me all the luck for the race ahead. His English was not so good, and neither was my Italian, but wow, I felt so elated.

Come race day, I wanted to slice up and wrap up the incredible Milanese atmosphere. Send it to all my friends as presents. The huge, ardent crowd filled up the stands as we took our places on the burgeoning grid. The noise of the race cars firing up, their exhaust fumes blending with the smell of rich Italian food floating down the pit lane. I was in heaven and couldn't have felt more positive.

As it happened, the actual race did not go entirely to plan. On the grid, a hand flew up into the air from the cockpit of the second

Centenari. For some reason, the Loic, Giovanna, and Marco's car would not fire up. Although our engineers raced over to help, the car would fail to start. We did and were making tremendous progress up through the field for the first three hours of this five-hour competition.

How I enjoyed this legendary circuit. Flat out, holding on for dear life through the famous Curva Grande at the end of the main straight. Swooping under the old circuit bridge at full throttle into the renown Ascari chicane. The blast down the very fast back straight and powering out of the sweeping and ever-increasing curve of the notorious Curva Parabolica, the fast bend that leads back on to the start line straight, kicking up the dust and grass on exit. Then, with a sudden boom, it was all over. The car silently rumbled to a stop on the verge with an exploded gearbox.

I still left Italy feeling very positive. The car was quick, the engines were strong, and the chassis well balanced. Centenari just required some more work done on the gearbox. Back in the office, Stuart was making progress with a potential Le Mans sponsor, Sony PlayStation. We were close to doing a deal as I left for the south of France. Round one of the International Sports Racing Series (ISRS).

Paul Ricard, the Grand Prix circuit, was the venue for the opening round of the ISRS. Set up in the hills, 50 minutes East of Marseille, this renovated state-of-the-art circuit, with its famed 200mph Mistral Straight, was another ultra-quick track which suited me down to the ground. In our car, we were down to run the same driver line up of Merzario, Ballabio and me. However, Fulvio Ballabio stepped down after the qualifying sessions because he was simply not up to speed. Fulvio is a lovely person, but I think his best days driving very quickly had passed. With more time in the car for both me and Arturo, we nailed it again and won our class. It was a great start to the championship push.

Next stop was Paris. Just a little North of the Champs-Elysees lay the head office of Sony PlayStation. Along with Stuart, Swedish ace Carl Rosenblad and former French Grand Prix driver Jean-Pierre Jarier, we were all there to attend the launch of our new Le Mans challenger. Attracting a lot of interest from passers-by, the fearsome, low-slung Sony PlayStation Porsche GT1 sat roped off outside the main entrance. It looked striking with its red, blue, and yellow logo shouting out of the car's all-black livery.

Inside, champagne and cocktails were being served to the many attendees. For some reason, these included the cast from a long-running French TV soap. Confident and loud, they all seemed to act with an over-exaggerated sense of importance. Of course, the funny thing was that to themselves and presumably the French, they were famous TV stars. I didn't know them from Adam, so the overblown effect they were all trying to portray was lost. I felt like the little boy in the story of the emperor's new clothes.

After drinks, we were all hurried downstairs to Sony's own private screening room. Feeling a little too self-evident wearing our brand-new Sony PlayStation racing suits, the drivers were asked to stand on a balcony at the back of the auditorium. Given small plastic hand controls, primitive to what is used today, we were all tasked to delight the audience with a racing lap of Le Mans shown on the big screen. Having never played a game on Sony PlayStation, I was left just to fumble around, attempting to get my car moving in the right direction. Fortunately for me, Carl and Jean-Pierre were little better.

After all the final executive Le Mans announcements were made, we were ushered outside next to the race car for an autograph signing session. I immediately felt much more at home. I had proved to a star audience I was useless at driving a lap of Le Mans, but at least I hadn't forgotten the ability to scribble down a signature.

Back in the Alfa Romeo, we took another podium at the undulating Czech circuit of Brno, but it was all change in the Centenari camp. Arturo Merzario had been replaced with Elf-supported rising star Xavier Pompidou, nephew of the former French President. For whatever reason, Arturo had chosen to walk away. I believe it was over a disagreement with Giovanni Centenari, but I never found out for sure.

It was sad in a way, as he ended up joining a far less competitive all-Italian team for the rest of the season. Ironically, with me securing a podium in the first round of the series and the keen and quick Xavier only starting in the second round, I solely led the class championship.

It was all change in the Le Mans camp as well. Securing two entries, the French Larbre Competition team were going to run the

Sony PlayStation Porsche GT1, but after major clutch problems in pre-qualifying, they chose to replace it with their faithful Porsche GT2 911. This, along with all their tyres and spares, matched their second GT2 car.

During qualifying at Le Mans, things within the team dynamic started to go wrong. I cannot remember what the exact issues were, but Stuart was very unhappy. He called for team members to attend an urgent meeting. He chose to hold it in the back of the pits during practice sessions. As many plastic chairs as we could find were duly pulled up around a plastic buffet table. All seated awaiting Stuart's arrival, he eventually blustered in.

Armed with his usual age-old leather brief case and an obvious bee in his bonnet, he immediately planted his rather large frame in the awaiting seat. With that, all four legs immediately snapped, turned up skywards, and the plastic seat with Stuart aboard crashed to the floor. I couldn't contain myself. With tears streaming down my face and in danger of cracking a few ribs, I lay squirming on the ground in fits of laughter. Meeting adjourned.

On the last day of qualifying, the car was quick. We were the fastest of a huge string of Porsche GT2 cars. The only marque ahead of us was the all-dominant, three-car works factory Chrysler Viper team. Jack Leconte, boss of Larbre, decided fourth in class was good enough. We might as well park the car up in the pit garage for the final nighttime session. Why risk it? And besides, there was no way we would gain any more time at night.

273

Work done for the evening, we adjourned to the team's hospitality tent and set about enjoying a relaxing dinner. I sat there with a number of team members, including Jean-Pierre Jarier. A little portlier than he was in his younger years, Jean-Pierre was a big star. He had won the Formula 2 championship before embarking on a Formula One career that spanned eleven years and impressive 135 Grand Prix starts.

Not one to take anything too seriously, he often wore a cheeky grin and had a mischievous twinkle in his eye. As tomorrow, Friday, was a day off for drivers, we ate and supped on copious glasses of red wine as he went about discussing what I *should not* do. Brake too late here, and 'you will be into ze trees'. Overtake on the wrong side here, and 'you will be into ze trees'. He went on, without a confidence lift, entering Indianapolis, you will be…. In harmony, we all hollered 'into ze trees'.

Jean-Pierre was opening another bottle of red when the boss, Jack Leconte poked his head in. Jack explained that Carl Rosenblad, the third co-driver, did not think the headlights were set quite right. You'll have to take it out for a quick spin and check, he told Jean. No problem, he said and with that, left for the pit garage. We just all sat there looking a little horrified. Jean-Pierre was taking out a 200mph racing car in the dark, having consumed what must have been a bottle of red or more. I quietly remarked to the remaining audience around the table that one small hiccup and Jean could be 'into ze trees'.

Half an hour later, a rather sweaty-faced Jean-Pierre strolled back into the hospitality tent. "Ze headlights are fine", he said as he poured the last dregs from the remaining bottle into his glass. What he forgot to mention was he split the Viper's time and was now the third-quickest GT2.

It was, however, a very grumpy Jean-Pierre who attended the driver's parade around the city centre on Friday afternoon. Sitting up on the back of open-top vintage cars, signing autographs to the hordes of fans that converge around the three-mile route was not his bag. He thought it a waste of his time. He said he would not have attended was it not for the fact the ACO, the governing body, fined 5,000 Euros for every non-attendee.

I looked at it differently. With a free day away from the racing while the mechanics fettled the cars, I have always found the parade fun. As well as the great carnival atmosphere created by the colourful extravaganza of theatrically costumed musicians and marching bands that intersperse the classic cars carrying the drivers, it is a way of giving back to the locals. Le Mans is not a wealthy city, and many locals cannot afford a race day ticket.

The 'Grand Parade des Pilotes' is sometimes the only celebration where they are free to get close-up to their heroes. Although the race is being held on their doorstep, a lot are forced to watch the race on TV. While Jean-Pierre had to spend a couple of hours huffing and puffing his way around, I thought it a very small price to pay.

The sheer explosion of the senses when the flag finally drops on race day never ceases to amaze me. Almost indefinable, the noise, smell, dust, crowds, and colours all collaborate to form a dynamic and ever-changing cocktail of aggression, speed and sound. As the sun sets, so it always becomes ever more surreal, more intense, sharper.

Out on the track, we were doing well. By midnight, fighting at the top of the GT2 field, we had forged passage into second place ahead of two of the three Vipers. I felt in control but could not or did not want to match the out and out pace of Jarier. He ran every lap as if it were the opening laps of a Grand Prix, and I think this might have caught us out in the end. Every high curb he could possibly mount, he did. This takes the huge demands made on the suspension to the absolute limit. By 3 am, we had clawed back time lost with a spin in a rain shower. By 3.45 am, we were out. It was all over. The suspension had finally let go.

Don't get me wrong, Jean-Pierre Jarier is a colossal talent. Always renown for being incredibly quick, some would say he was very hard on cars. His Grand Prix career was not without its fair share of accidents or retirements. But what did I know, at 52, not as young as he once was, he won the French GT Championship that year and the following year, too.

Going home after a very big race such as the Le Mans race is always a compromise to your system. Apart from anything else, you feel as if you could sleep and revitalise for at least a month.

However, two weeks later, I was in Italy for the next round of the ISRS Championship. Set on the east coast of the country near Rimini, the Misano circuit has always proved to be a friendly, happy, sunny venue.

Now, I really did not want to highlight this season, but it was extraordinary in so many ways. Now, with strong Elf Oil backing, the Centenari Alfa Romeo team entered three cars for this race. The avant-garde mix of drivers included Jacques Villeneuve. Not THE 1997 World Champion, but his uncle, brother of the much-missed Grand Prix superstar Gilles. We had Loic Depailler, son of French F1 Grand Prix hero Patrick. Former Italian Grand Prix driver Giuseppe 'Beppe' Gabbiani and ultra-talented rookie João Barbosa.

Later on, João would go on to win the legendary 24-Hour race at Daytona three times, as well as securing the American Sports Car Championship twice. I was back with Xavier while Fulvio had moved to another Centenari. However, last to join the driver line up threw us all. A very strange character that went by the name of 'Rael'. Wearing a white gown and armed with a well-trimmed goatee beard and receding hair pulled back into a neat bob, his appearance alone looked a little alien in the pit lane. After Rael had insisted the engineers place large UFO decals on the front of all three cars, we then heard his tale.

The story goes that French-born Claude Maurice Marcel Vorilhon aspired to be a racing driver after an early attempt at being a pop star. One dark, wintery night in 1973, he was driving along a quiet country road when his headlights picked up a beam of light descending from the sky. Parking the car on the side of the road, he hesitantly walked closer on foot to investigate when he was gently whisked up into a spaceship.

Apparently, the awaiting alien explained, in fluent French no less, that he had been chosen to be their ambassador on earth. His mission was to build an embassy on neutral ground in anticipation of the forthcoming arrival of these extraterrestrials. Seemingly, these aliens, known as 'Elohim', lived peaceably on a distant planet free of money, sickness, and war. 25,000 years ahead of us intellectually, they needed him to spread their word of peace and love.

Indeed, Claude was told he would follow in the footsteps of previous, Elohim-sent, extraterrestrial prophets who had visited earth in the past. These included the Buddha, Moses, Muhammad, and Jesus. All of which, which he said he was transported through space to visit in person a couple of years later.

True to his calling, Claude immediately changed his name to 'Rael' (messenger of the Elohim) and set about his given task with great gusto. He published several books and founded a religion called UFO. Courting controversy and lawsuits along the way, he launched a notorious series of publicity campaigns designed to shock, titillate, and capture the media's imagination. Soon, the new Raëlian movement became the world's largest 'flying saucer cult'.

With followers paying a tithe of up to 10% of their income I can only presume it was time for 'Rael' to go motor racing again.

Back on earth, we had a race to run. But first, we had to endure the arrival of 'Rael'. John Mangoletsi, the then series organiser, rolled his eyes into the back of his head as the chap's full entourage of followers trooped into the paddock. Various sized medallions hung down from their necks according to their position in the hierarchy. Clad in white, the men in gowns, the women in bits that just about covered their essentials but no more, banged their drums or blew their flutes as they all marched in.

However, a race that initially enjoyed so much initial promise didn't go entirely to plan. Sighting *force majeur*, we had to appeal to the stewards to start after the engine blew-up at the beginning of official qualifying. With a replacement secured and fitted in the nick of time, I was then black-flagged early in the race for not having my safety lights on.

On returning to the fray, I then suffered from engine management system problems. Nevertheless, Dr Clive's own superb management skills climbed us back in the mix. With one refuelling station between all three cars, he carefully engineered a way to not have us all filing into the pits together.

With everyone using up much the same fuel per stint, this was easier said than done. With our car at least salvaging 5th in class, the points accumulated were just enough to keep me in the class championship lead. Not the best day in the office, but certainly not the worst.

We didn't finish in the next couple of races at Donington Park in the UK or Anderstorp Raceway in Sweden, but I'll never forget that crazy sojourn to Scandinavia. Rael and his followers descended on Anderstorp, the former home to the Swedish Grand Prix, with the same tour de force as Misano. The only problem was they arrived three hours too late. By the time their grand parade had all strutted in, qualifying was over. All our grid positions already written in stone. Rael was beside himself as the organisers explained he was too late. After a lot of official deliberation, it was decided he could start at the back of the grid if he qualified by doing three laps in the lunchtime break.

We all stood around in the pit lane as Rael, dramatically revving the hell out of his car, sat ready for the off. He crunched it into gear, and as the lights turned from red to green, he let the clutch out and hit the throttle hard. We couldn't believe it as then, with great force, he shot off ...backwards. For the second time that year, I hit the ground screaming with laughter as my ribs nearly broke yet again. I was joined by most of the team, who uniformly couldn't control themselves either. He had one important task to start and stuck the bloody thing in reverse.

When we all managed to get up from the ground and brushed ourselves off, Rael had managed to do his three qualifying laps in forward motion. The next serious thing to do was go for the qualifying debrief and plan the race ahead. This was held in the meeting room at the rear of the team truck.

Fun over, this was usually a more stern, no-nonsense, deadpan affair. However, Rael put a stop to this as he continued to thump his fist down hard on the table. Trying to make a point, he resolutely said, 'why can't people take me seriously?' With that, game over. We all collapsed in fits of laughter. Another meeting irretrievably kissed goodbye. Oh, and we never set eyes on Rael again after Anderstorp.

Joining us for some of the later season races was Thorkild Thyrring, the Dane who drove the sister Callaway Corvette at Le Mans in 1995. He would arrive with a case full of large denomination Danish Krone. As part of a blind-eyed 'Elf Oil' deal I had, it would be my job to change the cash into Euros and pay the team for him. Still larger than life, 'Thorky' would hold court before the races by standing on an apple box in the paddock and demanding his sponsors and guests pay attention to him.

These orders were hollered out in his deep, stern, attention-drawing voice. Standing there, with what I always thought was his very bad-fitting hairpiece in place, he would expand on how difficult and heroic it was to be a racing driver of his calibre. Bearing in mind he was a star TV car racing commentator back in Denmark, he seemed to get away with it. In no uncertain terms he would announce how privileged they all were just being in his company. Woe betides anyone in the group not listening.

Bizarrely, by the skin of my teeth, I was still leading the drivers' championship in my class as we headed off for the last races. As I had won with Arturo Merzario at the beginning of the season before he was replaced by Xavier Pompidou, my points tally was always higher than Xavier's. The team had mechanical issues at Nürburgring, but we still collected some valuable points by finishing just outside the podium in 4th. Inwardly, I felt I gained some credence in the fact that outright 1989 Le Mans winner Stanley Dickens, driving the sister Centenari car that weekend, was a fair bit slower than me. Over the next couple of years, we became good friends, often propping up the local bar at Le Mans together.

Collecting more points at the following race on the 2.6 mile Le Mans Bugatti Circuit, with a strong podium finish, it was down to the wire with one championship round left to run. The only problem I had was it was at Kyalami in South Africa, and by then, my sponsorship had completely run out.

What was I to do? I had to win in Kyalami to stand any chance of taking the championship and there I was without a bean to get out there. Back in the UK, I did what comes naturally in times of calamity. I headed off to my local pub. Here, I bumped into James Martin, a friend I hadn't seen in a while. James was a friendly, light-hearted pal but one that had that Jeremy Clarkson effect on me for always being condescending to his buddies. He was street sharp, very clever but you never knew exactly where you stood with him.

As the drinks went down, I shared my woes with him. He said, 'no problem' he had a chum who could be willing to help out in my dilemma. James was a scenery creator for big blockbuster movies, so I was surprised when he suggested meeting up with a partner in a big property consultancy based just off the Ritz in the centre of London. How would he have friends there, I thought.

However, hesitantly, I arrived at the swanky offices of Montagu Evans in Dover Street, all suited and booted. Warmly welcomed by company partner Clive Riding, twenty minutes later, I walked out with half the funds I needed for South Africa and a large amount for the following Le Mans race. That was his real interest, as it was on his bucket list, and he could far more easily take his special guests there. I bought a large drink for my chippy pal James and promised to look after him if he came himself.

If I wasn't to spend the Le Mans cash, I needed to secure another sponsor keen on South Africa. The internet was in its infancy, but I somehow found Pinn Africa, a big insurance underwriting company twenty minutes from the Kyalami circuit. They were keen. They wanted to bring forty customers. They did not want to be involved with the incidentals. They just wanted the full works, a dedicated hospitality suite, all the VIP catering and customised tee shirts for all the guests. Of course, I said, no problem, then took a huge gulp. It was over a decade since I was there last.

True to form, they sent the funds, and it was now up to me to manage the rest. I flew out early and hired a lovely, coloured chap who spent a full three days driving around with me in his rather beaten-up old cab. I went and visited all the suppliers I had contacted before on the phone. I could not believe the barricades I had to endure just to get into their offices. Barbed wire at each stop and big yellow and black gun signs outside to say they were armed. Most had at least a double entrance.

You went through one door that locked behind you. Then another. The country itself is stunningly beautiful, but the rest needed a fair amount of work. Afterwards, I visited the Pinn Africa offices and acted like a local. Little did they know how long it had been since I was last in their country. I then paid my driver. I couldn't believe the small amount he was asking for. I paid him treble and still had enough cash for a McDonalds. Funny how you remember small things.

So, all set and confident, next stop was the race event itself. In qualifying we secured the class pole, so things were looking great. A clear run to the finish, and I would take the championship. All that effort was worth it. By then, the car was highly reliable, and at the end of a demanding season, the team were at their very strongest. What could go wrong? Well, just about everything.

I started. Shortly after taking over from me, Xavier had a clash with another car. Limping home, he eventually pitted before returning to the fray. Then the clutch packed up. Our arch-rivals, Tampoli, another Italian team, took the chequered flag and, by doing so, also secured the championship by just a couple of points. Vice

Champion just doesn't have the same ring about it. Devastated, all I could do was retire to the swish hospitality suite I had organised and party with the forty Pinn Africa tee-shirted clients who seemed totally oblivious of how important this was to me. Another *c'est la vie* moment. At least I didn't have to share the disappointment with 'Rael'.

Chapter Twenty-Six
Burning Orient

A new season beckoned, but I was getting tired at this stage. Where was I going? What did I hope to achieve? With so much promise, my career in racing had offered more low times than high. Every time I thought I was getting close, something would stroll up and quietly put a spanner in the works. I thought I at least wanted to sign off with one final Le Mans. Apart from anything else, I was committed to Montagu Evans. But where was I to go for a one-off? The answer came from the Far East.

Yojiro Terada was a past champion. Not only known for holding the record for the second most participations in the great race, but he had also scored class victories four times and was therefore seen as an absolute god in his home country of Japan. Nineteen ninety-nine would see his sixth time partnering Frenchman Franck Fréon. Franck was an Indy car driver who would later become a works factory driver for the mighty Chevrolet factory team. They needed their full set of three drivers to compete at Le Mans. At the 11th hour, I was hired to join the driver line-up, heading off for what would be my 13th participation.

Rebadged an AutoExe, in deference to Terada's parts company, to all intents and purposes our mount was a big Riley & Scott prototype. Outright winner of such celebrated races as the Daytona

24 Hours and the Sebring 12 Hours, this scary, multi-American title-winning beast was powered by a brutal six litre Ford V8 engine. Back in the top class, hopes were high for the big day. However, our faith in what could be achieved did not go entirely to plan in the first Wednesday practice session.

I must say, I loved this car from the word go. The confidence-generating stability and the way it just sat on the road was awesome. That and the speed, power and the braking ability left me smiling from ear to ear. So happy was I, I was leaving my braking later than ever to the point when closely following another big category car, I missed the last 100 metre marker board. Braking from well over 200mph into the second chicane on the Mulsanne, I sailed on. With stones raining down all around me, I went into a series of spins before nearly clearing the chicane's entire gravel trap. So confident I was with this car, I just chuckled to myself as I came to a halt, engaged first gear, and carefully egged the car slowly back onto the track. Worse was to come.

Franck followed next. Again, at over 200mph, his cockpit filled with smoke before flames began to lick up around him. Managing to stop at a marshal's post, he leapt out just in the nick of time. The cockpit, now devoured in a ball of fire, was quickly extinguished by the nearby marshals. Perhaps eyebrows a little singed, but no real harm done.

Franck returned to the pits 40 minutes later, shaken but not too stirred. The very sad-looking car arrived on the back of a trailer after the session ended. Taking one look, I naturally assumed it was all over and began to start thinking about whether it was worth staying at Le Mans or returning to the UK early.

What little faith. The mechanics rolled the blackened car into the pit garage and immediately dived-in to work. Half the engineers were hired from Sarthe-based Promotion Racing, and once the car was stripped down bare, they took various parts to one of their local workshops for repair. Burning the midnight oil, they worked solidly throughout the night and all the following day. Not surprisingly, the root cause was finally located to a faulty fuel tank. As we didn't have a spare, this was taken out and repaired as best as possible.

In the very short number of laps Franck was able to do before his smoky experience, he had set a very respectable time. Neither Terada nor I had. On the Wednesday, Terada went out first but only did an out lap and an in lap. I did three laps, but on my only flying lap, I missed the chicane entry and spun. With all three of us missing final qualifying on Thursday, we should have been packing up and going home. Our saviour Franck proved the car was fast. The ACO gave us special dispensation to start at the back of the grid. Whew.

We were not the only team enduring major problems. In the works factory, Mercedes camp engineers were at a loss as to what caused Mark Webber's qualifying accident. After the kink on the Mulsanne at the crest of the hill before Mulsanne Corner, Mark suddenly saw sky where there should have been a road. The car had

288

taken off like an aeroplane, flipped up backwards and crashed down in a heap of wreckage.

By Friday, our team was finally putting the finishing touches to a car that we thought was fully burned out just 40 hours before. The only official drivers' job we had to do was attend the downtown Grand Parade des Pilotes. This is normally a fun event and a way to relax with the ever-friendly crowds before race day. As we toured the city centre atop vintage cars, we waved to the vast audience that filed *en masse* into the streets of Le Mans and signed as many autographs as we could.

However, you could tell our minds were elsewhere. There was a feeling of angst-ridden anticipation between us all. Who was going to take the start? Normally, this esteemed job fell to the quickest driver of each team. The problem was Franck didn't want to take the risk. I was not overly keen, either. Climbing into what could be a 200mph lethal weapon is a calculated risk race drivers take every time they go out onto the track.

But what about this quickly refabricated fuel cell? How long would it last? Would it just burst into flames within a lap or two? After the parade, we were at the point of drawing straws when Terada stepped in and said he would take the start. After all, it was his car and his team. So, ultimately, his responsibility. We were all happy with this and at least Franck and I got a good night's sleep.

What I didn't know at the time was that it was decided I would do the early morning warm-up. A curved ball to throw if ever there was one. However, as I sat snug in the cockpit in the relatively dark pit garage, all strapped in and ready to go, I found something to relieve the intense anxiety I felt. In my tiny rear-view mirrors, I could see my Montague Evans sponsors all gathering around the mammoth rear wing of the car.

With a twinkle in my eye, I held back on pressing the starter button until the last moment. Then, as the guests were in touching distance, I quietly pushed it. The exhausts immediately delivered a deafening roar as an unbridled 600+ horsepower burst into life. As the lights turned to green and I joined the urgent pack exiting the pitlane, I couldn't help but chortle into my helmet with the picture of all my VIPs, still on their hands and knees, getting up after literally being blown off their feet backwards!

There was no need to go out on the edge during the warmup. Just a couple of laps to do all the necessary systems checks and to make sure the set-up was much the same as before the major rebuild. Of course, I also wanted to know whether there was any immediate concern of me becoming a high-speed BBQ.

With everything seemingly ok, I thundered down the Mulsanne Straight as happy as I could be. Approaching the hump at the end of the Mulsanne before the corner, marshals' yellow warning flags were being frantically waved. Over the crest, Mark Webber's Mercedes lay upside down in yet another crumpled heap. I came in the pits at the end of that lap but heard afterwards that the Mercedes had, again, mysteriously taken off 20ft into the air, flipped backwards, and had crashed down on its roof. This big, three-car team were now down to two and we hadn't even got to the start yet.

As the starting drivers took up their positions on the grid, former Grand Prix star Martin Brundle sat on pole at the front end of the grid. Yojiro Terada in our car at the other end. Although Franck was only a handful of seconds slower in the tiny number of laps he had managed in qualifying, it was the price we had to pay for Terada and I not setting a time but being allowed into the race. 4 pm finally arrived. Franck and I anxiously looked on from the pit wall. With the lights turning to green and the deliverance of a huge cloud of smoke and the immense sound and smell of approaching engines, Le Mans served up another dramatic start.

To our amazement, round and round Terada went. The work the engineers had hurriedly done on the fuel cell had worked. I was next out, and with everything going to plan, we thought the worst was over. It wasn't, and soon, clutch problems began interfering with our progress. So frustrating, as this was such a lovely car to drive.

On Franck's first stint, he had to stop at Indianapolis to wait until the clutch cooled down. Having lost 40 minutes, he finally got the car back to the pits, where even more time was lost replacing it. We clambered steadily on our way to midnight when, with a little too eager use of the throttle at the slow Arnage corner, I was sent spinning backwards into the barrier. Apart from a light tap to the rear wing, no harm was done.

Sadly, though, the next stint Franck undertook lasted less than a lap. He rolled quietly to a halt around the back of the circuit as the engine gave up the ghost. It was 2 am when we were pronounced the 6th retirement of the race.

A little earlier, around 9 pm, the Mercedes challenge had come to a much more dramatic end. Historically broadcast live throughout the world, one of the two remaining cars had yet another almighty accident. As the cameras rolled, the car driven by Scot Peter Dumbreck took off, again on the Very fast approach to Indianapolis. This was on the very slight crest over the second kink. The one I used to let out a confidence shriek to as the car went ultra-light at 200mph. Flying as high as the nearby bridge crossing the circuit, Dumbreck managed a triple backward somersault before clearing the trackside treetops and disappearing into the forest.

Aghast, everyone thought the worst. Thankfully, it became known later the car landed on its wheels the right way up. Once found and extricated, Dumbreck was taken to the medical centre but later released. That was finally enough for Mercedes, and they withdrew the remaining car there and then. The pit garage doors came down and to date, they have not been seen at Le Mans ever since. Whilst the fairly obvious aerodynamic issues they had with their cars became more apparent in the days and weeks that followed, few ever became aware of why Peter Dumbreck was so lucky.

The lady owner of the trackside house I had stayed in for many years when I raced at Le Mans explained the following day. She knew the local forester. He just happened to cut down a square patch of trees away from the picturesque tree line that sat alongside the Armco. They were cut down for logging reasons a few days before the race. Apart from a few tree stubs, the patch was left full of sawdust and little else. Out of all the many places Dumbreck could land, he came down slap bang in the middle of this cleared patch. Lucky in the extreme!

Having said my goodbyes to the team and still in my racing overalls, I felt a bit clammy as I bumped my way back in my hire car through the dark, unmade forest roads to the house. For some reason, I didn't fancy the delights of the funfair again. The chill that descends keeps the sweat damp, and I had to take the long and unmade-back road, as the front entrance to the house was trackside and so all barriered-up.

Once there, it was getting light and not at all sleepy, I wandered down to the front entrance to watch the race cars roar by, lights still blazing. Apart from out there on the track, where else in the world did could I possibly want to be?

Reflecting on the race, it was not the most auspicious outing I had encountered in the world's most legendary of all sportscar races. That said, the car, when it ran properly, was a delight and my passion that had almost withered away to a slow candle burn had all been fired up again into a flame.

Chapter Twenty-Seven
Green Hell

This was a flame easier lit than burned. Opportunities to race in the big one the following year were hard to come by. I consoled myself by being brought in to do outings in the ISCS International Touring Car championship. Run by SRS Motorsport and, at times, the GT Services team, my mount was always a BMW M3 that ran in the burgeoning Group N class. Not as big or powerful as the sportscars I had been driving, but with a much smaller footprint, no wing and skinnier tyres, they were still capable of speeds approaching 180mph.

We secured our first podium that year in the 6 hours of Barcelona on the Spanish F1 Grand Prix circuit just outside Madrid. I'm not sure what stood out the most. It was either the huge jeroboam of champagne I was awarded on the podium or the early morning street sweeper on Las Ramblas. The last hour of the race was totally engulfed in one of those climatic downpours. As I stood there on the podium on what was a rain-driven and windswept central stage, I could have so easily shaken the bottle, popped the cork and showered the fans.

The problem was most of them had already taken off and those that remained were hidden under umbrellas. I chose to keep the cork well and truly in place and took the fully intact bottle back down to the pits. Sharing with the team, we must have spent a good hour getting more and more tipsy as we sorted out the world as we knew it. After another tiny refreshment back at the hotel, it was decided that we would finish off our celebrations by taking a cab into the city centre.

After that, the memory goes in and out a little. Suffice to say, after what seemed like a Jurassic Lifetime, the entire team fell or indeed could have been pushed out of the Hard Rock Café around four in the morning. At the same time, a road sweeper turned up in his little two-stroke trailer van with all his brushes in the back. As he got out to begin cleaning that part of the road, one of our mechanics, the biggest of the lot, swayed and wobbled down the Hard Rock steps. This was the one who single-handedly lifted and then threw me out of the race car on urgent pit stops.

This giant gorilla of a man just walked directly to the two-stroke van, squeezed his big frame in, and then promptly took off down Las Ramblas. My lasting memory, before I must have been thrown into a cab, was of this small, moustachioed Spanish sweeper, broom still in hand and expressing a catalogue of Catalonian expletives, running down the road into the rising sun after him.

I scored another podium at the Vallelunga Autodromo. A great circuit very close to Rome. However, the race that really stood out for me that year was the Nurburgring 24 Hours. Hidden deep in Northern Germany's Eifel Forest, this celebrated event is held on the notorious Nurburgring Nordschleife. It is a race that combines the current Grand Prix circuit with the awesome northern loop to offer a mind-blowing 25km lap. With an unprecedented 170 corners, many fast and blind, and elevation changes of over 300m, this narrow and undulating circuit is a brutal challenge to both man and machine. Rightly nicknamed the 'Green Hell' by three-time World Formula One champion Jackie Stewart, this infamous circuit was declared unsafe for Grand Prix racing after Niki Lauda's fiery accident in 1976.

Although I did not get the chance to race at Le Mans in 2000, I did attend as I had VIP guests to look after there. I then spent a couple of days winding down with friends. Tim and Sara Line live in a picturesque village nearby. Without the pressure of racing, I enjoyed just sitting outside soaking up the sun in their big country garden. Here, I chewed the fat with my great friends and grazed on sumptuous, Sarthe-created Rillettes.

This was all washed down with copious amounts of the locally made white wine. At 4€ a bottle poured directly out of a big metal tank around the back of the nearby garage, the taste was divine compared to any Sauvignon you could buy on the shelves back in the UK. I said my farewells on the Tuesday night as I would be leaving very early the following morning, bound for the long drive to Germany and the Nurburgring.

After an eight-hour drive, having left before the sparrows could even wink an eye, I managed to enter the circuit gates around lunchtime. I had raced on the German Grand Prix circuit quite a few times but never, ever the fearsome Nordschleife. No problem, I thought. For a long time, I had heard you can pay a fiver a lap on public days to muscle your way around with everything from race cars to motorbikes to vans pulling caravans.

Weeks before, I had already planned it was a great way of quietly learning the circuit away from the competition, so on arrival, I duly found my way to the entrance gate. A chap who looked like a fearsome Gruppenführer in the SS but was only a local federal guard stood firmly at the closed barrier. He explained sharply, in pidgin English, that the circuit was closed.

The reason being they had a very big 24-hour race on the coming weekend and were duly making the necessary preparations. Oh boy, I thought. Would it help if I explained that I was in that big race he was so colourfully outlining? I did, and it didn't. Blimey, I thought. What was almost guaranteed as a true baptism of fire was about to take place in a day's time. With all its 170 corners, I would have to learn how to get around a 25 km a lap of the most frightening circuit on the planet, all in official qualifying.

The combined efforts of both SRS Motorsport and GT Services teams would run four identical BMW M3s. A total of 14 drivers and a supporting crew of over 50 staff. With 240 cars accepted to qualify, the F1 pit garages that would normally accommodate one Grand Prix car apiece had up to 8 cars crammed in nose to tail. Now, I was, by then, a veteran 24-hour specialist. However, what with the heaving numbers of people, the terribly cramped pit and paddock conditions, and the thought of what I was about to attempt to do, I felt as sick as a dog. The normal butterflies in my stomach felt like an overloaded hive of very angry bees.

Having still not seen any of this supposedly notorious Nordschleife, all was revealed, if not entirely remembered, come Friday's first qualifying. The Grand Prix circuit was fine, but instead of turning right at the last corner to go round again, you turn left onto the feared Nordschleife. Immediately, your aspect changes. The next 7-8 minutes are terrifying. With intimidatingly high pine trees bearing down at you from either side, it is narrow, bumpy, and uneven. A place where you can quickly feel very scared. It is also very, very fast, which surprised me from the circuit stickers I had seen on the rear windows of people's cars. Like so many on this track, the first three hills that kink either left or right, but only as you crest them, all have to be driven completely flat out and blind.

For my very first time here, I was fast enough but every so often found myself completely lost. A normal circuit you can learn within a few laps. The Nurburgring Nordschleife is more like golf. I am not sure if anyone apart from hardened local specialists could ever find anywhere close to the full potential it could deliver in any sensible amount of time. It is an extreme, one-of-a-kind.

And so it was that Ian Donaldson, closely following me in one of the sister team cars, who later said that it was by far one of the very biggest ever accidents he ever nearly saw take place. He was referring to my attempts to remember where I was going as I approached one of those earlier blind flat-out crests known as Schwedenkreuz. Did it kink left? Did it kink, right? I just couldn't remember, so I chose to crest in the middle of the track at around 170mph.

With a quick twitch on the steering wheel to the right, I suddenly noticed I had to be on the left. Another quick twitch, this time to the left, was enough to unsettle the car, which proceeded to dramatically spin round and round from virtually top speed for what felt like a lifetime. It had been raining earlier, and the minimal grass run-off was wet. Hitting this, it seemed to accelerate even quicker backwards. As the Armco barrier fast approached, head down, I could see what was coming.

I waited for the tremendously big bang. Surprisingly, it never happened. The car just veered to a final halt at what must have been less than an inch from the barrier. Silence. My heart was pumping so hard it felt as if it was thumping right out of my chest. I just sat there and waited for it to calm down. Unlike a race driver, I must have just waited a couple of minutes or more. Only when I felt it was firmly back in place, I quietly selected first gear and set off again. Unbelievably, and to my delight, all four cars had qualified. And qualified well.

Like Le Mans, a colossal amount of pomp, ceremony and parades featured in abundance during the lead-up to the 4 pm start. Because of the gargantuan number of qualifiers, 210 in total, the organisers start the race with three grids kicking off 30 seconds apart. Each grid of 70 cars followed their own individual pace car. After the first lap behind the pace cars, they exited down the pit lane. At the same time, the lights turned to green, and we were all off. Our class was in the second grid but closely surrounded by 70 of the 210 qualified starters; you could not help but feel in the thick of it from the very beginning.

On that first race lap, all was well on the Grand Prix circuit, but all hell broke out as soon as we hit the Nordschleife. Far too eager to impress, you had over-exuberant drivers trying to stamp their authority only to befall very early exits. By the time I had got to Aremberg, less than 5 kms around, there were cars all over the place. Some had launched over the barriers. Some had already thrown themselves into the trees. Those opening laps were mayhem. Ambulances came out, but unlike Le Mans, where you slowly file in behind a control car, here the marshals just waved a white safety flag, and you just passed at speed on the opposite side to the ongoing destruction. Crazy but, in a strange way, fun.

In the following laps, things began to settle down a little. I started to remember where I was for at least half the time. The rest was totally reactionary, to begin with. The M3 was timed at 178mph on the speed trap along the long straight that heads back to the pits, so not a slow car by any means. Taking on this mighty circuit when you are never 100% sure which turn happens next was a formidable undertaking.

However, certain corners get ingrained in your memory from the outset. The legendary Carousel or 'Karussell' in German is one of them. A big, ever-curving loop rather than a hairpin, it's steeply banked, and for some unknown reason, the continuous hugging apex is made up of concrete slabs. Like a monument to the past, they have been there forever and are exactly as seen on all the old, grainy black-and-white pictures of Grand Prix racing of a bygone era.

A lot is written about the numerous ways to get round this famous corner that substantially bumps and shakes both the car and driver in the quickest time possible. As well as the rest of the drivers sharing our car, I chose to take the long route around and miss the rumbling, body-shaking, chassis-breaking concrete slabs entirely. In a 24 Hours race, for the sake of a second, why take the risk? Traffic allowing, we just drove around the upper flat tarmac. It eventually would prove this was the slowest but ultimately the right way to go.

Our driving stints had to be kept to the official maximum of 2h10m. This seems a lot, but with a circuit this size, was only 11 laps per stint to safely get within this time. As night fell, the atmosphere became ever more rewarding. Bonfires and BBQs from the thousands of mostly Germanic campers egged us on by continually waving big BMW flags each time we passed their particular corner.

Even from a very sweaty cockpit, I could almost 'feel the love' as well as smell the sausages cooking away. I was learning the 170-corner circuit as fast as I could, but on occasion, I lost where I was.

This became a fair bit frightening, particularly when the rain started to come down in buckets. When you are travelling at some almighty speed, it's dark, and you don't know exactly what happens next; it tends to keep you on your toes.

On top of that, the radio from our team, Dr Clive in fact, came in to say most drivers were coming into the pits to take on wet tyres. Always a tricky situation, I was told, because with a circuit this size, it could be pouring down in one place and completely dry in another. I was told I could choose the same or stay out. Dr Clive also suggested the weather would break in the next 10-20 minutes. What was I to do? Come in like the rest of them, or stay out.

A calculated risk, but I chose to stay out. Sometimes teetering around on the brink, just waiting for a colossal accident to be involved with, we ended up OK. In fact, more than OK. Indeed, as the weather began to break, we had made-up a serious number of places by staying out.

In fact, I was really beginning to enjoy this Green Hell once the slick tyres started to offer some adhesion again, and I didn't feel as if I was attempting 170 mph roller skating on an ice rink. In fact, heartened by the ever-faithful BMW contingent that would congregate at various viewing points and fervently wave huge BMW flags in all weathers every time I went by, I inadvertently started to hum to myself.

Maybe it's an extreme concentration trait of mine. I had never noticed it before, but to my embarrassment, Dr Clive and anyone he chose to share his earphones with could hear my dulcet tones on my radio feed. Unlike the many sportscars I had driven, the radio button on the steering wheel was replaced by a simple switch. After radioing through to Dr Clive in the pits, I had to click the switch back to disconnect the feed. I forget.

As my stint was coming to an end, Clive was frantically trying to radio to me to say I had missed the 'in sign' last time round. Indeed, I missed it twice. I was over the maximum allowance for any one driver to be out. Completely oblivious to the panic in the pits, I was still merrily humming away. My rambling ditty was all he could hear. Fortunately, the officials didn't pick up on this small misdemeanour. This was good news because we were slowly climbing up the field in class positions.

As dark turned back into day, the sun started to beam down brightly. All the terrifying scariness of the very wet and slippery night quickly faded into memory. More to hum about, you would think. But shortly after getting back in the car for another stint, I thought my whole world was going to come to an end.

By this time, the cars still running were ridden with dirt, grime, and battle-weary scars. Like the rest of them, our car was not without blemish. Somewhere along the line, we had taken a hit to the front. The bonnet had been heavily gaffer taped down in a pit-stop as both latches were suspect.

I was heading down the straight to Tiergarten on the very fastest part of the circuit when there was a sudden, massive bang, and everything immediately blackened out. Taking a second or two to register, the high-speed air stream created must have got under the bonnet and had blown it up. The windscreen bore witness to this fact as it was now mostly in my lap.

Aside from that, I could hardly see a thing. I was not humming as, taking care not to hit anything, I somehow slowed the car down to a crawl. Undoing my belts, I squatted down in my seat so I could peer out of the inch of daylight, showing out from the slightly rounded shape of the still-hinged but now skyward-facing bonnet. Auspiciously, the pits were not too far away. Just the remains of that straight, a twisty chicane section and then the run-up to the pit-lane entry. I later heard I received more TV coverage than the ultimate outright winner during the time it took to safely get back to the pit garages. On arrival, the team had to move mountains to change both the bonnet and the windscreen before we could go out again. In record time, they did it.

As Sunday wore on, a major tussle took place over the best finisher of the two remaining SRS/GTS team cars. The other two having already retired. This was resolved when, with just an hour to go, Thomas Jacobitsch's class-setting pole position car blew up. As the chequered flag fell, we were the only   one to finish out of our four team cars that started 24 Hours earlier. To add even more substance to this, we scored an incredible third-place podium. Not a bad result for a rookie in The Green Hell I thought, as I undertook the long drive back to the UK the following day.

Chapter Twenty-Eight
Rimini Red Lighting

Not all the races I have done stand out. However good or bad the outcome, many are just locked away, hidden from view, in the depths of what is left of my forever-depleting memory banks. There are always a few that stand the test of time, not always for the best reasons. One such race meeting occurred in the early September of that year. Our destination was once more back at Misano, close to the Italian seaside shores of the sparkling blue Adriatic. Again, we were running a BMW M3 prepared by SRS Motorsport.

The latest car was now owned by my good pal, Dr Clive. The ISCS International Touring Car Championship was one we ducked in and out of. As we just cherry-picked the better events, we were not interested in the championship points. Also, by this time, feeling a little disillusioned with it all, I, for one, was not taking the event too seriously. I was going through a phase both on and off the track. I had been out of sportscars all year and, with no opportunities available, had to miss my beloved Le Mans.

Again, through no fault of her own, another fairly long-term relationship had gone south, and I was partying far more than I should. I had invited a severely good-looking, if somewhat wayward, younger girl, Natalie, to join us. If nothing else, I was determined to, at worst, to secure a late summer tan. At best, have some fun, Anything else would be a bonus.

I stayed on the shores of Cattolica, under 10 minutes' drive to the track, where the sun beat down every day, and the wine tasted delectable. I had turned up earlier than normal as pre-race testing was scheduled for mid-week. This was cancelled in favour of an unscheduled biker's day at the circuit. But 'hey-ho', I didn't mind. Waiter service on the sun-drenched Adriatic coast was something not too difficult to handle.

I indulged with great aplomb. I was then joined by Richard Cuene-Grandidier, one of the co-drivers I would be with for the race. Although his outstanding British BBC accent never gave the game away, he explained he was actually an ex-pat Frenchman. He smiled and said, 'Just call me Kermit'. From thereon, from and to this current day, I have called him Kermit. I knew we would become great friends.

We nattered about his past, how he used to own, run, and race under the name 'Kermit Racing' with his branded, all-green Group N touring car team. How his father was a French war hero who, after escaping from a Nazi POW camp, joined the French Resistance movement. Post WWII, his dad was awarded *France's* highest award - the Legion d'Honneur. Kermit came across as a very British aristocratic Frenchman. I was impressed.

Qualifying went well. No big surprise as, by this time, I knew the circuit quite well. The day before the race we discovered the local bar 'Giorgio's'. Although wonderfully Italian, it still reminded me of my local back home, 'Harry's. Natalie, affectionately known as Nat, and I, along with Kermit, indulged in the glorious spread of delectable nibbles Giorgio had offered us while we indulged in a glass or two. We then partied much longer than we should have. More than a tad weary, along with my new playmate Nat, Giorgio offered a place for us to stay down below in the beer cellar.

After a chilly and uncomfortable night, I awoke the next day, race day, not feeling so good. I felt bad. Where had I got to. Whatever race it was, it was something I would never have done in the past. I was not taking this job seriously enough. Making my way to the circuit I felt obliged to give myself a very severe talking to.

A few hours later, still not feeling 100%, it was up to me to take the start. Not being in the top class for this 6-hour race, the car was a few rows down as the grid formed. However, as the lights turned to green, I made a very good start was making healthy progress up the ranks. I was throwing everything into this effort, possibly in a wholehearted attempt to rectify the events of the recent past.

At one part of the circuit there is a corner where you can take full advantage and fully ride the curbs on the apex. I was riding the curbs with such gusto half the car was on the grass on the other side. Towards the end of my stint and clearly making up places, I started to feel dizzy. Everything began to go in and out of focus. Slowly nursing the car and myself back to the pits, I staggered out of the car only to promptly collapse in the pit lane. I was swiftly scraped up off the floor and taken away in an ambulance.

Having viewed the start from a vantage point above, Nat arrived in the back of the pit garages only to be told I had been raced away in an Ambulance. Finding the keys to my hire car in my racing bag I had left, she immediately drove to the nearest hospital. She was not insured, and I am not altogether sure she had ever driven on the wrong side of the road before, but that was Nat all over.

Not knowing a word of Italian, she was on a mission to find me. What she didn't know is that in the Rimini region there are a lot of hospitals. The main one is called Azienda but there are several of those spread along the coast. With due diligence, she scoured three hospitals, asking at the reception if they had a race driver recently admitted from the Misano circuit. When they said no, she asked for directions to the next hospital, most likely to receive one. Dismayed, Nat finally gave up and headed back to the circuit.

On arrival, she was shocked to find me standing in the pit garage, watching the race, and happily sipping from a hot mug of coffee. Feeling somewhat put out; she said where the hell have you been. I explained that they had taken me to the medical centre on the circuit. They put me on a drip for an hour or so. I feel as right as rain now.

Nat was about to divulge all the adventures she had had looking for me when the Tannoy system excitedly blurted out in Italian something that sounded serious. Although none of us knew what was going on to begin with, the race was suddenly slowed down under yellow safety flags. It soon became apparent there had been a huge accident. Word came through it was a BMW M3 being driven by Richard Cuene-Grandidier. Aka, our very own 'Kermit'.

Difficult to fathom from the Italian commentators, but as they started to talk slowly and quietly, it sounded very serious indeed. We all thought the worst. Kermit had gone head-on into the barriers at speed. An Ambulance was on the scene but so were several fire trucks. We heard later that the car had hit with such force that the engine had found its way into the cockpit, the steering wheel was pinned to Kermit's chest. It took an age for him to be carefully cut out of the wreckage and placed on a stretcher.

As we saw the ambulance leaving, I shouted to Nat, get in. With that we both jumped back in my hire car and stormed off after it. Soon catching up with the Ambulance, we sat right behind as, siren blaring and flashing emergency lights madly flickering on and off brightly in the night sky, we made ourselves in convoy along the busy main road to Rimini. I almost felt like Moses, as everything around parted like the Red Sea waves as we ploughed ahead, without stopping through more and more red lights entering the city centre.

On arrival, Nat quickly recognised she had been here before, no more than three hours ago. Kermit, on a stretcher, was rushed through a separate door as we made our way to reception. Looking more than a little confused, the same nurse who had spoken to Nat earlier said, well, he's just arrived. Nat replied that one was Richard, the one she was looking for was Robin and he was standing right next to her.

Now you want to know about Richard the nurse asked. Completely discombobulated by then, she just let out a huge sigh in resignation. You could see in her eyes she was desperately hoping her shift would very soon draw to a close. I think a lot of this, for ever more bizarre evening, was getting lost in translation.

As we saw the top halves of the medics disappearing along a semi-glass-fronted corridor, taking Kermit to surgery, there was nothing much else we could do there. The nurses were not going to share his diagnosis other than to say he was fine and in the right hands, so after hesitating, we left. A very sore Kermit would phone the following day. They were keeping him in for a couple of days. He had ruptured his spleen, had done something severely adverse to his downstairs bits, and had incurred a few broken ribs.

Quietly driving back from the hospital, we dropped into the circuit to pick up our belongings. We conveyed what little news we had on Richard to the team as they struggled to get what remained of the totally wrecked car back into the transporter. With that, we retired to Giorgio's for one last, more sensible, late-night tipple. As we clinked glasses, Nat said, "To Kermit". "To Kermit", I replied.

Chapter Twenty-Nine
Kings Man Chaos

So, what can I really say about my 14th and final participation at Le Mans? By then, I was a seasoned veteran of this hallowed event. At the time, I was featured in history books as one of the drivers to have appeared the most. I was still not in the same league as your Derek Bell's and Yojiro Terada's, but I was still up there. I had thought that my 1999 Le Mans would be my last. That said, that would have meant 13 participations in total. That number is unlucky for some, and with my spirit all fired up again, I was certainly ready for another shot should the opportunity arise.

Again, it was Stuart who came up with the goods. Both he and I had some small sponsors to help out, and there was also big support that came from FAT Turbo Express. They were a well-known and respected French transport company who loved to spend far too much money sponsoring the cars at Le Mans.

Stepping back yet another class, the car would be a Porsche 911 GT3 running in the LM GT category. Still a 180-190 mph car, to many enthusiasts, the road-going GT3 version is a supercar. The status of a GT3 race car is several steps up from that. However, I still felt in an odd position. I suppose I had begun to reason why, yet again.

The race car was being run by my old Playboy colleague Alfonso de-Orleans-Borbon'. It was actually owned by his uncle. As mentioned before, this happened to be a certain Juan Carlos, the then-King of Spain. However impressive it might read on paper, entering the biggest and most prestigious Sports car race in the world with a new car, as untried as the King's nephew's ability to run the team, did not fill me with instant positive vibes. To then hear I was the only real pro' in the driver squad did not help either. As I always do, I rallied to the cause.

For this race I would be partnering two American amateur drivers. One was Terry Lingner, a chap who knew Le Mans well but not from the driving seat. He was president of a production company that worked closely with ESPN and Speedvision and in that role, had been here a number of times before. He had raced historics and had moved up to the U.S. IMSA sportscar championship. The other was Chris MacAllister.

Chris owned a giant Caterpillar dealership in Indiana and owned numerous historic race cars. He had also raced in contemporary cars, coming 12th overall and 3rd in class in the Daytona 24 Hours race a couple of years before. He would go on to win his category (Grid 6) in the Le Mans Classic, driving his Gulf Mirage M6 in 2014.

As Le Mans tradition sometimes has little to do with the most practical method, the venue for scrutineering, the place where all the technical and safety checks occur, is always held in the city centre at the beginning of the week. To the delight of the locals, it has all the razzamatazz of a carnival. The race cars have to leave the circuit in their team transporters for the 20-minute trip, unloaded and then have to be wheeled into what is effectively a showground surrounded by fast food stalls and merchandise stands.

Mechanics then push these silent monsters to numerous marquees where every part of the car is individually checked. The seats, the belts, the extinguishers. The height, the width, the ground clearance and so on. The final marquee is where they are awarded their Le Mans technical check pass. These passes, which come in the form of decals, are placed on the cars with great ceremony. We received ours as well, but the car was found to be in need of a diet. It was seriously overweight.

Drivers had to be there, too. After signing-on, they have their helmets and race wear checked thoroughly to ensure it is all up to date. They are then interviewed on stage by the official multi-lingual host and the press before autograph sessions begin. The last stop is for both cars and drivers to appear for the official team photo. The entire process takes around 4-5 hours. All of this could be done at the circuit in next to no time. However, the crowds love to be up close and personal for their once-a-year, celebratory 24-hour week. Tradition can sometimes be, and often is, all about show business.

Just before practice began, we received a surprise visit from the King himself. He arrived in the pit garage surrounded by a plethora of armed guards, all looking like they had walked out of central casting for Men in Black. All with dark suits with ties, sunglasses, and radio earpieces. Everyone, even the Fonz himself, politely stood to attention as he individually shook our hands and wished us well. All the while, his entourage, armed with serious frowns, whispered into their collars. And with that, he was gone; the rotors of the nearby helicopter had already fired up, awaiting his swift retreat.

With multiple teething problems, Wednesday qualifying was a disaster. With the weather on the turn, Thursday showed little more promise. Not only was the heavy car slow, but none of us had qualified for the race under the 110% rule. Something extraordinary had to be done.

As lead driver, it was down to me to make a mark. We were not going down without a fight. It was now or never, and as I climbed into the cockpit and got belted up, the Fonz told me the weather forecast was bleak. I had maybe two or three laps before the next shower was due.

With that, I was off. I can hardly remember the lap that followed my out lap. It felt as if I held my breath all the way round. It was as hard, if not harder, than any qualifying lap I had ever done before. I was so focused on at least making a point, my concentration was as intense, if not more than ever. Forget the front row when I was in one of the fastest cars a few years before; somehow, squeezing into this race was all important. On the following lap, droplets of water spitting onto the windscreen was enough to suggest it was all over.

To my astonishment, I had qualified this elephant of a Porsche for the race. I had set a time faster than twelve of the Porsche drivers in the same class. That quick moment of joy dissipated as quickly as it had arrived as I heard Terry was borderline, and Chris was nowhere near the qualifying time required. Like last time back in 1999, we had to lobby the ACO to allow us to race. For what I thought was such a severe organisation they agreed we could run. 'Wahey', although at the back of the grid, we were in the race.

Friday was again the driver's parade through the city centre. I did all the right things. I smiled and joked all the way round, waved, and signed autographs, but the thought of the following day felt intimidating. I had that odd, uncomfortable feeling looming in the back of my mind. I wouldn't go so as far to say impending doom, but I felt something imminently foreboding was out there on the horizon somewhere. A sleepless night followed.

After the air displays, revelry, and jamboree of the pre-race festivities, it was time to ready myself for the race ahead. As I had qualified quickest, the team agreed it best I start. Our garage was placed about halfway down the pit lane, and it seemed like an age to walk all the way down to where the Porsche was positioned, right at the back of the mighty grid. As I stood beside the car, I donned my helmet and took a brief glimpse upward at the darkening, overcast sky. Wow, I thought, that really does look bleak and threatening. I then slid into the cockpit as one of the team helped belt me up and ensure my radio was fully connected. He closed the door, and there I was, alone. After all the combined effort it takes to get a race car like this onto the grid, for a while at least, the rest would be up to me.

Amongst the hustle and bustle of marshals clearing the grid of mechanics, press and officials, the piercing sound of countdown sirens going off, and the animated crowd cheering down from the stands, there I sat, still in my seat. Beyond the windscreen lay totally silent. It was as if the world outside was working in some parallel dimension. Again, all I could hear was the sound of my own heavy breathing filtering its way through my fireproof Nomex balaclava and helmet. My focus was entirely on the grid ahead and what would come next.

With a thunderous roar of engines firing up, the entire grid burst into life. The marshals waving flags and gantry lights suggested we were off on our rolling lap. So far back, all I could do was press the starter button and head off in the same direction. With ever-blackening skies, I was on slick, non-treaded tyres, as was most of the rest of the party, leaving the safety of the stadium.

Keeping position, we edged forward as fast as the safety car leading the grid would allow. Hitting the Mulsanne, we all began to insanely weave from left to right to warm up our tyres. A skill in itself, as I have known of cars coming off in the process. The 8.5 mile/13.6 kms lap, normally accomplished in well under 4 minutes at racing speed, seemed to take a lifetime behind the safety car.

Finally, I then rounded the Porsche Curves, and headed for the Ford Chicane, the final corner before the main start-line straight.

The safety car rushed into the entry of the pit lane. With the front end of the grid-keeping formation, until the start line gantry lights turned green and the starting flag was waved, I knew when to hit the throttle. We were off.

As was inevitable, all hell broke out by lap 4. As the gloom descended to ground level, the heavens opened and deposited an inordinate amount of wet stuff on the track. Not everywhere but it did include the western boundaries such as Indianapolis Corner, Arnage and the Porsche Curves. One car was off at Indianapolis and another at Arnage. Missing those, I skittered and splashed my way down to the entry to the Porsche Curves, only to be met by a chaotic scene. Out of half a dozen cars, not one was facing in the right direction.

A couple were bouncing back onto the circuit, having already hit the barriers. With no grip, some were wildly spinning like tops right in front of me. Taking evasive action at over 150mph was totally reactionary when it was not clear who you might hit on the rebound. Finding the little available black piece of tarmac, I managed to slalom around all the carnage.

Not long afterwards, with warning lights urgently flashing, the first of the safety cars were deployed. These to dramatically slow the pace down and provide marshals time to clear up all the havoc created all around the circuit. After just 15 minutes of racing, the race was under control of the pace cars for the next half hour.

On arrival at the pits, the scene was nearly as chaotic. Pretty much everyone had pitted at the same time for rain tyres. The scene was one of sheer pandemonium. The entire pit lane was crammed full of tyre men changing tyres, mechanics doing hasty repairs, and team managers screaming orders. Race cars were all over the place, either coming in, up on air jacks and being frantically set about with wheel guns or attempting to find a clear space to join the queue to get out. The pit lane exit lights were being kept on red until the safety car had passed, and they could join the back of the crocodile's tail.

Going out again, I finished my stint and handed over to Terry. As there was a break in the weather, he reverted to slicks. Apart from a lurid spin at Indianapolis, Terry completed his turn and passed the mantle over to Chris. With neither one being particularly quick or stretching the limits of their stints, I felt as if I should try and sharpen up the pace next time out. As I climbed back into the cockpit it was little more than 8 pm.

However, the ever-blackening skies cast a nighttime shadow over the remaining daylight as the rain turned from a gentle spit to another full-on downpour. Just before firing up, the car was put back onto rain tyres. Right, I thought, let's just see what this old heavyweight can do.

With the bit firmly in my teeth, I set off as the rain lashing down got progressively worse. Always good in the rain, I was thinking that maybe I could make up some long-lost time. On my first full lap, I could tell by the surrounding cars in my class we were gaining.

That said, I was getting wheelspin going up through gears, even when changing into top.

On the Mulsanne, I got caught on the standing water, the car felt light as if to aquaplane, and the front end nervously twitched. I snatched it back but still travelling at nearly a football pitch a second, my heart must have missed a beat or two in the process. Sliding out of the second chicane and hammering up through the gears, I was just approaching the final stretch of the Mulsanne when my luck finally ran out. The torrential rain was now of monsoon proportions.

By then, the rain was bouncing a foot or more off the ground. Again, the car aquaplaned, but this time, there was no coming back. All control was lost. The Porsche was hurtling towards the barrier at monumental speed, and I was convinced it had no choice other than go right up and over the Armco.

You are taught at the racing school that if all else fails, take your hands off the steering wheel and brace yourself for impact. Very much easier said than done. My hands stayed firmly on the only thing I knew could offer some sort of resistance to what might come next. In that millisecond that followed, I knew it was all over.

Like that day I crashed my Hillmen Imp so many years before, a great calm befell me. A what would be, would be, moment. With what seemed like the mightiest of bangs, the car rocketed into the barrier on the right. It then immediately ricochetted to the left of the circuit and hit the other side with almost as much force. Hands still firmly clenching the wheel, I was helplessly attempting to control something I had no command of.

As a mere passenger, I was then thrown back to the right, side-swiping the armco yet again to land broadside at the top of the hump where the Mercedes took off a couple of years back. I just sat there looking out of the side window as two Audis, heading straight for me, jumped to the left and right at 200mph. More cars followed, but by then, furiously waved marshals' flags were telling ongoing traffic to slow down.

The marshals then managed to push both me and the car to safety. Radioing to the pits, all I got back was abuse from Alfonso. Obviously unimpressed, I had virtually destroyed his uncle, the King's car. Out of the car, blood started to slowly trickle from both hands, as with adrenaline still flowing, I tried to pull the crunched-up front bodywork away from the wheels. When that failed, feeling a bit bewildered and befuddled, I got a lift back to the pits, only to receive even more abuse from the team manager. There was not one 'oh, I'm glad to see you still alive' gesture.

Never mind. As a working driver, I had promised to attend a late-night interview hosted by former Le Mans and F1 driver Perry McCarthy. The audience was held in a big marquee for about 1,500 fans who regularly attend Le Mans with a company called Chequered Travel. By this time, my left hand was all bandaged up, and my right sporting plasters.

320

Perry is very good at asking questions, so much easier for me to casually answer, often incurring a laugh or two. By the end, my hand was throbbing like hell, but no matter, I would be going home in a day or two. Also, contrary to my belief at the time, I was still allowed back in Spain again.

Chapter Thirty

Schoolboy Dreams

It was about six months later I was told by my own Doc' that I had indeed broken my hand. It had healed to a certain extent, and as I had never caught up with him before, there was not a lot he could do with any condition that might occur in the future. But what was my future?

My short-term future became trekking to Everest Base Camp then climbing a number of big Himalayan peaks. A year later, I clambered to the top of Mount Kilimanjaro. All scary in different ways, but nothing like the racing. Soon after Le Mans, I drove on the M1 on a rainy day and got scared by a light aquaplane feeling, but by the end of the year, I did yet another Vallelunga 6 Hours. In the pouring rain, starting 33rd on a huge grid, I was 8th into the first corner, way above what my class in the field would normally have realised.

I had certainly got over my rain issue. I competed in several other touring car races and also did a one-off in the Le Mans Classic. More rain and wheelspin at 190 mph. My last race was again back at my revered Vallelunga. As I confidently slid out of corners, just clipping that small piece of grass on the exit, I remember thinking how much I was only ever really good at two things: one was art, and the other was racing. I was so good at it, but however much I loved this sport, what rewards had it actually given me back?

Thinking back now, when I was racing, everything played out in bright Technicolor, whilst normal life for me has always been a far more in a drab black-and-white affair. Only out on the track in a race car did I fully feel alive. Was that not reward enough in itself?

Approaching fifty, I finally got hitched. I met and married the lovely Anne, always Annie to me, in a picturesque village church known as St Michaels just on the outskirts of St Albans. As completely serene and stunning as she looked on her arrival, I must have looked very nervous. It wasn't so much the dramatic change to my life that was about to happen but more the fact that unbeknownst to her, I was waiting for a vast transporter to park up next to the church.

One of our wedding guests, affectionally known just as JHB, John Harwood-Bee, was a major benefactor of Stuart's company, Project 100. Soon to become the chairman, I had known John for years. With a charmingly friendly and jovial demeanour and a powerfully resonant voice, he was also as sharp as a knife business-wise. Without too much outward fanfare, John had purchased our front-row winning Gulf Porsche car I raced with Derek Bell back in 1994. Although a lot of money at the time, that Le Mans scrutineering pass in the cockpit acted as a passport to the future, and we all hoped would do him well when he eventually sold it. A few years on and passing through a number of owners since, that car is now worth $6 Million today. I forever pondered why Le Mans drivers don't go up in value as much as the cars they drove. Sadly, they don't. Coming back to the wedding and hidden out of view just around the corner, that massive transporter contained JHB's car, my precious 'being Steve McQueen for the day' permit of ten years past. Gone were the driver decals for both Jürgen Lässig and Derek Bell. Although mine still stood proudly along with the Union Jack, I had the other two replaced by the now-married name of my gorgeous new wife alongside the blue and white flag of Scotland, her country of birth.

Spits of rain droplets threatening a light shower were the last thing I felt as a single man. Fully clad in the kilt I was allowed to wear, I then walked through the church doors and marched myself swiftly up to the altar. As my glorious bride came forth and presented herself beside me, the vicar started saying things like, will you, won't you, do you, don't you. Old habits die hard, as I was just thinking wet or dry tyres.

After the deed was done, we eventually managed to get her and her flowing wedding dress into the cockpit of the open car. It had been quietly pushed to the church entrance. The team had decided on slick, not treaded tyres. Firing up and loudly blipping the throttle in what I thought was an impressive celebration of our commitment, the first embarrassment of married life was when I then proceeded to stall it.

Happy with my second attempt, I completely illegally drove my new bride out of the church grounds and down the narrow village street. With astonished passers-by looking on, we passed the 16th-century Six Bells Inn and the equally characterful Rose & Crown pub before going up and over the quaint humpback bridge. Passing the duck pond, we only came to a halt when we arrived at St Michael's Manor, where our reception was being held.

Many years on, I am still happily married to Anne, and I spend most of my spare time walking my beloved Golden Retriever dogs. The road-going sportscars I had once owned are all gone now. I drive an old Range Rover. With the woofers in the back destination dog walk, this is now driven at 'Driving like Miss Daisy' speeds. I now thoroughly appreciate the blueness of the sky and the greenness of the fields. I take most pleasure indulging in the simple delights, unbelievably free for everyone. The forests and the rivers. The hills, dunes and the beaches. I am at peace with myself. And I survived.

That is not to say I have given up Le Mans entirely. For almost too many years to remember, I still return every year where I now look after VIP guests, teams and sponsors at the 24 Hours. As a director of an auto-events company, Dettaglio, clients have included everyone from Porsche, Ford and Ferrari to TAG Heuer, Gulf Oil and Vodafone.

With no family investment whatsoever and no particular urge to much more easily make a name for myself in lower categories of racing, I had managed to haul myself up from nowhere to start on the front row of the legendary Le Mans grid. A venue where hundreds still aspire to get to and where thousands and thousands look on in awe. I had competed against many of my heroes.

In true competition, I had taken on the likes of everyone from Mario Andretti to Michael Schumacher. I had shared race cars and held my own with ex-Formula One Grand Prix drivers such as Arturo Merzario and Jean-Pierre Jarier. That would never, ever be forgetting five-time outright Le Mans winner and former Ferrari F1 driver Derek Bell. What more was there to achieve? A little boy with a dream and no funds at all had grown up to do the very best he could. To this day, not a wealthy man in pure monetary terms by any means, but I believe I have lived a life. I have to believe my bounty has come from the epic journey I experienced along the way. Some would say the stuff of schoolboy dreams.

In closing, I thought it best to leave you with a small speech made by a much wiser man than I. For a lot of reasons, I took a certain warmth from the words he said over 100 years ago:

"It is not the critic who counts, not the man who points out how the strong man stumbles or where the doer of deeds could have done better. The credit belongs to the man who is actually in the arena, whose face is marred by dust and sweat and blood, who strives valiantly, who errs and comes up short again and again, because there is no effort without error or shortcoming, but who knows the great enthusiasms, the great devotions, who spends himself in a worthy cause; who, at the best, knows, in the end, the triumph of high achievement, and who, at the worst, if he fails, at least he fails while daring greatly so that his place shall never be with those cold and timid souls who knew neither victory nor defeat."

—Theodore Roosevelt

Speech at the Sorbonne, Paris, April 23, 1910

THE END

Photograph Credits

To illustrate this book, I started with a big box of pictures, randomly given to me over the years. They sat for years gathering dust amongst the cobwebs in my loft. To attempt to source all the original photographers was harder than I ever could have imagined. Especially when most pictures were taken on film, and not digitally recorded as they are today. That said, wherever possible I have endeavoured to secure the credit to each photograph chosen. In some instances, however how hard as I have tried, a few cannot be located. Sadly, these I have had to mark down as unknown. You will also find a fair amount listed under 'Authors Collection'. These were mostly supplied by family, friends or team members taking their own pictures on the day. For every photographer who took it upon themselves to record my journey (listed or not), I remain forever extremely grateful.

1. Front cover: Jeff Bloxham
2. Page:
3. 106: Top & middle: Authors Collection. Bottom: Martin Lee
4. 107: All: Authors Collection
5. 108: All: Authors Collection
6. 109: All: Authors Collection
7. 110: All: Authors Collection
8. 111: Top: unknown. Middle: Authors Collection. Bottom: unknown

9. 112: Top: Motorsport Images. Middle: Authors Collection. Bottom: unknown

10. 113: Top: Unknown. Middle left: Authors Collection. Middle right: Autosport. Bottom: Authors Collection

11. 114: Top: Ken Wells. Middle left: Christian Vignon. Middle right: Ken Wells. Bottom: Motorsport Images

12. 115: Top: Authors Collection. Middle left and right: Motorsport Images. Middle bottom: Michel Picard. Bottom: unknown

13. 116 Top: Project 100. Middle right: Alee Hoy Sports. Bottom: Project 100

14. 117: Top: Project 100. Middle left: unknown. Middle right: Project 100. Bottom: unknown

15. 221: Alee Hoy Sports. Middle: unknown. Botton left: Project 100. Bottom right: Autosport

16. 222: Top left : Project 100. Top right: Jeff Bloxham. Middle: unknown. Middle insert right: Gulf Oil. Bottom insert: Authors Collection. Bottom: John Brooks

17. 223: Top: Jeff Bloxham. Middle left: Authors Collection. Middle insert: Gulf Oil. Middle right: Authors Collection. Bottom right: Project 100. Bottom right: Jeff Bloxham

18. 224: Top: Christian Vignon. Middle left insert: Authors Collection. Middle: John Brooks. Middle right insert: Vincent Laplaud. Bottom left & right: Authors Collection

19. 225: Top: Vincent Laplaud. Middle left: Christian Vignon. Middle right John Brooks. Bottom: Christian Vignon

20. 226: Top left & right Clive Calcutt. Middle: Studio Alquati. Middle insert Scandinavian Raceway. Bottom: Clive Calcutt

21. 227: All: Clive Calcutt

22. 228: Top left & right Project 100. Middle left & right John Brooks. Bottom: John Brooks

23. 229: Top and middle left: Unknown. Middle right and bottom: John Brooks.
24. 230: Top: John Brooks. Middle left: Authors Collection. Middle right: Christian Vignon. Bottom: Motorsport Images
25. 231: All: Authors Collection
26. 232: All: Authors Collection
27. 233: All: Authors Collection
28. 234: Top, middle left insert, and bottom right: Clive Calcutt. Bottom left : Authors Collection
29. Back cover: Milan Sames

Index

C

T

U

www.ingramcontent.com/pod-product-compliance
Ingram Content Group UK Ltd.
Pitfield, Milton Keynes, MK11 3LW, UK
UKHW020940011025
463461UK00002B/4

9 781967 679591